A HANDBOOK OF SERVICES FOR THE HANDICAPPED

A HANDBOOK OF SERVICES FOR THE HANDICAPPED

Alfred H. Katz
and
Knute Martin

GREENWOOD PRESS
Westport, Connecticut • London, England

Library of Congress Cataloging in Publication Data

Katz, Alfred Hyman, 1916–
    A handbook of services for the handicapped.

    Bibliography: p.
    Includes index.
    1. Handicapped — Services for — United States — Hand-
books, manuals, etc. I. Martin, Knute. II. Title.
HV1553.K37 362.4′0458′0973   81-20314
ISBN 0-313-21385-2 (lib. bdg.)   AACR2

Library of Congress Catalog Card Number: 81-20314
ISBN: 0-313-21385-2

First published in 1982

Greenwood Press
A division of Congressional Information Service, Inc.
88 Post Road West
Westport, Connecticut 06881

Printed in the United States of America

10 9 8 7 6 5 4 3 2 1

CONTENTS

FIGURES AND TABLES

FIGURES

TABLES

THE SITUATION OF THE HANDICAPPED IN THE UNITED STATES

The purpose of this volume is to discuss a number of aspects of the lives of disabled persons in the United States in the light of recently developed knowledge and of remedial programs that can help overcome their problems. The book is thus designed to provide a general overview of common problems and needs of the handicapped, and of the resources available to help meet those needs and overcome those problems. The book is addressed both to nonspecialist academics and students, who seek an accurate general account of disability in the United States, and to handicapped persons, their families, and others interested in improving their welfare and status in our society.

The intent of the book is thus practical and informational, rather than theoretic. Many unresolved questions, frequently of a technical nature, surround particular approaches, therapies, and techniques, and there are many political issues. Although these issues will be touched on when appropriate, the work's major goal is not technical, political, or polemical, but essentially pragmatic.

There is no claim or intent to be exhaustive or encyclopedic in the treatment of any of the major topics the book addresses. Instead, our purpose has been to select key factors in the life of almost all disabled persons, to describe their ramifications and interrelationships, and to outline the remedial programs society has devised to assist in their melioration or resolution. Particular disabilities or disease categories are only discussed illustratively, and the book's emphasis is on the common problems faced by disabled people, regardless of the symptoms, causes, severity, or treatment of their particular disability. We hope that this approach will result in the book being useful to the maximum number of readers. More detailed and specialized discussions of particular disabling conditions are available elsewhere in the literature.

Historians remind us that a salient criterion of a civilization's progress is the way it treats its "marginal men," of whom the physically and mentally handicapped are prototypical examples. On that score, the United States is becoming more civilized, but it still has much to achieve before it can be classed as a truly humane and equal society. A highly technologized and achievement-oriented culture does not offer much nurturance, or even tolerance, for those who are born with or acquire some physical or mental limitation unless it makes massive efforts. Before the modern age, such persons were regarded as burdens on the able-bodied, as objects of pity or charity, and as the unfortunate products of sinful behavior or malign forces. The handicapped were surrounded by a mist of myth, misconceptions, folk belief, or mystical awe, any or all of which prevented the recognition and acceptance of their membership in the human species and an objective assessment of their assets and deficits as human beings.

The sweeping biological, technical, and educational/psychological revolutions of the nineteenth and twentieth centuries have gone far to dispel the myths and replace them with facts, but not far enough to revise and reformulate irrational public attitudes and practices regarding the handicapped. Biomedical advances have brought refined understanding of the causes, nature, and duration of many disabling conditions; some can even be prevented. Restorative medical techniques and treatments, methods of psychological assessment, and educational technologies have made it possible to relieve much suffering, restore much functioning, and arrest or control the course of development of particular disabilities, but the massive consequences of an inferior social status still affect most disabled people in our society.

It is a scientific truism that the conquest of infectious diseases, the improvement of the environment, better nutrition, greater understanding of the risks of pregnancy and childbirth have resulted in the survival of many persons, albeit with some physical or mental deficits, who would formerly have died. Furthermore, the technical achievements that have brought about the conquest of formerly lethal or crippling diseases have also brought in their train new hazards — radiation, chemical pollutants, and other environmental hazards, which have contributed, in ways not fully although increasingly understood, to the pool of surviving infants who bear some deficit or defect. Finally, the conditions of modern life, including high mobility, rapid transportation, hazardous occupational and even home exposures, have also contributed to an accident and injury rate that further swells the total of those suffering a disability.

Although exact data are lacking, Table 1 presents statistics that give an overview of the extent, scope, and situation of the disabled segment of the U.S. population at the end of the last decade.

Table 1

Disabilities in the U.S. Population, 1980

Total persons with activity limitation caused by chronic physical or mental impairment	37,536,000
Percentage of U.S. population with activity limitations	17.2
Disabled children under 17 years of age	8,350,000
Disabled persons 17–44 years of age	7,979,000
Disabled persons 45–64 years of age	10,412,000
Disabled persons 65 years of age and older	10,795,000
Disabled children 3 to 21 years of age receiving special education	4,030,000
Disabled persons receiving public vocational rehabilitation services	1,442,000

SOURCES:

Gearheart, Bill R., *Special Education for the '80s* (St. Louis: The C. V. Mosby Company, 1980).

Kovar, Mary Grace. "Health Status of U.S. Children and Use of Medical Care," *Public Health Reports*, Vol. 97, No. 1, U.S. Department of Health and Human Services, HRA 82-605 (USPH 324-990) (Washington, D.C.: Government Printing Office, January–February 1982).

Select Panel for the Promotion of Child Health, *Better Health for Our Children: A National Strategy, Vols. I, II*, U.S. Department of Health and Human Services, Public Health Service, Office of the Assistant Secretary for Health and Surgeon General, DHHS (PHS) Publication No. 79-55071 (Washington, D.C.: Government Printing Office, 1981).

Sunshine, Jonathan, *Disability: A Comprehensive Overview of Programs, Issues, and Options for Change* (Washington, D.C.: President's Commission on Pension Policy, December 1980).

U.S. Department of Education, *"To Assure the Free Appropriate Public Education of All Handicapped Children," Second Annual Report to Congress on the Implementation of Public Law 94-142: The Education for All Handicapped Children Act*, Office of Special Education and Rehabilitative Services (Washington, D.C.: Government Printing Office, 1980).

U.S. Department of Health and Human Services, *Current Estimates From The National Health Interview Survey: United States, 1980* (Vital and Health Statistics, Series 10, No. 139), Public Health Service, Office of Health Research, Statistics, and Technology (Hyattsville, Md.: National Center for Health Statistics, 1981).

This table indicates the surprising proportion of the U.S. population that is disabled. *Over 37 million persons*—or about 17.2 percent of the total population—was so affected in 1980. Fourteen percent of all children and about 11 percent of preschool children suffered a disabling or limiting condition. In addition, there is a wide and probably increasing gap between the numbers of those persons who need remedial services and those who actually receive them. Although many of the previous causes of disability have been eliminated or nearly so—tuberculosis of the bones and spine, for example, formerly a main cause of orthopedic defects in children—*new* causative factors have arisen so that the number of disabled persons does not shrink, but is actually growing. Nor are the figures in Table 1 merely numbers—each of the table's totals is composed of *individual* sufferers, and in addition to them there are their families, others who are important to them, their social networks, all of whom are in some way affected by their condition. So the number of "patients" and their affected intimates is both very great and almost incalculable.

Of course, degrees of disability vary greatly, both within specific categories and from one disability to another. Moreover, the definitions, standards, and classifications of disability used for technical assessment and legal purposes change. The case of the blind is an example: there were 525,136 legally blind persons in 1980 and about 1,500,000 additional classified as having "severely impaired vision." The standards alter so that members of the latter group may at times move into the former. Deafness has never been satisfactorily or permanently defined: 551,550 persons, in 1980, were called totally deaf, but 15.6 million additional persons have hearing impairments in one or both ears sufficient to impede their communication.

A highly problematic area of classification is that of mental retardation, despite many decades of scientific study and conceptualization, with successive terminologies and classification schemes being proposed and adopted about every twenty years. In 1963, President Kennedy's Commission on Mental Retardation proposed the adoption of the scheme that is still widely used—with the four categories of mild (IQ 52-68), moderate (36-51), severe (20-35), and profound (below 20)—but there is much questioning of this scheme. There have been extensive criticisms of the inherent biases of the intelligence tests employed, and some important scholars, such as Jack Tizard in England, have concluded that it is impossible to devise a culture-free IQ test. Many U.S. scientists decry the use of the mild category of retardation and believe it should be abandoned, since, in their view, it reflects primarily the absence of social opportunity and discriminatory labeling of the socially deprived.

It is generally proposed that classifications of degree of disability should be based on functional or performance criteria, rather than on predetermined diagnosis or purely physiological indicators. A functional view of disability is essentially a dynamic one. Changes in performance ability may reflect growth and development, the effects of therapy, or social-psychological changes resulting in heightened motivation. Much of the social stereotyping of the disabled has arisen from diagnostic assessments that were essentially static and did not allow for changes from any or all of these assessments.

This book was conceived and a good deal of it written prior to the November 1980 elections. As is well-known, the subsequent health policy directions and recommendations to the Congress of the Reagan administration involve a major philosophical shift and call for massive decentralization and rollbacks of many federal programs and agencies. Financing of personal health care services, of many social service programs such as food stamps and school lunches, of programs to regulate environmental and occupational health hazards, of social-behavioral research, of health professional training, and many others have been reduced, with administration of them shifted to the states. In addition to the immediate reductions and reorganizations, the Reagan administration has announced its intention to abolish the federal Department of Education, which, since 1978, has administered and financed many of the programs for disabled persons that will be discussed in this volume. As of this writing, not all these proposals have been effectuated by congressional action, but their general thrust is clear, and they will certainly be implemented to some extent, although debate and negotiation about them will continue.

In such a volatile and changing political and economic climate, it is difficult to present definitive materials about the current status of the publicly-financed programs. A number of the federal services for disabled persons are now to be administered under the "block grant" concept, which permits each state to allocate monies to particular programs and to determine the type and level of services provided. It is not yet possible to know in detail how the disabled in the United States will fare in general or in individual states, yet it is already clear, from the changed political climate in Washington, D.C. and in many state capitals, that they will generally receive less money and fewer services in the immediate future than in the decade preceding the Reagan administration.

A HANDBOOK
OF SERVICES
FOR THE
HANDICAPPED

PHYSICAL CARE SERVICES FOR THE HANDICAPPED

1

For nearly two hundred years attempts have been made in this country to devise effective medical programs that would restore health and functioning to seriously handicapped members of the population. For over sixty years centralized governmental leadership has been directed toward this goal. Only during the past few decades, however, have notable strides been made in developing medical rehabilitative services that are remotely comparable with the achievements in other phases of medicine.

The current vitality can be traced to several sources. Renewed interest originates principally from national attention given to hundreds of thousands of wounded veterans returning from World War II and two subsequent military conflicts. Immense gains in medical technology and disease control are partly responsible; yet paradoxically, these advances have resulted in the creation of new problems. Lengthened life span and decreased early mortality have resulted in a larger segment of the population with continuing disability.

Recent governmental concern has been prompted because the enormous drains incurred in supporting over twenty million disabled Americans have jeopardized the soundness of state and federal generic income-maintenance programs. Other responses have occurred in the components, specializations, and organization of medicine. New disciplines have emerged, some largely independent specialties, others closely allied to the medical profession. Hospital organization has diversified, and new departments of rehabilitation and home care are commonplace. An entire new industry of professionally staffed nursing homes has been established, and in 1981 over 20,000 disabled people obtained rehabilitation services from these skilled nursing facilities each day.

The surge in public awareness, medical advances, and community needs has been paralleled by alterations in the concept of rehabilitation itself. From its original designation and acceptance simply as the "third phase of medicine," rehabilitation has become recognized as a multidimensional activity, necessitating a holistic approach to disability. Important though the various elements of care are, the fundamental need of a disabled person is first to survive and have stabilized health. This chapter will outline the normative ways by which chronic disease or impairment may be detected, and the medical, or physical care services that people will use when they become disabled and, in all probability, that they will continue to need.

DEFINITIONS

Activities of daily living, or ADL, is the ability to carry out, unassisted, personal activities such as eating, toileting, dressing, moving around, and bathing. This ability is also known as *self-care* and *functional independence*.

Diagnosis consists of the analysis of a problem or condition, identifying it by name, recommending or prescribing a course of treatment, and predicting the likely outcome or prognosis.

Direct care means any service given directly to a disabled person during the rehabilitation program.

Equipment refers to mechanical aids such as beds with motor controls, hoists, adapted kitchen equipment, special chairs, and remote control apparatus.

Inpatient is an individual who is hospitalized.

Medical services include any type of care or treatment that is given or prescribed by a physician.

Orthotic device is an orthopedic support, usually a corset or brace. A person who provides such a device is known as an *orthotist*; the appliance is called an *orthosis*.

Outpatient is anyone who receives treatment or care at a hospital but does not stay there on a twenty-four-hour basis. The site of care is known as a hospital *outpatient department* or *clinic*.

Personal physical aids are usually small items that assist in activities of daily living. Examples are special eating utensils, bath and toilet aids, adapted household gadgets, and modifications in clothing.

Physical care is a broad term describing all services and activities designed to improve a disabled person's medical condition. It includes diagnosis, treatment, prostheses and orthoses, and any aids and equipment that will help the individual resume or acquire physical independence.

Physical rehabilitation describes all activities and therapies required to restore functioning. It includes special treatments such as hydrotherapy and range-of-motion exercises and many other passive and corrective therapies.

Prosthetic device is a substitute or replacement for a missing part of the body. Artificial arms or legs for amputees are, for example, known as *prostheses*. A specialist in this field is known as a *prosthetist*.

Psychological rehabilitation consists of personal counseling, psychotherapy, and social support. The goals are usually self-acceptance, cooperation in the rehabilitative effort, and adjustment to the problems of disability.

Rehabilitation is the systematic process that occurs between the onset of disability and the acquisition of maximum self-functioning.

Rehabilitation services or care includes the entire array of help needed to attain or restore physical, mental, social, and vocational functioning.

Rehabilitation team includes all medical and nonmedical people who assist the disabled person in reaching goals of independence. The team may include an internist, surgeon, physiatrist, psychiatrist, social worker, speech therapist, psychologist, work evaluator, and rehabilitation counselor.

Secondary disability is a medical problem that occurs as the result of the primary injury or disease. Examples are bedsores, incontinence, and mental depression.

Social rehabilitation is assistance aimed at improving a disabled person's relationships with other people and adaptation to community life.

Therapy is synonymous with treatment. A therapist is an individual who gives treatment, either on a person-to-person basis or in groups.

Vocational rehabilitation means any service that will help a disabled person get a job. This rehabilitation may involve counseling, testing, job training, and sheltered workshop experience. A person skilled in this specialty is known as a *vocational rehabilitation counselor* or *rehabilitation counselor.*

DEVELOPMENT OF PHYSICAL CARE GOALS

Medical goals in the treatment of disabilities are divided into critical, acute, and long-term categories. Each is descriptive of specific patient need and also relates to a phase of care. Commonality is shared in three respects, through stabilization of physical condition, restoration of lost functioning, and prevention of secondary disability. The direction and degree of emphasis expended on each concern depend on the extent of the physical damage sustained and the specific medical technology and specialized skills needed to maintain life and promote healing of the lesion. Emphasis continually shifts as successive levels of recovery are reached.

CRITICAL-CARE GOALS

At the most crucial level of patient need, the uppermost goal is to stop a perilous physical condition. Accidents and injuries require emergency procedures that usually preclude a thoughtful assessment of long-term physical effects. The slower manifestation of chronic disease, however, permits an evaluation of which medical and surgical interventions will lead to the highest quality of life for the disabled person. This goal is achieved through specific objectives that are medically feasible, technically sound, acceptable to the patient, conducive to independence, and cosmetically and socially acceptable.

ACUTE-CARE GOALS

At the post-surgical level of patient care, the predominant goal is to assure recovery and the continuation of body processes. Medical and nursing efforts are the same for patients who face permanent disability as they are for any acutely ill person who has undergone radical medical or surgical intervention. In most hospitals, when a patient improves, he is moved from a specialized department, such as a critical care, cardiac care, or intensive care unit, to one that is less technically oriented. Goals are then established successively in relation to the disabled person's progress in recovering from the critical phase of care.

LONG-TERM CARE GOALS

The primary goals at this level are to prepare the patient for hospital discharge and return to a normal environment. The skills the patient should attain are established by a multidisciplinary team, which should include the patient and important family members. The team writes a rehabilitation plan, giving goals intermediate objectives, and a time sequence for achievement of the agreed upon goals. The list of goals may be long or short, depending upon the functional abilities the disabled person still retains. Invariably, goals are developed commensurate with need. They follow a sequential pattern that can be graphically illustrated as progressively leading from a status of dependency to ultimate functional and social self-sufficiency. See Figure 1.

LEVELS OF PHYSICAL CARE

In all of the nation's nearly seven thousand hospitals, patients are categorized by their particular needs and the specialized services, medical, surgical, or rehabilitation that they receive. Wards or departments are also classified by identical, or similar, terminology, thus denoting the type of services

FIGURE 1. FROM DEPENDENCY TO SELF-SUFFICIENCY

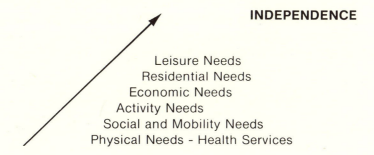

INDEPENDENCE

Leisure Needs
Residential Needs
Economic Needs
Activity Needs
Social and Mobility Needs
Physical Needs - Health Services

DEPENDENCE

needed by a patient and provided in a particular hospital unit. When a patient is hospitalized for a disabling condition, an additional set of subcategories, or levels of care is used; however, neither the number of ascribed levels nor their terminology is consistent from hospital to hospital. This adjunctive classification system is presumed to specify a patient's level of recovery. When the system was established, the theory was that new therapies could be added only after a certain level of recovery had been reached. In practice, a patient's progress or regression to a different level alerts medical personnel to be watchful for new physical problems. However, the complexities of, and the rationale behind, this multiple classification scheme are understandably confusing to disabled people who are hospitalized. *Levels of care and the designation of rehabilitation as a defined service area are anachronisms that go back many years.* Today they appear largely irrelevant. Although rehabilitation services may be considered distinctive or special, that is only because they deal with long-term impairments. *There is no valid basis for isolating either the field or the patients therein from a hospital's customary range of services. Modern conceptions of rehabilitation properly consider all forms of care as logical components of general medical care, and from the inception of a problem the aspects of restoration, maintenance, and prevention should be an ongoing part of a patient's life.*

The levels of rehabilitative care described here, critical physical intervention, restoration to functional capacity, and continued support of functioning, are composites of what is usually observed.

CRITICAL PHYSICAL INTERVENTION

The onset of chronic disease and disability, unless of congenital origin, is typically a slow process beginning with symptoms that, over time, provoke the suffering person to seek diagnosis and relief. If symptoms are ignored, recognition of illness may await a dramatic and decisive manifestation, making medical attention imperative. Serious injury usually provokes immediate, urgent problems requiring professional aid and intervention. Care at the critical level of physical intervention is concentrated on the immediate application of medical and surgical measures to save life, restrain the spread of lesion, and repair organic damage.

The kinds of care required depend upon several factors. Uppermost is the extent of physical injury or "insult," the organs affected, and the prognosis for recovery. Although basic measures may be started in a physician's office, at home, or in a hospital emergency room, the full range of technical equipment and professional assistance needed is available only in the specialized facilities of hospital medical and surgical wards. Hospitalization is mandated when physical damage is extensive or profound.

Although survival and physical improvement are obvious and fundamental concerns, attentiveness to the acute aspects of patient care does not preclude simultaneous and equal attention to subsequent patient needs. Modern concepts of total patient care stress the importance of early instruction in order to obtain and ensure the best results from rehabilitation. Not all, nor perhaps the majority of disabled people, need a formal, distinctive hospital rehabilitation program. However, when basic rehabilitative *activities* are not prescribed for chronically ill patients as part of early treatment or at diagnosis for persons with handicapping conditions, that absence is detrimental and regrettable. Experience indicates that early implementation of such activities significantly broadens the scope of maximum functioning and hastens its achievement. If a disabled person is to be restored to a condition where he can resume a normal life, rehabilitative activities should commence parallel to, rather than following, acute medical and surgical care. Even in severe or acute cases, some passive activities, designed to maintain function and prevent deterioration because of immobility, are appropriate.

RESTORATION TO FUNCTIONAL CAPACITY

At the intermediate level of recuperation, a comprehensive rehabilitation plan is developed, and patients can expect a wide range of therapies to be instituted. This phase is the most closely identified with rehabilitation, and it is chiefly responsible for the perception of rehabilitation as a separate area of medical concern. When the patient progresses to this level, attention can be aggressively focused on the patient's restoration and gaining of new skills. For most patients, the period is characterized by ambivalent feelings of futility, depression, and alternately, hope. The terminology that hospitals have created for this phase includes "disability limitation," "preventive rehabilitation," "short-term ADL training," "physical retraining," "vocational readjustment," "secondary prevention," "tertiary prevention," and the contrasting terms "limited rehabilitation" and "intensive rehabilitation."

The primary goal is for a patient to develop sufficient independence to enable him to return home, reestablish customary routines, and resume normal social behavior. Therapeutic programs are tailored to individual needs. Several may be implemented simultaneously and vigorously. The regimen will consist of programs designed to encourage adaptation to the disability and to prevent secondary disability. Although numerous activities may be involved, the major ones are designed to maintain vital functions, limit disability, strengthen residual capacities, and develop mobility and self-care skills. Activities aimed at maintaining vital functions and limiting disability apply most directly to patients whose long-term goals do not extend beyond bed care or restricted mobility. Activities involving physical and occupational therapy, which have a more universal application to disabled people, will be reviewed here.

STRENGTHENING OF RESIDUAL CAPACITIES

"Rehabilitation," to paraphrase a standard axiom, "is achieved with what remains after disability." Objectives at this level are to restore anatomic and physiological function. If restoration through natural recovery fails, corrective physical therapies are employed to develop compensatory body mechanisms. Exercise is the basic component in these therapies and is part of the rehabilitation plan of every disabled person. When a disabled person is confronted with a tedious and often frustrating exercise regimen, he is likely to rebel or consider it nonessential, and all active therapies are interspersed with relaxation therapy. Therapeutic exercise is medically prescribed and rigorously supervised by a physician, and all therapies are based on the sequential development of muscle strength and neuromuscular coordination.

DEVELOPING MOBILITY AND SELF-CARE

If a handicapped individual is to resume a normal social status and return to a home environment, he must be able to care for himself without assistance. Through training in functions of self-care or functional independence, he must learn to move about, eat, dress, go to the toilet, and care for body cleanliness. Hospitals and rehabilitation centers separate training in self-care into several components. Usually, they include assessing residual abilities, identifying physical limitations, evaluating potential and creating a work plan, and finally, initiating methods to restore self-care. This process, which is known as an "activities of daily living" or "ADL" evaluation, is likely to be started soon after surgery and is conducted by a physical therapist, a social worker, and sometimes a vocational counselor. The evaluation is important for economic, as well as therapeutic reasons, since all public agencies and private insurance companies require a self-care assessment before releasing financial or medical benefits.

Special equipment is required in many instances of disability. Some aids, such as artificial limbs, are medically prescribed and fitted during surgery or soon after. Other mechanical aids, such as enlarged door knobs and tongs for reaching articles, facilitate the performance of ordinary tasks. Equipment is divided into several overlapping categories of therapeutic aids, transportation devices, aids for daily living, working tools and household equipment, and housing modifications. (See Chapter 2). The simplest are those used in developing personal care skills. Plate guards, for instance, are usually indispensible in relearning how to eat and handle solid food, and extensions to comb or toothbrush handles simplify grooming problems. More complex and sophisticated apparatus, designed to improve mobility and movement, has resulted from bioengineering achievements. Misleading inferences may be drawn from the publicity and acclaim heralding these technical advances, however. The use of electronic and sensory-stimulated prostheses is far less common than popularly assumed. Although cost is a major deterrent, the majority of handicapped people do not require radical devices. Highly complicated equipment and aids are prescribed only when medical treatment has failed to restore full physical function and intact body parts are unable to compensate for the injured ones.

CONTINUED SUPPORT, OR
MAINTENANCE, OF FUNCTIONING

Acute medical intervention and restoration to functional capacity may be viewed as preliminary steps in the rehabilitation process. Particularly for the severely disabled, discharge from a formalized hospital-based program represents merely the conclusion of structured rehabilitation. The third or final level of physical care, maintenance of functioning, designates those ongoing activities and supports that will maintain physical strength, prevent regression, and stimulate new gains.

Several terms are used to describe this phase, including "preventive rehabilitation," "tertiary prevention," and "maintenance care." The last term is somewhat objectionable because of its connotation of helplessness, but its use continues, largely because the terminology is used by many government agencies. Another term, "long-term care," is unsuitable because it now carries the implication of institutional placement. Nearly all hospitals provide services called "discharge or post-discharge planning," "after-care," or "follow-up." In large institutions and specialized rehabilitation facilities, these activities may be extensive, but they are usually minimal.

In its largest sense, the maintenance of functioning consists, as the term implies, of maintaining and attempting to improve the level of physical function already achieved by rehabilitation. The underlying conviction is that professional help should not end with discharge from the institution, but should continue as an integral part of patient care in all settings. The goal is to provide uninterrupted or continuous care to the patient after discharge to home as a means of assuring growth and preventing deterioration. Supportive assistance is also required, in most instances, to help the disabled person's family cope with the adjustments and changes accompanying disability. The range and scope of continuing assistance needed for the patient and his family is determined before he leaves the hospital. Assessment usually includes the answers to several questions, such as the following:

1. What help is needed in working out problems of adjustment to home life?
2. Does the physical environment need to be changed?
3. What are the pressing financial needs and where can assistance be obtained?
4. What equipment or special aids are necessary to promote movement and comfort?
5. Does the family need any special instruction?
6. What additional resources are necessary to meet medical, transportation, housing, educational, vocational, social, and recreational needs?
7. What types of specific health care will be needed, now and in the future, and how can they be obtained?
8. Is regression likely? How can it be avoided?
9. Is there a clearly understood mechanism for providing information, follow-up, and referral?
10. Will the hospital take responsibility for maintaining continuity of care? If not, what agency will?

Unfortunately, although continuity of care is a well-established principle, it remains the weakest link in most rehabilitation programs. Contemporary hospital practice assigns the responsibility for uninterrupted care to other agencies. Disabled people will find that many agencies — public, private, and voluntary — are involved in providing continuing care.

DISABILITY DETECTION

The combined causes of birth defect, organic illness, and accident accounted, in 1981, for nearly two million Americans becoming disabled. At any one time there are an estimated ten million people who could achieve a higher degree of rehabilitation. For most, some form of medical care is necessary either as a transitory episode or as a prolonged requirement. The question arises as to how handicapping or potentially disabling conditions are detected and how treatment services are obtained. This section will examine the methods by which a person becomes aware of disability and subsequently obtains medical diagnosis and treatment.

Definitive diagnosis and physical care, or treatment, are provided only by a physician. "Self-referral" is the term often used to describe the act of one's taking direct personal action to obtain medical diagnosis, advice, and aid. Motivation for self-referral is usually the result of personal physical symptoms, but frequently it is initiated by a referral agent. Referral agents are individuals and organizations that occupy strategic health vigilance stations in our society. Individuals may be teachers and school nurses whose work duties include health assessment. Other agents are social and health service organizations that conduct disease detection screening activities. The methods of detection will be reviewed, since key factors such as the stage of the disability when discovered, the age of the person when identified, and the promptness with which treatment is commenced, are all directly related to the outcome of rehabilitative efforts.

SELF-REFERRAL

Self-referral, or personally obtaining medical assessment and care, is the most common method for discovering chronic disease or impairment and for securing medical treatment. Most people seek medical help because of acute and persistent health problems. Progressive disease and disability are usually discovered as a result of acute conditions or because of deviations in health patterns that necessitate medical consultation, through periodic medical examination, and through disease screening tests. Less often, hospitalization for an acute condition reveals other conditions that may cause subsequent disability. Congenital disabilities are regularly detected by physicians in hospitals at the time of birth, or during the mother's pregnancy, since home delivery is no longer the norm and most expectant mothers receive some measure of medical care during the prenatal period.

PHYSICAL EXAMINATION

The chief value of a physical examination is in discovering incipient disease or disabling conditions. Despite massive public education efforts, periodically scheduled health examinations are not common in our society for either children or adults. Of the nation's 57,775,000 children under 17 years of age in 1980, half had not been examined by a physician in two years. Adults under age 65 obtain medical examinations even less frequently. The exceptions to this pattern, for both groups, are members of health maintenance plans, or when medical examinations are provided as an employee or executive health service. The costs of a thorough examination, including tests and physician services, are not usually covered by health insurance and present financial barriers to those in lower economic brackets. Most people in America do not see a physician until alarmed by a symptom or ever-worsening health problem. Alternative detection methods, such as community-based programs to discover people-at-risk, have developed as a response to this reality.

HEALTH SCREENING SURVEYS

Screening for the presence of disease or its precursors has always been an integral part of health care. Testing of newborns, a particularly effective form of screening, is routinely conducted in hospitals at the time of birth. Some kinds of screening tests, such as vision testing in the schools, have long been performed by personnel other than physicians. In a screening survey, single or multiple tests are applied to a selected group of people to determine those who have evidence of, or who have a high risk of incurring, certain diseases or disabling conditions. The most common screening tests are those designed to detect specific conditions such as diabetes, vision and hearing problems, hypertension, and cervical cancer. Mass screening programs are conducted by voluntary health agencies, public health departments, community hospitals, self-help and consumer groups, and public schools. Screening programs are directed at diverse populations or target groups. Surveys may be conducted using mobile units in neighborhoods or industries, among school children, children who are public welfare recipients, or among residents of nursing homes and other long-term care facilities. They may be infrequent and occasional or continuing services offered by public and private agencies at specified locations. Large business corporations frequently provide employees with a range of health tests, either as a condition of employment or as a benefit offered, and often in conjunction with a local health organization. Although well-baby clinics and even school health programs are declining nationwide, the screening services given by these agencies in the past have decisively improved the life course of thousands of children whose disabilities would otherwise have remained undetected and untreated.

Shared employee and employer concern over the problems of long-term disability has resulted in many screening programs for the early identification of handicaps. These preventive and detection services have existed since the 1920s, preceding those offered by public health departments. Organized labor, however, has been the strongest influence in making employee screening programs a common part of every community's health structure.

As a rule, screening is not conducted specifically for union members, except in sizeable local organizations that maintain a special health department or office. The bulk of union effort has been in financially underwriting the costs of detection provided by voluntary health agencies and in taking a national leadership role in the development of comprehensive health plans. Health insurance costs may be paid from membership dues, or employers may prepay them as part of a labor contract. If the insurance plan is with a private insurance carrier, union members have three options. They may select their own physician; the union will provide a roster of recommended physicians; or the union will refer the member to a specific practitioner or physician group. Union members and their families are encouraged to obtain regular physical examinations.

There is no uniform pattern in the screening services provided by business and industrial organizations. The range varies by company size, medical and personnel policies, benefits of employee health plans, work hazards, and the availability of other community resources. Large national corporations usually have a medical department or nursing unit at their central and regional offices. Although the services offered are not comprehensive, some degree of screening and disease detection is generally provided. Either single-disease testing or multiphasic screening programs may be available, and the technology tends to be sophisticated. Test results are usually reported to the employee by a physician or nurse. If there is evidence of disease, "company referrals" are usually explicit in recommending specific private physicians who may be consulted, and periodic follow-up will be made to assure that this occurs.

Over the past decade, many local and state departments of public health developed large-scale applications of a combined battery of several screening tests, or multiphasic screening, as part of their community health programs. Generally, screening is done to detect sensory impairments, coronary or hypertension problems, pulmonary function disability, anemia, and delays in childhood development. The number of these programs has greatly diminished in the past two years because of decreases in government financial support. Departments of public health now largely restrict their screening activities to participants of a federal program, Early and Periodic Screening, Diagnosis, and Treatment (EPSDT).

This nationwide screening program started in 1967 when Congress amended Title XIX of the Social Security Act. States were required to provide "early and periodic screening, diagnosis, and treatment" to all children under 21 who were eligible for Medicaid, primarily recipients of the Aid to Families with Dependent Children (AFDC) program. EPSDT was enacted at the recommendation of a Department of Health, Education, and Welfare task force that had been appointed to review a Selective Service study reporting a high prevalence of chronic handicapping conditions among young men. More than 15 percent of 18-year-olds had been rejected for the draft because of hearing, vision, dental, orthopedic, emotional, and developmental problems. The Department estimated that over 60 percent of these conditions were preventable and correctable through comprehensive and continuous care and at least 33 percent through a program based on early-age periodic screening. The latter was chosen as the most cost-effective route.

In 1972 Congress, concerned over the sluggish implementation of EPSDT, required all states to screen children who were receiving AFDC payments. States and local counties were permitted to contract with local departments of public health and other local organizations to provide outreach, screening, diagnosis, treatment, case management, and transportation. The Department of Health and Human Services, formerly DHEW, reported in 1980 that over 2.1 million children had been screened that year.

As with all screening programs conducted under any auspice, testing conducted by departments of public health as an ongoing or "crash" program, or as a Medicaid service, is not diagnostic but suggestive of the presence of disability. When individuals' tests are positive, a nurse at the public health agency advises them, usually by mail, to obtain more definitive medical assessment. This notification of positive findings is usually called an "agency referral," and the phrase is used widely in the medical community. The popularity of its usage is based on two interpretations which, in turn, are assumed to evoke two responses. Agency referral implies, first, that the evidence of disease, or its potentiality, within a person has been discovered by an "official" agency. The other is that a governmental agency is responsible for recommending that the individual obtain more thorough examination from a private doctor. When informed by an official agency that disease is suspected, participants in screening programs are believed to infer a sense of urgency about their condition and thus promptly seek medical care. Private physicians, and their office admitting personnel, are expected to be equally impressed and preemptively admit as a patient someone who comes as an "agency referral."

All health screening concentrates on distinct and overt physical problems, and, as a consequence, conditions that tend to be diffuse and unspecific in their effects will likely escape detection. Experience with Medicaid's EPSDT program shows that one-time screening programs identify only existing health problems and fail to discover those that reveal themselves over time. Concern has also been expressed over the specialization of screening programs that focus on specific diseases or conditions and over the necessity for consolidating services into an inclusive assessment program. Such questioning is relevant, but the benefits derived from surveys must also be acknowledged. In the absence of nationally supported comprehensive health surveillance programs for the entire population, few other disease detection services are available to the majority of people.

The merit of any screening and detection programs depends on the adequacy and diligence of the sponsoring agency's follow-up efforts to obtain comprehensive medical examination for individuals who have been tentatively identified. Screening itself is only the first step toward the goal of minimizing disability. Definitive diagnosis and treatment, the next steps, need to be obtained.

DISABILITY DIAGNOSIS AND TREATMENT

Symptom diagnosis, confirmation of screening test results, and treatment are performed by physicians in private practice or by physicians who serve on a hospital outpatient department or emergency room staff.

PRIMARY CARE PHYSICIANS

Most people receive medical service by going to a primary care physician, usually an internist or general practitioner, where they are examined, diagnosed, and, most often given treatment or a prescription. When a medical condition is complex or symptoms are diffuse, the process becomes more intricate and includes a series of medical referral points. Although most people, and particularly those who are disabled, are aware of the medical referral process and its origin in medical specialization, the process can be perplexing and disconcerting to a prospective patient and his family if not clearly understood from the outset.

Referral points literally involve referring a patient to another physician, whose specialization is appropriate to his or her needs. More than one referral may be made. If a patient's disability manifestly requires substantial medical care, the primary physician may enlist the diagnostic and curative assistance of several other specialists or consultants. Unless the patient requires immediate hospitalization, he is expected to meet individually with each referred specialist. Each specialist reports diagnostic findings back to the primary physician, and eventually treatment is started. If the patient is hospitalized, the consultants are brought in.

When treatment begins, several approaches may be taken. The primary physician may conduct the treatment, often, again, with the advice of specialists. Full responsibility for the patient may be transferred to another physician, whose specialty most encompasses the patient's medical problems, or a team approach may be used, with one specialist assuming patient supervision and liaison. Responsibility for medical follow-up generally follows a similar pattern.

Medical or physician referral is pervasive in Western medicine in general, but it is particularly characteristic of the American medical system. It is rooted in the basic proclivity of physicians to specialize in their activities, perhaps for enhancing their skills and keeping abreast of advancing technology. Specialization, or overspecialization, as this predominant tendency is sometimes termed, has resulted in the segmenting of total health care into special areas of concern. For physicians, specialization may concentrate on the study of specific organs, as in dermatology, otolaryngology, or ophthalmology; categorical body systems or functions, as in neurology and urology; technical abilities and skills, as exemplified by the various surgical specialties and radiology, anesthesiology, plastic surgery, and physical medicine and rehabilitation; phases or aspects of human life, as in pediatrics; disease entities, such as oncology or allerology; or a combination of body process and organic structure, as in obstetrics and gynecology. Many subspecialties, such as cardiology, occupational medicine, and geriatrics, have also evolved. Specialization is acquired through advanced study and training over and above the regular medical curriculum. A physician is certified as a diplomate after passing an examination for proficiency in a certain area of medical care. Recognition of specialty areas, the study and training involved, and the certification of diplomate status are carefully regulated by the American Medical Association.

The pervasiveness of specialization in medical care is not confined to physicians alone, but is also evident in the proliferation of medically related professions and in the development of special hospitals and specialized departments within general hospitals. However, physicians alone are responsible for diagnosis, prescription, and the entire medical management of a patient. Although members of many professions are part of a rehabilitation team, their roles are subsidiary to that of the doctor. Referral to a specialist is, with few exceptions, made solely on a physician-to-physician basis, and definitive entry into a diagnostic and treatment system is effected only by a physician.

HOSPITAL EMERGENCY ROOMS AND OUTPATIENT CLINICS

Although a personal physician is still normative, hospital emergency rooms and outpatient departments are being used increasingly as a source of diagnosis and treatment. In the past, low-income people were the major users of these health care resources, but this is no longer the case. Today use of these facilities is more related to the severity of symptoms and the greater awareness nationally of the emergency room as part of the medical care system. However, acute illness, accident, and injury still account for most emergency room admissions.

Patients visit hospital outpatient clinics for a constellation of medical, economic, and social-psychological reasons. Predisposing medical conditions tend to be those that have not yielded to standard forms of treatment or home remedies, are resulting in progressive impairment, are generalized in nature, or divergently, are specific in their effect and body locus. Reasons attributable to personal attitudes, community beliefs, and public perceptions are difficult to determine. However, clinic care is now frequently viewed as a chosen option and not as an economically unavoidable recourse; and although outpatient care is generally regarded as a less costly substitute for private care, clinic patients often see it as being of equal or superior quality to private care. Convenience is another factor in its selection. The nearness of general and specialized clinics in adjacent hospital buildings reduces transportation problems, time off from work, and the physical exertion and expense involved in seeing various private specialists in different locations. As a result of media coverage and informal information sources, the general public has increasing knowledge about what constitutes appropriate medical care, how it is procured, and how medical systems operate. When deciding on disability diagnosis and treatment by clinics or by private practitioners, people consider (a) the likelihood of being accepted as a patient, (b) the number of patients with similar problems the clinic or doctor has seen, (c) the clinic's or doctor's reputation for success in cure or recovery, and (d) the willingness of doctors to care for people for whom "cure" in the usual sense may not be an objective.

SETTINGS OF PHYSICAL CARE TREATMENT SERVICES

In 1980, the year of most current reporting, over eight million Americans between the ages of sixty-five and seventy-four were hospitalized for problems caused by chronic disease. During the same year, over a million other Americans of all ages required hospital services because of extensive disability. Whereas most people's chances of being hospitalized increase as they age, disabled people share the likelihood that they will require hospital care at various periods throughout their lives.

For everyone, whether or not disabled, being hospitalized, even when it is anticipated because of advance medical warning, provokes some degree of anxiety and apprehension. These normal concerns are compounded by the strangeness and the complex impersonality of the hospital environment. The provision of continuing health care after hospital discharge is equally intimidating, and if special living arrangements are necessitated, new problems arise. In the United States, physical care for the disabled involves a multiplicity of systems, agencies, and facilities for treatment, continued support, and residence. No single pattern predominates, since the sites of care are influenced by economic and geographic factors and availability as well as by the type and extent of impairment. The following review of the normative services and sites will include those variations and alternatives most frequently encountered.

HOSPITAL-BASED SERVICES

Other than in the use of emergency care facilities, acutely ill patients do not have complete latitude in selecting the hospital where they will be treated. Hospitals only admit patients directly for emergency room care or, if warranted, for a few hours of observation. Admission for diagnostic studies, treatment, and surgery is made by a physician who has privileges to practice in a particular institution. If a patient requires critical medical interventions and does not have a private physician, a member of the hospital's house staff will examine the patient and then admit him and assume responsibility for medical care. Most physicians have privileges in several hospitals, but if a patient prefers a hospital where his physician has not been granted privileges, he must either go to some other hospital or obtain another physician.

There are many kinds of hospitals throughout the nation. Hospitals are classified by service type, average length of stay, and by ownership. Service types include general, acute, psychiatric, mental retardation, TB/respiratory diseases, OB/gyn, rehabilitation, orthopedic, chronic disease, and eye, ear, nose and throat hospitals. A few others, such as children's hospitals, are restricted to specific age groups. Length of stay indicates whether the hospital is long-term or short-term. Ownership varies among hospitals which are owned and operated by the federal government or by state and local governments, investor-owned, and nongovernmental not-for-profit. The term community hospital means institutions which are nonfederal and provide acute-short-term services. They may be nongovernmental not-for-profit, investor-owned, or owned by state and local governments. The majority of all hospitals are publicly or privately supported not-for-profit, and church-related nonprofit facilities. The kind of ownership, however, only indicates tax-exempt or profit status and has little relationship to the costs of care.

Critical care for most acutely ill people is given in a short-term general, or community, hospital, either in the medical and surgical wards or in the emergency treatment room. Most patients are discharged after six or seven days, but patients with serious impairments may expect three or four weeks of hospitalization. Various types of rehabilitation training may be started during this period. The scope tends to vary with institutional size. Most of the nation's 5,904 short-term hospitals offer some physician and other therapist-provided services plus medical social work assistance. But a comprehensive rehabilitation program will be provided only in one of the approximately seven hundred hospitals that have a full range of therapies.

Although the length of hospitalization varies with the extent of disability and the patient's rate of recovery, it is also based on how the hospital costs are paid. Hospital care is expensive, and basic daily charges, exclusive of ancillary charges and professional fees, nationally hovered around $400 in 1981. In some states the average daily cost is higher; and, of course, costs dramatically soar with a patient's need for intensive and specialized care. For most people who were admitted to a hospital in 1981 for nonintensive procedures, their average bill upon discharge was $2,500. In an effort to curtail costs, governmental programs such as Medicaid and Medicare restrict payment to a maximum number of days and there are current proposals to make further reductions. Private insurance plans and health maintenance organizations, such as the Kaiser-Permanente Health Plan, discourage prolonged hospitalization through the use of a "financial disincentive." That is, a patient is responsible for an increasing share of payment as the hospital stay continues, and even the period of shared payment is limited. The expense of hospitalization and the development of new concepts in patient care have resulted in innovative methods for continuing rehabilitation and medical care after the acute phases of treatment and recovery have ended.

Contemporary rehabilitation practice emphasizes the ultimate return of a patient to his home, but at the point of discharge from a hospital, there may be several intermediate possibilities: a convalescent hospital, a long-term rehabilitation hospital, or a short-term rehabilitation facility. The first two may also be used for permanent placement or for a series of temporary stays. Placement sequences may follow various patterns:

Acute hospital → home
Acute hospital → convalescent hospital
Acute hospital → convalescent hospital → home
Acute hospital → convalescent hospital → rehabilitation hospital
Acute hospital → convalescent hospital → rehabilitation hospital → home
Acute hospital → rehabilitation hospital
Acute hospital → rehabilitation hospital → home
Acute hospital → rehabilitation hospital → convalescent hospital
Acute hospital → rehabilitation hospital → convalescent hospital → home

The selection of successive or permanent placement sites is determined by the patient's need for continued specialized treatment, the availability of outpatient rehabilitation services from a hospital or community agency, and the willingness of the patient's family to adapt themselves and the home environment to the patient's rehabilitation needs. Selection of a placement site is a collaborative decision made by a patient and his family, with recommendations from the physician and hospital rehabilitation staff. The majority of disabled people leave medical and surgical wards, return home, and continue rehabilitation on an outpatient basis. If home care is not feasible or if it must be delayed until recovery has improved, one of the above patterns will be followed.

OUTPATIENT SERVICES

One-third of all hospitals in the United States offer some type of basic outpatient rehabilitation care, and seven hundred conduct comprehensive programs. Most of the latter are situated in the east and west coast states, but well-rounded services may be found in large hospitals of any sizable city. Hospital rehabilitation centers, as such outpatient departments are some-times called, now constitute the major resource for rehabilitation throughout the nation. Annually, over 350,000 disabled people obtain services from them, making an aggregate of 76 million outpatient visits.

In contrast to outpatient *diagnostic* clinics, rehabilitation treatment is usually given in a single, unified department. When necessary, specialized techniques, equipment, and the professional personnel of all hospital departments will be utilized. As a rule, outpatient departments bearing the name "rehabilitation center" are capable of meeting the needs of severely disabled patients. All disabled patients, hospitalized or discharged to home or another type of residence, share the same rehabilitation facilities, therapies, and professional services. A great value of outpatient care lies in the assurance of continuous care from the original hospital source.

CONVALESCENT HOSPITALS

Continuity of care can also be ensured by partial hospitalization. Generally, such hospitalization is in convalescent hospitals or, as they are now called under licensing and certification requirements, "skilled nursing facilities" or simply "SNF's." These institutions differ from acute-short-term hospitals in that they do not have facilities for diagnosis or acute and emergency medical care. Rather, their emphasis is on continuing nursing and other supportive care under medical supervision.

Many types of small facilities are confusingly included under the general term "convalescent hospital," but they have little similarity to a skilled nursing facility. Traditionally family-operated, their business names usually include phrases such as nursing home, rehabilitation home, and, frequently, convalescent home. Particularly in the past, they had the pejorative reputation of being either a lifetime residence or permanent depository for the severely disabled. In most instances, these small businesses operate as a long-term boarding house for the aged and infirm.

Skilled nursing facilities serve two distinct functions: short-term rehabilitation and long-term care. In either capacity, a facility must be licensed by a state agency if any part of its revenue comes from federal programs. To qualify for governmental financial reimbursement, the facility must have a written agreement with at least one acute care hospital, providing for transfer of patients between them. Each year, an increasing number of hospitals develop long-term patient care facilities of their own. Currently, about a thousand hospitals operate skilled nursing homes.

REHABILITATION HOSPITALS

Shifting concepts of care for the treatment of disability have greatly reduced the number of long-term and specialized institutions that once flourished throughout the nation. Most long-term hospitals now are for the mentally retarded or psychiatric patients, and they tend to have a custodial function. The few remaining hospitals specialize in orthopedic, alcoholism, children's, respiratory, chronic disease, including cancer, and eye, ear, nose, and throat, conditions.

Chronic care and rehabilitation hospitals are designed for severely disabled patients. All, or various types of, handicapping conditions may be treated, or treatment may be confined to a specific disability such as spinal cord injuries and amputations. Disabled patients require these specialized facilities when life-support and attendant care is necessary or an extensive and profound disability requires a highly technical rehabilitation program. In the United States, there are now 73 inpatient rehabilitation hospitals and 56 that specialize in the treatment of chronic diseases. On any day they are occupied by some thirty thousand patients. The use of these alternatives as a successor to an acute general hospital is not based, however, only on patient need, but also on geographic factors. Most of these hospitals are located along the eastern seaboard, and the overall number of such specialized facilities has declined nationwide since 1975. This reduction is a result of, and a stimulus to, the expansion of community hospitals into this once-specialized role and the development of private agency and governmental home health care programs. Unfortunately, there is mounting evidence that the federal government's financial support of home health care services will be decreased by the present administration.

COMMUNITY-BASED TREATMENT SERVICES

For the severely and multiply handicapped, living in a community is a realistic possibility only if various therapies provided by skilled personnel are systematically available in the home and from near-at-hand sources. Some of the services that must be available include physician care; nursing; dental care; medical social services; laboratory assessments; nutrition monitoring; aids and equipment; physical, occupational, speech, audiology, inhalation, and other therapies; homemaker or health aide assistance. In addition, day health or outpatient hospital care may be required, and home-delivered meals and special transportation may be needed on either a constant or intermittent basis.

Community living is often hindered by the elaborate and varied organization and auspices of rehabilitation care in the United States, by the uneven geographical distribution of facilities, and by the need to rely upon the mixture of public and private efforts. The person who must unify many separately provided and fragmented community services into a comprehensive support system for rehabilitants will find the task demanding and challenging.

Hospitals, of course, provide the range of physical care services needed by the severely disabled. In addition, some other resources are available, but their limitations must be kept in mind.

This section will discuss community-based facilities that are not directly linked to a hospital. Such services are provided by three types of organizations: tax-supported agencies, private or voluntary organizations, and commercial enterprises. Each type of organization is involved, to some degree, in the provision of long-term rehabilitation. The organizations are also interrelated by funding and shared programs. Government agencies, for example, purchase professional services and rehabilitation equipment from voluntary health groups and private businesses. Through contractual arrangements or direct purchase, state and national medical programs delegate patient rehabilitation care to local practitioners, agencies, and hospitals.

VOLUNTARY HEALTH AGENCIES AND
EDUCATIONAL SERVICES

All voluntary health agencies provide some ingredients of rehabilitation care, but these services are typically piecemeal and often in rudimentary form. Generally the range of services available is directly related to the size of the agency, whether it is voluntary or privately owned, and to the population of the community. For the most part, disease-specific voluntary health agencies (such as those devoted to cancer, heart disease, and respiratory impairment) tend to place more emphasis on public education, prevention, and professional training than on direct therapeutic assistance.

Most of the few comprehensive rehabilitation centers existing nationwide that are not hospital-related and do not require membership in a health maintenance organization are operated by chapters of national voluntary health agencies that were originally established to meet the rehabilitative needs of handicapped children. Physical care assistance is an essential program of most affiliates of the National Easter Seal Society, United Cerebral Palsy Association, and the Association for Retarded Citizens.

When one attempts to discover where and what help is available, his search can be expedited if he inquires from information and referral services of public social service or welfare departments or at the nursing division of the local public health department. Classified telephone directory listings under "rehabilitation" indicate generic voluntary and for-profit organizations in the community or region, but they usually omit governmental programs. Individual practitioners are listed under "physical therapy" and "occupational therapy."

HOME HEALTH AGENCIES

For disabled people who are living independently, with family members, or in communal living arrangements, home health agencies are a limited but valuable source of physical care, providing many of the comprehensive therapeutic and nursing services required in rehabilitation. The term "home health agency" is confusing, however, since it has both a generic and specific reference. Home health agencies developed as a consequence of Social Security Act amendments in 1965 establishing the national Medicare and Medicaid programs. At that time, the majority of agencies were the already well-established visiting nurse associations and the nursing units of county public health departments. In 1981 there were about 2,500 home health agencies; however, under the present federal administration the likelihood of continued growth is doubtful. The original participants have been augmented by newly formed hospital-based programs, and many proprietary or for-profit organizations have incorporated as home health agencies. Classified telephone directories list these agencies under the general heading.

The number of home health agencies is not a precise reflection of the range and accessibility of services. Nursing care is the primary service. Other in-home services, such as physical therapy, home health aide services, nutritional advice and instruction in food preparation, social work consultation, and speech therapy are not as readily available. Staff size frequently affects the services provided; about one-half of the agencies have three or fewer professional staff members.

DEVELOPMENTAL SERVICES

Developmental training is the aspect of physical care service that is the most readily available throughout the nation. Generally, developmental programs have two divisions: sensory or sensorimotor development for children and physical training for adults. The former is more commonly found, largely because its sponsorship is more diverse. Developmental programs for children with disabilities are conducted by informal groups such as parents of disabled children, by health departments, by hospital pediatric departments, by nursery schools, and by professional associations of nurses and psychologists. Affiliates of national health agencies concerned with permanent disability, such as the United Cerebral Palsy Association, regularly conduct programs for both age groups.

Sensorimotor experience for infants and young children consists of physical manipulation and exercise and the development of discriminatory responses to various stimuli. Physical development for severely disabled adults emphasizes the acquisition of daily living skills and utilization of community transportation systems, or, as it is called, mobility training. In most communities, these programs are designed for the developmentally disabled, but they are open to people with any type of long-term and severe impairment.

FINANCING OF PHYSICAL CARE SERVICES

The financial impact of severe disability is immediate, cumulative, and devastating. The enormous immediate costs of critical medical intervention are enlarged by the consequences of long-term impairment, which invariably brings loss of income and family disruption. The United States remains alone among all industrialized Western nations in failing to have national medical protection for all of its citizens. Landmark federal legislation in

1965, amending the U.S. Social Security Act, was a breakthrough toward a national health insurance system. Yet the programs that were initiated, Medicare and Medicaid, not only have been inadequate and problematical but now are threatened with cutbacks in funding and benefits under proposals of the Reagan administration. The utility of the programs has been counteracted by surging medical and hospital costs, increasing premium payments, and reductions in benefits. Simultaneously, older people require an increased amount of medical and hospital care.

More than 182 million Americans have obtained private insurance protection, either as a total form of coverage or as a means of fortifying against the gaps left in government-sponsored programs. The full range of protection plans is exhaustive; over 1,200 private insurance companies provide individual or group health insurance. Combined federal, state, and local government programs include the two main national programs and those for military personnel and dependents, the Civilian Health and Medical Program of the Uniformed Services (CHAMPUS). Others have been formed for federal civilian employees, veterans' medical care, Indian health services, workers' compensation medical care, and crippled children. With the exception of the native American program and the state-operated workers' compensation medical services, each of these national programs could be adversely affected by the present Administration's efforts to balance the federal budget. Many major financial reductions, included in the 1982 budget, have already diminished the scope of these health programs. Characteristics of the three basic types of programs will be discussed.

PRIVATE INSURANCE

More than eight out of ten people depend entirely or in part upon private health insurance for protection against the financial risks of medical and hospital care. The majority of these, or 167 million persons, are under the age of 65. An additional 15 million older citizens hold private health insurance policies to supplement benefits available through Medicare. Private health insurance coverage is made available in various forms by several different types of insurers. These include commercial insurance provided by indemnity companies, hospital and medical service plans such as Blue Cross and Blue Shield, and group medical plans operating on a prepayment basis, or health maintenance organizations.

DESCRIPTION

Private health insurance coverage falls into two basic categories: insurance against medical expense and disability-income insurance. The first is a reimbursement type of coverage and provides broad benefits, covering virtually all expenses connected with hospital and medical care. Frequently, coverage is only provided for in-hospital services. For a higher premium, both inpatient and outpatient care from either a hospital or private physician will be covered.

Disability-income insurance partially replaces income lost as a result of accident or illness. The amount of the benefit varies, depending upon whether disability is total or partial and the duration for which benefits are payable. There are, in turn, two types of coverage: short-term and long-term. Short-term policies provide benefits from as few as 45 days up to two years. The duration of long-term policies is indefinite, but they are, of course, an expensive option.

During several recent presidential administrations, emphasis was placed on the development of health maintenance organizations. These are agencies that provide comprehensive health care services to members for a fixed periodic payment. In such plans a group of physicians, surgeons, dentists, or other health professionals such as optometrists, furnish needed care as specified in the contract to subscribers.

Group health insurance coverage is also available by plans provided by employers or labor unions, fraternal societies, or consumer health cooperatives. Usually the extent of protection is tailored to the amount desired and affordable by a specific group of people. Benefits tend to be more generous than those provided by private, or individual, insurance policies.

BENEFITS

Nearly all insurance policies require partial payment by the person insured, usually a fixed amount each calendar year and then a percentage thereafter of all costs. The basic amount is frequently called a deductible, and the percentage clause in policies is called coinsurance or deductible as well. Benefits for medical expense are structured into four categories: hospital, surgical, physician, and major medical. Frequently, plans may contain a combination of benefits.

HOSPITAL EXPENSE INSURANCE

Hospital expense insurance usually provides full protection for a wide range of services, for a specified number of days in a hospital, and for emergency care in the outpatient department. If the length of hospital confinement exceeds the days for which full payment is made, insurance coverage is reduced or benefits discounted. The extent of benefits varies with plans and with their costs. The customary types of covered service are:

Inpatient Services

- Semiprivate room, board, and general nursing care
- Use of operating and recovery rooms and equipment

—Laboratory, x-ray, and other examinations

—Oxygen and anesthesia

—Drugs, medicine, dressings, and plaster casts

—Blood transfusions

Outpatient Services

The number of outpatient visits and types of service are always specified, but will include:

—Care for sudden and serious illness

—Treatment for accident and injury

—Minor surgery

—Presurgical tests

SURGICAL EXPENSE INSURANCE

Insurance for surgical expense covers the costs of surgical procedures performed because of accident or sickness. Benefits may be paid according to a schedule of maximum allowances or insurance companies may simply determine if a physician's fee is "reasonable and customary." Types of benefits can include:

—In-hospital physician care

—Surgical services

—General anesthesia

—In-hospital consultations by specialists

—Diagnostic x-rays

—Laboratory tests

—X-ray, radium, and radioisotopic therapies

—Physician home visits for acute illness

—Home health agency services

—Emergency medical aid

PHYSICIAN'S EXPENSE INSURANCE

The term "physician's expense insurance" is new. Formerly it was called regular medical insurance. This insurance tends to be expensive, since there is a likelihood that patients will require physician assistance more frequently than hospitalization. This type of policy may help pay for:

—Physician's fees for nonsurgical care in a hospital, home, or doctor's office

—Diagnostic x-ray

—Laboratory expenses

MAJOR MEDICAL EXPENSE INSURANCE

Major medical insurance protects against the large, unpredictable medical expenses that inevitably accompany catastrophic illness. Maximum benefits range from $100,000 per person, over a lifetime, to as many million dollars' worth of benefits as an insuree wishes to purchase. This type of plan is usually a supplement to other basic insurance coverage. It may be combined with other insurance in a single policy and is then called a comprehensive plan. Benefits can include all care and treatment prescribed by a physician both in and out of a hospital, such as:

—X-ray and laboratory services

—Prescribed drugs and medications

—Nursing care by a professional nurse

—Ambulance service

—Physician's and surgeon's charges

—All hospital services, whether inpatient or outpatient

—Anesthesia

—Surgical services

MEDICARE

After many years of debate, Medicare became effective in 1966 as the nation's first major program for providing hospital and medical insurance to a large part of its population. Medicare is considered "insurance" since participants share in the payment of costs. It was established as an amendment (Title XVIII) to the national Social Security Act and is closely linked to that system for financing and for determining enrollment eligibility. Revisions in major features of the program dealing with eligibility, benefits, and government share of an elderly or disabled person's health costs, have been proposed by the Reagan administration.

DESCRIPTION

The original purpose of Medicare was to give basic hospital and medical protection to persons over 65 who were eligible for Social Security retirement and disability support. Amendments in 1973 eliminated age restrictions in certain instances and extended coverage to additional groups that had been receiving Social Security benefits or were entitled to them. For the first time, eligibility was also extended to people with a specific medical need. The 1973 amendments provided coverage for Social Security beneficiaries, of any age, who had been receiving Disability Insurance benefits for two years and family members who required dialysis treatment or a kidney transplant because of permanent renal damage. Approximately 26 million aged and 3 million disabled Americans, the President's Office of Management and Budget estimates, will be enrolled in the Medicare program during 1983. The federal expenditure is expected to total $55.3 billion, and the president has urged Congress to reduce the scope of the program.

Medicare is separated into two plans: hospital insurance (HI) and supplemental medical insurance (SMI). The hospital portion is always identified as Part A, and the medical as Part B. For each, enrollment procedures, benefits, deductible or coinsurance payments, and, to some extent, eligibility requirements vary.

HOSPITAL INSURANCE ELIGIBILITY

Eligibility for hospital insurance, or Part A, is determined by age and entitlement to Social Security income-maintenance benefits. Most of those who are eligible automatically receive hospital insurance because of "credits or work" accumulated under the basic Social Security system. HI coverage is automatic for:

1. Anyone 65 or over who is eligible for any type of Social Security benefit, either because of contributions made to the system as an employee or because of contributions made by a spouse.
2. Disabled people of any age who have been receiving Social Security or Railroad Retirement Board disability benefits for two consecutive years.
3. Disabled widows or widowers, 50 and older, who have been receiving Social Security checks.
4. People insured under Social Security or the Railroad Retirement Board, and their immediate family members, who require maintenance dialysis or renal transplant.

Someone who is over 65 but ineligible for regular Social Security benefits can purchase hospital insurance.

SUPPLEMENTAL MEDICAL INSURANCE ELIGIBILITY

Eligibility for Medicare hospital insurance implies eligibility for Part B, or medical protection. This insurance is not free, however. It is an option that must be purchased. The enrollment process becomes involved when an individual initially has Part A coverage only and subsequently desires medical insurance. Medicare restricts the period when "partial enrollment" can be accomplished to January, February, and March of each year. Coverage begins the following July. The complexity grows if a person who is 65 but *ineligible* for regular Social Security benefits wishes to purchase Medicare. Part B can be purchased separately, but Part A, hospital insurance, cannot be purchased without Part B.

COSTS OF ENROLLMENT IN MEDICARE

Hospital insurance premiums are deducted from the Social Security checks of people who are receiving benefits from either the Retirement and Survivors Insurance or Disability Insurance portion. People over 65 who are not in these categories can purchase coverage at $113 a month during 1983. Part B, or medical insurance, costs $12.20 monthly, and for people who receive Social Security payments it will be deducted from their monthly check. People over 65 who are not covered by the Social Security program pay the premium directly. Rates for 1983 increased 11.2 percent over the 1982 premium costs. New rate changes go into effect July 1 of each year.

COSTS OF COINSURANCE

HOSPITALIZATION

Medicare HI benefits and charges are based upon a span of illness known as a benefit period. A benefit period begins when a patient first enters a hospital and concludes 60 days after being discharged to home or a skilled nursing facility. A hospital inpatient is responsible for $260 as a basic payment or deductible for each benefit period. If more than 60 days of hospitalization are required, a patient is billed $65 by the hospital for each additional day. When hospitalization extends more than ninety days, a new cost cycle is entered. This cycle involves the "use of lifetime reserve," a bank of 60 available hospital days. Each day of lifetime reserve used costs a patient $130, and Medicare pays all additional expenses. The reserve is nonrenewable.

PHYSICIAN AND MEDICAL COSTS

In addition to premiums, enrollees in Part B pay a base annual cost of $75. Afterward, Supplemental Medical Insurance pays 80 percent of "approved charges" for most services. "Approved charges" is a critical issue in Medicare. Payments are limited to 80 percent of what is considered allowable, and, if a patient's bill is higher than the approved, or allowed amount, he will have to pay the difference in addition to 20 percent of the approved amount. Through an "assignment of claim," a provider agrees to accept the rate approved by Medicare.

BENEFITS — HOSPITALIZATION (PART A)

The major services covered by hospital insurance include:

1. A semiprivate room
2. Meals, including special diets
3. Regular nursing services
4. Costs of special care, such as intensive care and coronary care
5. Drugs provided by the hospital
6. Laboratory tests included in the hospital bill
7. Blood or units of red blood cells
8. X-rays and radiation therapy
9. Medical supplies
10. Use of wheelchair and other appliances
11. Operating and recovery room costs
12. Physical, occupational, and speech therapies and other rehabilitation services

Hospital insurance does not cover physician services, even though these are given in the hospital. Such costs are paid by Medicare through the medical insurance plan.

SKILLED NURSING FACILITY CARE

For patients whose recuperation requires hospital-related care, the hospital insurance program provides twenty days in a skilled nursing facility for each benefit period. If a longer stay is required, a patient must pay $32.50 daily and Medicare pays the remainder. After 100 days Medicare payment ceases and the patient must pay all expenses. Entry into this service is rigorously guarded, and, in addition to the initial medical reasons for discharging a patient to the facility, Medicare requires continuing justification for its use. The services Medicare pays for are:

1. A semiprivate room
2. Meals, including special diets
3. Regular nursing services
4. Rehabilitation services, such as physical, occupational, and speech therapy
5. Drugs furnished by the facility
6. Blood transfusions furnished by the facility
7. Medical supplies such as splints and casts
8. Use of appliances such as a wheelchair

HOME HEALTH CARE

Since January 1982 either hospital insurance or medical insurance can pay for an unlimited number of home health visits. Visits consist of part-time nursing care or physical and speech therapy provided by a home health agency. These services are provided by Medicare only when a patient is confined to home and a physician prescribes them. The services are:

1. Part-time skilled nursing care
2. Physical therapy
3. Speech therapy
4. Occupational therapy
5. Part-time home health aide services
6. Medical social services
7. Medical supplies and equipment

The home health services excluded by Medicare are full-time nursing care, drugs and other medications, home-delivered meals, homemaker services, and blood transfusions.

BENEFITS — SUPPLEMENTAL MEDICAL INSURANCE
(PART B)

The major services covered by medical insurance for patients requiring either hospitalization or office care are:

1. Medical and surgical care, excluding routine physical examinations
2. Outpatient surgery
3. Diagnostic tests that are part of treatment
4. Radiology and pathology services for hospital inpatients
5. Drugs and medications that cannot be self-administered
6. Blood transfusions
7. X-rays received as part of treatment
8. Physical therapy and speech pathology services
9. Medical supplies such as splints and casts
10. Emergency room or outpatient clinic services
11. Laboratory tests
12. Ambulance transportation
13. Prosthetic devices, including heart pacemakers
14. "Durable medical equipment," including oxygen equipment, wheelchairs, and home dialysis systems

New laws implemented in 1982 have somewhat expanded services. For example, while optometric services for prescribing or fitting eyeglasses continue to be excluded, Medicare now pays for an optometrist's examinations involving aphakia, the absence of the natural lens of the eye. Other limited services newly available are:

1. Pneumococcal immunization
2. Podiatric services for the removal of plantar warts
3. Dental care involving surgery or the setting of jaw or facial fractures
4. Chiropractic spinal manipulation to correct a subluxation that can be demonstrated by X-ray
5. Outpatient treatment of mental illness up to $250 a year

Medicare also pays for patients to obtain a second doctor's opinion before undergoing surgery. Patients may obtain names and phone numbers of participating physicians by phoning Medicare's Second Opinion Referral Center, 1-800-638-6833 (in Maryland 1-800-492-6603).

MEDICAID

Title XIX of the Social Security Act is a program of medical assistance to low-income individuals and families. Known as Medicaid, it became federal law in 1965 and was implemented in the following year. The services provided reflect a blend of joint governmental financing, since they are a combination of those mandated by the federal government and options that states may choose to provide. Services differ among the states, and this disparity is apt to increase as a result of current governmental policies. Restrictions in the nation's Aid to Families with Dependent Children program have already resulted in the disqualification of many thousands of children who previously received Medicaid health care. State participation in the Medical Assistance Program is voluntary; Arizona has elected not to participate.

DESCRIPTION

Medicaid specifically accommodates the medical and rehabilitation needs of persons who are eligible for two categorical income-maintenance programs of Social Security: Supplemental Security Income (SSI) and Aid to Families with Dependent Children (AFDC). These people are termed "categorically needy." In addition, Congress permitted states to extend coverage to the "medically needy." These are individuals whose family income exceeds the amount allowed by SSI or AFDC, but who otherwise would qualify because of their age or disability, and are unable to pay all or part of their medical expenses. Many states extend Medicaid to another group

known as the "medically indigent." Generally, these are the working poor
who have no health insurance and little material worth and who are not
eligible for other public assistance programs. In 1983, over 22 million people
are expected to receive Medicaid services because they are categorically or
medically needy, at a cost to the federal government of $17.1 billion. Medi-
caid services to the medically indigent are financed entirely by state funds at
an estimated additional cost during 1983 of $15.5 billion. California has the
largest number of Medicaid enrollees in each category. In 1982 nearly
3,020,000 persons received categorical coverage under that state's Medicaid
program, or Medi-Cal as it is termed. An additional 343,500 beneficiaries
were medically needy, and 364,000 were medically indigent.

The original legislative directive was vague, giving states near autonomy
in determining eligibility, residence requirements, and types of services
offered. Subsequent reductions in state and federal support have further
widened state variations in the national Medicaid program.

ELIGIBILITY

Generally, people are "presumptively eligible" if they are receiving cash
benefits from SSI or AFDC. In 1981 about two-thirds of the states also
included the medically needy and medically indigent groups; however, many
states are now considering eliminating coverage for these people because of
budget difficulties. Financial eligibility for the medically needy and indigent
is nearly parallel to that of the Supplemental Security Income Program.
Personal property must be "spent down" through payment of medical expenses to the SSI level of $1,500. Personal property includes all cash or
cash-convertible assets, with the exception of clothing, a house, or an
automobile if used for work. Eligibility redeterminations are usually made
on a monthly basis since a recipient's income is likely to fluctuate. Monthly
income in excess of a comparable SSI allocation must be used to "share the
cost" of medical services with Medicaid.

BENEFITS

In most states, Medicaid pays for health care services that are "necessary
and reasonable." This determination is not subjective. Medicaid payments
for care are based on a formula, devised by each state, which is usually
called a "schedule of maximum allowances." The schedule is frequently a
contentious issue between providers of care and the Medicaid programs,
since states usually retain a rate schedule over several years in an attempt to
control program costs.

Federally mandated services are inpatient hospital care; outpatient hospital care; laboratory and x-ray services; skilled nursing facility and home
health services for individuals over 21 years of age; family planning services;

physician care; and early and periodic screening, diagnosis, and treatment (EPSDT) for children and young people. Many additional, or "optional," services are given in thirty of the states, such as chiropractry, audiology, psychology, occupational or speech therapy, physical therapy, podiatry, hemodialysis, medical transportation, aids and equipment, eyeglasses, drugs and medications, blood transfusions, and periodic physical examinations.

MEDICAID AND MEDICARE

Medicaid and Medicare were enacted during the same session of Congress, and they are interrelated in various respects. If, for example, an individual is eligible for both programs because of age and income, Medicaid pays (a) hospital coinsurance, or deductibles, under Medicare's Part A, (b) premiums for Part B, medical insurance, and (c) copayments for physician care.

NEXT STEPS IN PHYSICAL CARE SERVICES

Rehabilitation potential is achieved through the confluence of many medical, social, and supportive mechanisms. The process of growth is sequential and dependent upon attaining at least minimal physical restoration. For most of the nation's disabled people, this fundamental objective has been delayed or attained only in part.

Encouraging trends have appeared during the past twenty years. Reliance upon long-term institutions has been replaced by new concepts of care. Public enlightenment has resulted in acceptance of people whose appearance and physical limitations differ from the norm. Buildings and streets have been altered to accommodate wheelchairs and walkers. The proliferation of hospital rehabilitation programs has brought care closer to home than ever before. And advances in technology and treatment have made minimal restoration a clear possibility and brought maximum functioning within sight.

Yet, for people who are disabled and for those who will become so, the prospects of a full and rewarding life are thwarted by basic problems which remain unresolved. Impairment and rehabilitation are costly; the former in terms of lost social productivity, the latter because of the necessity for comprehensive and individualized services. Efforts to improve the situation of the handicapped require more than the building of new facilities and the training of highly skilled personnel. In fact, the nation appears adequately endowed with both. Rather, progress in physical recovery will be determined largely by the amount of therapeutic service that can be afforded.

Growth toward providing any substantial degree of rehabilitation hope for America's disabled has been a slow but persistent process. Now, after fifty years of progress in creating national programs of support for those least able to support themselves, even these few gains are in jeopardy. A reordering of national priorities need not be accomplished at the expense of the most vulnerable members of society, because much still remains to be done for them. The pressing issue in physical rehabilitation is the need for a public insurance system that will finance specialized services within the home.

BIBLIOGRAPHY

American Hospital Association. *American Hospital Association Guide to the Health Care Field.* AHA Catalog No. 010081. Chicago: American Hospital Association, August 1981.

Brody, Elaine M., ed. *A Social Work Guide for Long-Term Care Facilities.* Department of Health, Education, and Welfare. Publication No. (ADM) 76-177. Washington, D.C.: Government Printing Office, 1976.

California Hospital Association. *Hospital Fact Book 1981.* Sacramento: California Hospital Association, October 1981.

Goldenson, Robert M., ed. *Disability and Rehabilitation Handbook.* New York: McGraw-Hill, Inc., 1978.

Health Insurance Institute. *Source Book of Health Insurance Data 1979/1980.* Washington, D.C.: Health Insurance Institute, 1980.

Stolov, Walter C., and Clowers, Michael R., eds. *Handbook of Severe Disability.* U.S. Department of Education, Rehabilitation Services Administration. Stock No. 017-090-00054-2. Washington, D.C.: Government Printing Office, 1981.

Stryker, Ruth Perin. *Rehabilitation Aspects of Acute and Chronic Nursing Care.* Philadelphia: Saunders, 1977.

Wright, George Nelson. *Total Rehabilitation.* Boston: Little, Brown, 1980.

2 | HOUSING

It is difficult to separate the problem of housing for the disabled from the general housing situation in the United States. Poverty, discrimination, and lack of facilities wreak as much havoc in the lives of the more than one in five families in urgent need of housing as they do in the lives of disabled persons. Massive rebuilding programs, the restoration of a sensible housing market, the reduction of inflation and interest rates, a return to the construction of public housing projects, the improvement of income and employment opportunities, all these are required constituents of a move toward better housing for the population-at-large, including the disabled.

Some European countries have notably surpassed the United States in this area as well as in providing other services for the disabled. Yet there is growing recognition here of some special housing needs, and programs for the particular situation of the disabled are being developed. Although, in proportion to our wealth and population, U.S. efforts look pitifully meager in the housing field, some worthwhile and imaginative ideas have been tried in the past twenty years. There is now a body of experience, both from this country and others, regarding the advantages and limitations of various types of housing for disabled persons.

The purpose of this chapter is to review the special housing interests and requirements of the disabled, present examples and summarize the characteristics of various housing adaptations and arrangements that have been tried, and present information about existing programs to provide housing aid for the disabled.

HOUSING AS SYMBOL AND REALITY

Satisfactory, convenient, and affordable housing arrangements constitute an important part of independent living in general. They are especially important for disabled people. Disabled adults who, against their own choice, live in the homes of other persons emphasize the psychological significance of dependency on others. Although the others may be parents or other close relatives who offer physical care, love, attentiveness, and support, the situation can be stifling to independence and initiative. Although overprotection begins during the period of childhood, parents and other relatives, including parents of "normal" children but especially parents of the handicapped, may find it difficult to recognize their childrens' need for independence. Yet there is in the United States an expectation of a "normal" progression toward increasing independence as one grows up, and this expectation extends to housing. It is the norm for college students, if their families and they can afford it, to live away from home. Whether marrying or setting up a bachelor establishment, one is expected to establish his own household. Sociologists remind us that the old pattern of the multigenerational family living under one roof, as was typical in the rural areas of an earlier United States, has long and irreversibly disappeared. Thus independent housing is highly important in the minds of disabled people for both the reality and the symbolic meaning of "normalization."

However, not only are the psychological barriers to independent living formidable, the physical and economic ones are even more so. The unavailability of suitable housing may support and perpetuate the inappropriate dependency of disabled adults, who, for lack of alternatives, have to continue in the homes of parents or other relatives. Housing, of course, involves more than a mere dwelling place. The feasibility of the particular neighborhood, including the possibilities of transportation to work, school, clinic, social center, stores, and services must be considered. Also included is the idea of choice of living arrangements. The handicapped might choose to share living quarters with companions, maintain a single household, or live in group apartments with some common services or personal attendants for the severely disabled. For the disabled, extra ingredients are often required — training in everyday living skills, special employment or other sources of income, transportation to work or school, and opportunities for social life and recreation.

The severely disabled may also require assistance with the essentials of living by a personal attendant and mechanical equipment to compensate for, or at least adapt to, the loss of mobility. Thus housing considerations also include technical adaptations that can make vital working areas, such as the kitchen, feasible for occupancy by persons in wheelchairs or with other serious limitations. The key concept in housing for people with a disability is individualization and individual choice related to personal needs. Ideally, housing patterns should enable disabled individuals to choose among many alternative living arrangements, with the possibility of easy change from an arrangement that is not convenient or satisfying. Under current U.S. conditions, however, this is a utopian and impractical ideal. Still the possibilities should be reviewed, both to give an account of their range and characteristics and to provide a perspective and platform toward which all interested persons can aspire and work.

Since the aim of this book is primarily to discuss services and arrangements that can facilitate *community* living for disabled persons, this chapter will not discuss institutions as a form of housing. However, there is a strong trend within institutions to apply the normalization principle to humanizing the physical environment and living arrangement. The resident's feelings, needs for privacy and individual choices, aesthetic reactions, and other reactions are beginning to be recognized. Excellent discussion of these approaches are available in recent publications, and their analyses of disabled people's living needs are also applicable to noninstitutional housing.

Since World War II there has been considerable interest in and study of ways to assist in the deinstitutionalization of disabled persons. Especially since the Medicare legislation of 1965 (Title XIX) many elderly disabled persons, who could not be cared for at home, were placed in nursing homes or other institutions. With disabled persons themselves and their relatives taking the lead, many types of community housing arrangements, cutting across a wide range of disabilities and types of projects, have been demonstrated. Examples include group homes, hostels, halfway houses, foster homes, mobile homes, sheltered living arrangements, and group apartments. Such facilities reflect particularly the residents' needs for protective and supportive services and for training in living and growing to greater independence.

Spurred by the initiatives of voluntary agencies and demonstrations and lobbying by organizations of disabled persons, legislators passed several important pieces of legislation in the 1970s. New possibilities for services, housing, and the removal of architectural barriers were opened through the Rehabilitation Act of 1973, the Housing and Community Development Act of 1974, the Rehabilitation Act Amendments of 1974, and the Social Services Amendments of 1974. All this legislation signalized an increased consciousness of human rights and needs. Academic and professional groups produced studies of principles and specific programs leading to a barrier-free environment for the disabled. Taking their cue from the federal legislation, a number of states also studied the problem and produced reports that analyzed every phase of the environment—civil rights, architecture, transportation, street mobility—as it affects the disabled. These reports provide a treasure trove of useful, practical information, although implementation of the recommendations has been exceedingly varied and spotty.

Although this chapter cannot review details of all the successful adaptations of housing style and mechanical equipment that have evolved, it will discuss a number of the considerations that should be kept in mind when upgrading the accessibility and usefulness of a specific housing arrangement.

SOME NEEDED ADAPTATIONS FOR DISABLED PERSONS

ENTRANCES TO HOMES

The average wheelchair is about 2 feet, 1 inch in width, but some motorized chairs are 2½ feet wide. Walks and approaches to a door or entrance should, therefore, be 3 feet wide, as should individualized ramps. Ramps need a gentle rather than a steep slope. They do not need to protrude from a house, but can be adapted to a side entrance driveway or concealed behind shrubbery or vegetation. Since climbing an extremely long ramp is tiring, ramps should not be more than 30 feet long, and they should also have guard rails to prevent the person from rolling off.

Wheelchair elevators, which have been widely developed, can be used, instead of a ramp, for access or within a house.

Since persons with reduced hand function may have difficulty using the conventional key or the conventional round door knob, the shape of door handles and door keys should also be considered. Lever knobs, which are frequently used outside of the United States, might be easier to use than round door knobs.

KITCHENS

Kitchen adaptations are, of course, a major concern in housing for the disabled, since the disabled need to be able to manage their own food preparation if they are to be independent. The number of kitchen adaptations is infinite, involving pantries with vertical up-ended drawers that rest on the floor, and lowered sinks or counters, and push-button turntables for plates, cutlery, and other equipment. There are also adaptations of cutting, chopping, opening, baking, and peeling equipment for use in food preparation. An extensive bibliography of helpful brochures and literature exists, many of them published by the organizations discussed in the next section. The most useful publications are included in the bibliography at the end of this chapter; some are mentioned in the next section.

BATHROOM

Bathrooms are frequently the most inaccessible room in an apartment or house, either because the door is too narrow or, if the door is wide enough for a wheelchair, because the open space in the bathroom is too small to allow for turning and closing the door. Obviously, proper access should be provided. The height of sinks and toilets should also be adapted to the needs of the disabled individual. Showers should be free of curbs and have enough space inside them, and tubs should have handrails or a lift. Medicine chests, mirrors, and wall electrical outlets need to be within reach. Floors should be slip-proof, and there should be an alarm system for calling when assistance is needed. There are numerous adaptations of telephone or personal alarm systems designed for use by a person who is in some difficulty or requires assistance.

A BRIEF HISTORY
OF FEDERAL HOUSING LEGISLATION

Historically, American political leaders have considered housing and community development to be problems best left to individual homeowners, business interests and the "market place." It was felt that individual initiative, combined with the laws of supply and demand, would provide housing and related facilities necessary for all people.

In response to the Great Depression of the 1930s, the New Deal administration of President Franklin D. Roosevelt formulated policies that departed radically from this philosophy. As in many other fields, for the first time the federal government determined to intervene in the housing and community development processes in order to make them conform more closely with clearly recognized social and economic needs.

In the early 1930s, Congress sought to encourage the construction and rehabilitation of housing in the private market by stimulating the flow of mortgage money. The Federal Home Loan Bank System was established by the Federal Home Bank Act of 1932 (Public Law 72-304)* and the Federal Housing Administration (FHA) was established by the National Housing Act of 1934 (Public Law 73-479). These Acts made it more profitable and less risky for lenders to invest in home mortgages by insuring those mortgages against default, while at the same time creating standards to be met by each mortgage insured and by each housing unit constructed or purchased with an insured mortgage. At the same time, Congress endeavored to increase the amount of money deposited in banks and thus made available to be invested in mortgages. This was done by creating the Federal Deposit Insurance Corporation and the Federal Savings and Loan Insurance Corporation. These measures were designed as much to stimulate the construction industry as to provide adequate housing. Later, it became clear that additional types of intervention would be necessary if low-income people were to afford decent housing. Thus, the United States Housing Act of 1937 (Public Law

*Public Law numbers were not constructed in this way until the mid-fifties. Before that, this Public Law would have been written Public Law 43, 72nd Congress. However, for reasons of clarity, brevity, and uniformity, the modern notation will be used throughout this module.

75-412) was enacted, creating the United States Public Housing Authority (PHA) and authorizing for the first time large-scale, publicly-subsidized, and publicly-owned housing. These two types of government intervention, namely the manipulation of the mortgage market (as represented by FHA) and direct subsidy of housing for the poor and disadvantaged people (as represented by PHA), formed two parallel trends that have evolved over four decades into the present programs of the Department of Housing and Urban Development.

The 1940s saw a number of significant changes in housing programs. Among these changes was the establishment of two additional federal agencies which guaranteed mortgage loans—the Veterans Administration (VA) (Public Law 78-346), an independent agency, and the Farmer's Home Administration (FHmA) (Public Law 79-731) in the Department of Agriculture. However, the most important housing legislation enacted in the 1940s was the Housing Act of 1949 (Public Law 81-171). This act established a five-year goal of 810,000 additional housing units. In addition, it also contained urban renewal and slum clearance provisions that marked the beginning of federal community development efforts.

During the 1950s, the urban renewal portion of the housing program was extended and elaborated into an overall community development policy. FHA loans were made available, along with capital grants, to support community development projects. Partly as a result of the displacement of families by urban renewal, a number of programs were initiated that were targeted upon particular disadvantaged groups. For example, the Housing Act of 1954 (Public Law 83-56) made liberal mortgage insurance available for low-income families displaced by urban renewal. Low-income elderly families or individuals were made eligible for admission to low-rent public housing through the Housing Act of 1956 (Public Law 82-1020). The Housing Act of 1959 (Public Law 86-272) expanded access through the Section 202 direct loan program, and the Section 231 insured-loan program for rental housing for the elderly under private sponsorship.

The 1960s, particularly the period 1964–1968, were marked by the establishment of a stream of new programs. President Johnson's "Great Society" domestic programs and the "War on Poverty" produced a number of new agencies, including two new cabinet departments, involving the federal government in the total design of American society in ways unheard of in previous administrations. *As a result, handicapped persons began to be recognized as a group that could benefit from special services.*

The 1965 Housing and Urban Development Act (Public Law 89-117) increased authorization levels for the Section 202 direct loan program—to include the handicapped as well as the elderly—and initiated a rent subsidy program. Later in that same year, the Department of Housing and Urban Development Act (Public Law 89-174) was passed, placing the housing and community development programs under a Cabinet Secretary. The 1968

Housing and Urban Development Act (Public Law 90-448) created additional programs targeted upon low-income, displaced, and handicapped people. These programs included Section 235, which provided lower interest rate subsidy assistance for home-ownership by lower-income families and Section 236, which provided for rental housing assistance for lower-income families.

Under the Nixon administration, which came into office in January 1969, some relatively small-scale legislation was enacted. For example, one provision of the Housing and Urban Development Act of 1970 (Public Law 91-609) was the inclusion of congregate housing for the elderly and the handicapped in the Section 221 and Section 236 programs that provide interest-subsidized insured mortgage loans for multifamily projects. In 1973, President Nixon suspended all subsidized housing programs and ordered a review of their cost-effectiveness and administrative efficiency, as well as the possible conflict of purpose among programs. During this time, Congress debated a number of proposals for changes in the assisted housing and community development programs. This debate, along with considerable negotiation between Congress and the administration, finally produced a monumental piece of legislation—the Housing and Community Development Act of 1974 (Public Law 93-383).

The Housing Authorization Act of 1976 (Public Law 94-375) amended Title I of the 1974 Act to include "centers for the handicapped" among facilities that may be constructed. It also amended the Section 8 housing assistance payments program to provide that rent subsidies under that program may not be considered as income in determining eligibility for or calculating the amount of Supplementary Security Income (SSI) payments under Title XVI of the Social Security Act.

The most recent housing legislation is the Housing and Community Development Act of 1977 (Public Law 95-128).

SOME EXAMPLES OF HOUSING ARRANGEMENTS

LONG-TERM RESIDENTIAL FACILITIES

Since World War II, dozens of nonprofit organization and church groups have created long-term residential facilities that provide one housing alternative. One program that has existed since 1948, the Occupational Home of the Christian League for the Handicapped in Wisconsin, is particularly notable and representative of such facilities in the United States. Starting with a camping facility, the home grew gradually to meet the needs of the community and now offers individual and group apartments, employment, transportation, recreation, therapy, and attendant services as well as the possibility of leasing apartments on a lifetime basis with attendant care as

*Congregate housing is defined as housing with central dining facilities where not all individual units have kitchens.

needed. The entrance age limits are 18–50 years; about 100 persons are now housed by the League, and expansion according to need occurs regularly.

THE SWEDISH FOKUS SYSTEM

For some disabled persons, the shelter of a long-term residential facility is too confining and isolated from the general community. For them, special adapted city apartments, where additional services are provided by an organization, could meet their needs. In 1964, such a system known as the Fokus System was originated by a paraplegic in Sweden as a comprehensive, innovative program. It will be presented in detail.

All of the Fokus apartments are located in regular residential areas near cultural, shopping, and business centers and in communities with employment opportunities and educational programs. A fundamental principle of Fokus is that every tenant should have his own apartment. Apartments vary from one room with a kitchen and bath for a single disabled person, to two and three rooms for disabled individuals who are married and for families with disabled members. Experience has shown that the best combination for integration and services is ten to fifteen apartments at one site. In high-rise buildings, these apartments are located near the elevators with only one or two on each floor to minimize segregation.

When first planning the apartments, the Fokus Society sets up a task force consisting of architects, rehabilitation experts, consulting engineers (for heating, ventilation, sanitation, and electrical equipment), and disabled persons. This task force studies the design of dwellings as well as the surrounding environment, plans common-use facilities, and works out details such as an emergency signal system. Such task forces have concentrated on communication and the two main problem areas in dwellings, the bathroom and kitchen, and the flexible designs they have produced are adaptable to a wide variety of disabilities.

With electrical controls, the Fokus tenant can open doors, call for assistance, talk on the house telephone, and turn lights and electrical appliances on and off. These controls are centered in portable boxes that are small enough to be carried on a wheelchair. All apartments are connected to a staff room by an intercom system. Most tenants have their own telephones. Every apartment has a smoke detector, and all the elevators have automatic door openers.

The kitchen and bathroom cabinets and fixtures can be located to suit an individual's needs. Their height can be adjusted, and the position of the shower and basin can be changed so that the tenant can transfer to the toilet from the right or the left. Undercounter cabinets in the kitchen are all on rollers so that they can be moved to allow more space for a wheelchair. The water faucets are designed for easy operation by arthritic or paralyzed hands; sinks can be raised or lowered.

In the Fokus buildings, certain common rooms can be used by both the disabled and the nondisabled tenants: physical therapy rooms, laundry, sauna, and the lounge, lobby, and dining room. Most of the Fokus sites have special parking stalls for cars of disabled tenants or carports equipped for wheelchair use outdoors.

The tenant has to furnish his own apartment, although Fokus will help obtain the capital if the tenant has insufficient funds. All tenants must pay for their own food, but they can have an evening meal in the common dining room, if they so wish.

The Fokus System provides a variety of services on a twenty-four hour basis. Each individual is assessed for his need based on what he can do with special mechanical devices. Every tenant who needs more than occasional help can have an individual attendant, who will come every day for one or more hours to take care of his personal needs, such as cleaning, cooking, laundry, and shopping. Although personal services vary from one site to another, the basic unit includes a special staff that works an eight-hour shift. Someone is on duty around the clock. Staff members are provided with staff rooms as well as an office or duty room. The disabled tenants can call the duty room for any service they need at any hour of the day or night—to be dressed, to be turned over in bed, to be fed. Help with dressing and toileting is needed by 70 percent; 30 percent need assistance in eating; 25 percent must be turned over at night. Wheelchairs are used by 80 to 90 percent of the disabled tenants. Half of these are electric wheelchairs; some are operated by sucking or blowing remote controls.

In addition to the services performed by the staff in the apartments, the local governments also provide various services to the Fokus tenants such as major house cleaning, shopping, or general assistance to the aged and ill. The helpers providing this kind of service are usually housewives with special training. They work three to five hours a day and are paid by the local authorities. If the tenant can pay, he is charged a small fee. Some young people substitute for their military service by working as assistants to the disabled for a year; they are paid by the government for their services. Whenever services are provided by other persons, even a relative or a spouse, they are paid.

A special transport system has also been developed for Fokus sites. Buses specially equipped for wheelchairs and trained drivers are available to drive the residents to work, church, or recreation. The prices are the same as those charged by the regular municipal transport system.

The total cost of a Fokus apartment with service was estimated in 1976 at $6,000 a year for each disabled individual (one-third for rent; two-thirds for services). The Swedish government subsidizes the cost of adapting the apartments for the disabled, including intercoms, flexible kitchen and bathroom equipment, special communal rooms, and so on. The government pays these costs directly, and they are not included in the rental. The flexible Fokus concept has been adapted for use in a number of other countries such as Germany, Holland, and Canada.

Fokus launched these apartment facilities by contacting the builder of a new housing project when it was in its planning stage and renting ten to fifteen apartments in advance. Just ten years after founding, the Fokus Society stated: "We have about 300 disabled tenants and 260 Fokus flats. In addition to these tenants, there are, of course, nondisabled in the flats. There are thirteen Fokus units in thirteen cities and we have estimated the total need for Sweden as about 2,000 flats or almost 10 times the present availability" (from report of Fokus Society, Stockholm, August 1974).

HOUSING ARRANGEMENTS FOR THE
SEVERELY PHYSICALLY DISABLED

The severely physically disabled (SPD) are those whose mobility or functional impairment makes them significantly dependent on other people or mechanical devices for the satisfaction of basic life needs. Suitable living arrangements for the SPD must include life support systems or services, and SPD persons often need the care of an attendant, who will assist them in a variety of tasks of daily living ranging from dressing to meal preparation to personal hygiene.

During the 1970s, under the Housing and Community Development Act (1974), the federal government supported eight projects to demonstrate and study different models of independent living arrangements (ILA) for the SPD. These are located in Los Angeles, Toledo, Seattle, Omaha, Fall River, Fargo, Columbus, and Houston. Some of the most innovative projects were carried out by the Texas Institute for Rehabilitation and Research in Houston. Four of the Houston models—Independent Lifestyles, Spring Tree, Free Lives, and Cooperative Living—provide examples of possible independent living arrangements. These incorporate many of the experiences of the Swedish Fokus program.

Independent Lifestyles, a nonprofit corporation, provides housing and services for the thirty residents, each of whom is responsible for his own apartment and for meal preparation. A staff of attendants, supervised by a resident manager, provides physical assistance, and attendants are generally available to help with meal preparation. All physical activities are scheduled. The corporation, which owns a van and employs a driver, provides transportation to the residents on a first-come, first-serve basis. The residents contract for services on a monthly basis, and the charge depends on the extent of the services needed. The monthly charge, including rent, ranges from $600 to $740. Most residents support themselves, although some receive service subsidies from the state Division of Vocational Rehabilitation. A Board of Directors, made up of elected resident representatives, advises the resident manager.

At Spring Tree, a medium-sized apartment complex that has been remodeled to be wheelchair accessible, apartments, located near each other, are available for twenty-four SPD persons. The SPD residents share a twelve-person staff of attendants who assist them with all aspects of their physical care. An attendant manager schedules the staff's time. Residents, who assume full responsibily for their own personal welfare, schedule routine care activities and voluntarily assist the attendant manager. The service provided by the staff is augmented by a private contractor, who serves residents that qualify for state-subsidized transportation. Apartment rent in the complex is modest, and the state Department of Public Welfare pays attendant salaries for the residents, all of whom qualify for Homemaker and Chore Services (attendants) of the Department. Each resident contributes a few dollars per month to a fund that is used for parties, gifts, and so forth.

At another independent living arrangement, Free Lives, one wing of Independence Hall, a 292-unit FHA 236 project for the handicapped and elderly, is reserved for SPD persons. Eleven people live in the wing, each in his own apartment. They subscribe to a cooperative attendant service and schedule routine physical care activities. A chief attendant manages the twelve-person staff. The complex provides cafeteria service, but some residents can use their own kitchens. Houston Goodwill, the apartment sponsors, provides prescheduled transportation and charges according to mileage. Apartment rents and attendant services are subsidized by the state Division of Vocational Rehabilitation and Goodwill. A resident administrator and an elected grievance council interact with the attendant manager and the project management.

In a more institutional group ILA, Cooperative Living, twelve SPD persons live in separate dormitory-style rooms at a hospital facility that is shared with the Texas Institute for Rehabilitation and Research. The residents elect four residents to a management council, which shares the management responsibilities, and they manage and share their own attendant services. Cafeteria service is available in the facility. However, residents also own and share a microwave oven, and some residents have refrigerators and hotplates and prepare meals in their rooms. The group owns a large van and employs a driver and schedules all transportation, as well as routine attendant service, a day ahead of time on a first-come basis. Monthly room fees and attendant services are modest and subsidized; transportation and other occasional service charges are based on the amount of service received. Residents receive subsidies from the local housing authority, the state Division of Vocational Rehabilitation, and Supplemental Security Income.*

---

*Quoted with the permission of the Lex Frieden from *Independent Living Arrangements for Severely Physically Disabled Persons*, Papers Given at the First National Conference on Independent Living, 1975. Texas Institute for Rehabilitation and Research, Houston.

Since the early 1970s, there have been programs in the United States that assist the disabled in locating apartments and personal attendants and that sometimes provide transportation, counseling, and referrals to social and welfare programs. One of the most important and influential is the Center for Independent Living in Berkeley, California, whose membership comprises blind, deaf, and wheelchair individuals. The services of the center cover every aspect of independent living, ranging from ensuring the provision of curb ramps throughout the Berkeley area; providing transportation by van to the public transit system, wheelchair repair, and attendant registry; and helping to locate accessible apartments and assisting in adapting them through bathroom and kitchen alterations. While the Center for Independent Living does not at present have a residential facility, with the aid of architects it is planning one. In the meanwhile its consultation on the modification of existing apartments and training of disabled persons in independent living skills has made it possible for hundreds of the formerly institutionalized to live in individual and group community apartments. The example of the Berkeley Center sparked the growth of dozens of similar organizations in California and throughout the country, most of which render similar housing aid; some are also planning their own apartment projects.

SOURCES OF HOUSING AID FOR THE DISABLED IN THE UNITED STATES

Since it serves large numbers of disabled persons in its hospitals and domiciliaries, the Veterans Administration (VA) is interested in facilitating their transfer from institutions to the community. The Spinal Cord Injury Service, of the VA Central Office in Washington, D.C. has pioneered a house-call program through which individual patients receive specialist services in their homes. Several VA centers now have apartments within the hospital, where disabled veterans and their families can practice living together, receiving guidance in practical problems of home living.

A voluntary group, the Eastern Paralyzed Veterans Association, with aid from the New York City Housing Authority, has established a network of modified and subsidized low-cost apartments known as Rogosin Houses, in which quadriplegics live independently, receiving professional services as needed from the VA Hospital-Based Home Care Program.

Housing aid for wheelchair veterans is provided under Title 38, United States Code, Chapter 21, in the form of financial assistance to buy land and build or remodel an existing house so that it becomes medically feasible for the veteran's occupancy.

Between 1967 and 1974, the Department of Housing and Urban Development (HUD) supported eight projects with a total of 1,085 units designed wholly or partly for occupancy by persons with disabilities. (Between 1958 and 1974, in contrast, HUD supported 500,000 units for the elderly.)

HUD'S ROLE AS THE MOST IMPORTANT
FEDERAL AGENCY

The Department of Housing and Urban Development thus provides by far the most significant and the largest number of federal programs for housing disabled and elderly persons. Its programs have gradually evolved, with many legislative and organizational changes, since it was established by passage in 1968 of the Housing and Urban Development Act (Public Law 90-448). That act affirmed the national housing goal of "a decent house and living environment for every American family." Each successive Housing Act of the 1970s has added to the range and coverage of HUD programs for the disabled; and the 1977 Act sparked the creation of a HUD Office of Independent Living for the Disabled in June of that year.

The major HUD housing programs are:

1. *Section 8.* Direct payments to housing owners to reduce disabled tenants' rent. Can also pay mortgages.
2. *HUD Traditional Public Housing.* Nonprofit organizations may lease facilities for the disabled, with HUD area office approval.
3. *Section 202.* Direct government loans for new construction or rehabilitation.
4. *Section 231.* HUD-insured private mortgage loans for handicapped or elderly.
5. *Section 232.* HUD mortgage insurance for skilled nursing homes and Intermediate Care Facilities.
6. *Section 235.* HUD-insured private mortgage loans. Useful for handicapped people seeking single-family homes.

While a few examples of HUD-supported projects for disabled people have already been presented, these separate programs will be discussed seriatim.

SECTION 8 IS KNOWN AS THE
HOUSING ASSISTANCE PAYMENT PROGRAM.

Under Section 8 disabled persons who are unemployed or earning less than the area's median income can receive financial assistance, enabling them to rent suitable housing at an expenditure of no more than 25 percent of income. This program takes into consideration the expenses of disability and has an extended cut-off period for those whose income increases past the median.

For leased housing, families eligible for Section 8 assistance must apply to the local public housing authority (PHA) administering the program in order to receive a certificate of family participation. This specifies the applicable fair-market rent for the size unit appropriate for the family and the maximum amount the family can pay for rent. It is then up to the family (or an agency operating in its behalf) to find a standard-quality dwelling unit that the owner is willing to rent at an established contract rent, no higher than the fair-market rent. When a suitable dwelling is located, a "request for lease approval," signed by the owner, is submitted to the PHA. After the PHA approves the unit, a leasing contract is made. It may be for up to three years. This leasing program is only applicable where Section 8 contract authority has been allocated.

The Section 8 program is intended for lower-income families. However, the law defines "families" to include elderly or handicapped households consisting of:

—a single elderly or handicapped person living alone;

—two or more elderly or handicapped persons living together;

—one or more such individuals living with another person who is essential to their care or well being; or

—a person who was living with an eligible elderly or handicapped person at the time of that person's death.

TRADITIONAL PUBLIC HOUSING PROGRAM

A number of local housing authorities have utilized the traditional public housing program to develop housing for handicapped persons. The reactivation of new construction under the traditional public housing program provided opportunities for construction and substantial rehabilitation of housing for handicapped and disabled persons under the public housing program.

SECTION 202 PROGRAM

Probably the most important financing program for rental housing for the handicapped is Section 202 which provides a direct federal loan for construction and permanent financing, with an interest rate below commercial rates (thus helping achieve lower rents). The Section 202 construction loan must be combined with the Section 8 housing assistance payments program to further reduce rent levels and, therefore, to serve families or individuals with limited income.

The congressional intent for the Section 202 program is that it serve as the primary vehicle for the production of housing for the elderly or handicapped by nonprofit private sponsors and developers. It covers both new construction and substantial rehabilitation of permanent housing, and it cannot be used for the production of hospitals, nursing homes, intermediate care facilities, or transitional facilities.

SECTION 231 (HUD-INSURED MORTGAGE LOANS FOR HANDICAPPED OR ELDERLY)

Under this program, the Federal Housing Administration (FHA) insures lenders such as banks or mortgage companies against loss on mortgages in order to facilitate financing of rental housing for the elderly and/or handi-capped. Mortgages are insured by FHA to build or rehabilitate multifamily projects consisting of eight or more units. The maximum mortgage limit for private sponsors is $12.5 million. For public sponsors the limit is $50 million. Sponsors may include nonprofit and profit-motivated organizations, builders and developers, quasi-governmental bodies such as housing author-ities, state housing finance and development agencies, and redevelopment agencies. Handicapped persons and all persons who are 62 years of age or older may occupy units insured under this program.

SECTION 232 (HUD MORTGAGE INSURANCE FOR SKILLED NURSING HOMES AND INTERMEDIATE CARE FACILITIES)

Through this program, the FHA insures mortgages for the construction or rehabilitation of facilities to provide care for individuals who either require skilled nursing care or related medical services, or who need minimum but continuous care provided by licensed or trained personnel.

The purchase of major equipment needed to operate the facility may also be financed through use of this program.

Nonprofit and profit-making organizations which are licensed by the state to accommodate convalescents or persons requiring skilled nursing care or intermediate care may qualify for this mortgage insurance.

SECTION 235 (HUD-INSURED PRIVATE MORTGAGE LOANS)

This program provides interest subsidy and mortgage insurance to enable public or private agencies to purchase and rehabilitate housing for resale to low-income families, including the handicapped.

Under this program, FHA insures mortgage loans made by private lenders to private- or public-sponsoring agencies to reduce interest rates as low as 5 percent. These sponsors acquire and rehabilitate dwellings and sell them to low- and moderate-income families. This program has been especially useful for handicapped people seeking single-family homes.

Eligibility for the HUD programs of housing aid for disabled persons is defined in the following composite statement taken from regulations of the 1974 Housing and Community Development Act.

Eligible for federal housing assistance are any physically handicapped or mentally retarded persons who have limited or substantial permanent handicaps to employment or who may be unemployable. This definition covers all impairment levels, including the severely mentally and physi-cally handicapped who require multiple services over an extended period of time. Also eligible are the developmentally disabled who suffer from physical disabilities, mental retardation, or a combination that affects a normal level of functioning. All physical or mental handicaps must be of such nature that ability to cope and improvements in quality of life could be promoted by suitable housing and needed services.

The entire range of the physically handicapped, from minimal to maximal handicapping conditions, are included, whether or not the recipients may expect to be employable. Under the Housing and Community Development Act of 1974, a like range of mildly to profoundly retarded persons (or the developmentally disabled with both physical and retarded conditions) are also eligible for housing.

EXPERIENCE WITH HUD PROGRAMS

As already noted, between 1967 and 1974 eight HUD-assisted facilities with 1,085 units were designed and built. These small projects in a sense were pilot demonstrations, from which both HUD and community groups interested in the handicapped gained valuable lessons. Although HUD's learning was steady from the mid-1970s on, the agency could not quickly overcome its preconceptions that all disabled people required very special and exceptional housing designs and equipment. The result was that housing aid to handicapped persons has never represented more than 10 percent of the total of the various HUD programs. During 1977, a total of 388,413 units were constructed or rehabilitated under Section 8 and traditional public housing authorizations of HUD. About 36,000 of these were for disabled persons, an additional 8,000 for disabled elderly persons. In 1978, of the total 326,026 units, 29,415 were for the handicapped, and 3,800 for the disabled elderly. In 1980, of the total of 240,392 units, 2,218 were for the handicapped. (Source, Rental Housing Hearings, Sub-Committee on Housing and Urban Affairs, United States Senate, March 20, 1980, p. 175).

THE REAGAN ADMINISTRATION'S PROPOSALS

President Reagan's fiscal 1983 budget calls for a major shift in housing policy that would scrap most subsidized programs in favor of cash vouchers for the poor and limit new construction to units for the elderly and handicapped. "The (subsidized) housing construction programs are being terminated because they are very costly, provide too large a subsidy to too few people and do not address the nation's current housing problem." (Major Theme and Additional Budget Detail, Budget of the United States Government: Fiscal Year 1983, p. 10).

Under the proposed cutbacks, 39,000 Section 8 units of new construction were to be cancelled in 1982, along with an estimated 20,000 units of cancellations under public housing. For 1983, new construction subsidies would be limited to 10,000 units for the elderly and handicapped.

Changes were made in the 1981 budget reconciliation legislation to authorize increasing rents under the Housing Assistance Payments Program from 25 percent to 30 percent of tenant income by 1986. Tenants involved with new housing or moving into new housing in 1982 automatically pay 30 percent of their adjusted income, while existing tenants would be increased 1 percent a year, from 25 to 30 percent.

Other specific programs have also been reduced or eliminated under the Reagan and reconciliation budgets. For Section 235 or Home Ownership, no new financial commitments were accepted after March 31, 1982. No funds have been set aside for public housing for fiscal year 1983.

These drastic changes—in philosophy and funding—constitute serious set-backs to the expansion of demonstration concern for the housing needs of disabled people that marked the 1970s—especially the latter half of the decade.

Whether the American people and their political leaders will be content to let these regressive changes occur, or will seek to reverse them, is still unknown.

OTHER PUBLIC PROGRAMS

STATE HOUSING FINANCE AND DEVELOPMENT AGENCIES

State housing finance and development agencies are quasi-public agencies that vary from state to state in structure and financing authority. Generally, they provide mortgage loans for builders of rental or sale housing for the elderly or the handicapped. Although financing terms vary, loans are long term with low down payment and low interest rates.

FARMERS HOME ADMINISTRATION (FMHA) RESOURCES

FmHA Section 515. Direct government rural rental housing loans (fifty-year term) 100 percent for nonprofit and 95 percent for others. For new construction, purchase, and substantial rehabilitation of existing housing in small town and rural areas.

FmHA Section 502. Direct government loans to low or moderate income persons in rural areas (thirty-three-year term). For new construction, rehabilitation, or purchase.

FmHA Section 504. Direct government loans (up to twenty-year terms). To very low income persons, including the elderly and handicapped, mainly for repair or improvement of homes with health and safety hazards.

Community Facilities Loans. Direct government loans to small rural communities or counties. For construction or rehabilitation of public facilities. Nonprofit organizations are eligible, if financially capable. Can be used for small group homes.

USEFUL SOURCES OF INFORMATION

ISSUES RELATED TO HOUSING AND
BARRIER-FREE ENVIRONMENTS
FOR HANDICAPPED PERSONS

Two reports published in 1975 by the HEW Architectural and Transportation Barriers Compliance Board, *Freedom of Choice*, Volumes 1 and 2, provide the results of two days of testimony before the board in June 1975 and all housing recommendations emanating from the testimony.

The March 1975 issue of *HUD Challenge*, the monthly magazine of HUD, is devoted entirely to a discussion of issues in housing for handicapped persons. It includes illustrated descriptions of types of housing for physically handicapped persons throughout this country. It may be requested from Superintendent of Documents, Government Printing Office, Washington, D.C. 20402.

DESIGN GUIDES AND STANDARDS

An excellent source on this subject is a study, *Into the Mainstream — A Syllabus for a Barrier-Free Environment*, by Stephen A. Kliment. Funded by the HEW Rehabilitation Services Administration and published in 1975, this study is available from the American Institute of Architects, 1735 New York Avenue, N.W., Washington, D.C. 20036.

Also of interest is *Center for Human Awareness*, edited by J. Tector, a report of the fall 1975 architectural programming studio project at the School of Design, North Carolina State University, Raleigh. Write to the school, Post Office Box 5398, Raleigh 27607.

The Central Mortgage and Housing Corporation in Ottawa, Canada, provides a comprehensive guide to designing for the mildly or moderately handicapped person. Entitled *Housing the Handicapped*, this guide is replete with practical and dimensional drawings. It followed three years of intensive research in Europe, the United States, and Canada and reflects the broad experience of each country. For information, contact the corporation, Montreal Road, Ottawa, Ontario KIA OP7.

Barrier-Free Environments, Inc. (Post Office Box 3446, Fayetteville, North Carolina 28305) has available slide shows for training and public awareness as well as the following publications: *An Illustrated Handbook of the Handicapped Section of the North Carolina Building Code*, 1976, edited by R. L. Mace, AIA, and Betsy Laslett, and *Accessibility Modification: Guidelines for Modifications to Existing Buildings for Accessibility to the Handicapped*, 1977, by R. L. Mace.

Other sources of materials on this subject include the National Center for a Barrier-Free Environment (8401 Connecticut Avenue, Chevy Chase, Maryland) and state offices and agencies in North Carolina, Massachusetts, and Minnesota. These three states are among those that have developed programs in recognition of the housing needs of handicapped persons.

Design Principles and Considerations for Community Residences for Developmentally Disabled Persons, Including the Mentally Retarded. Perhaps the best source of information on planning housing for the mentally retarded is the *Standards for Residential Facilities for the Mentally Retarded* (5th edition, 1975), published by the Joint Commission on Accreditation of Hospitals, 875 North Michigan Avenue, Chicago, Illinois 60611.

RESOURCES FOR INFORMATION ON BARRIER-FREE ENVIRONMENTS

Several organizations provide information on architectural adaptations for the handicapped:

Architectural and Transportation Barriers Compliance Board (ATBCB)
330 C Street, S.W., Room 1010
Washington, D.C. 20201
Telephone: (202) 245-1591
TTY: (202) 245-1592

The Board develops and distributes a selection of public awareness materials to the general public, including the following publications:

- *Architectural and Transportation Barriers Compliance Board*, a pamphlet outlining the board's responsibility under Section 502 of the Rehabilitation Act of 1973.
- *Access America: The Architectural Barriers Act and You*, (1978), an explanation of how to file a complaint about any inaccessible facility under the board's jurisdiction.
- *Freedom of Choice*, a report on 1975 hearings dealing with the housing needs of the handicapped. The report makes recommendations for the improvement of housing for handicapped individuals.
- *Access Travel: Airports*, a twenty-page brochure, published in 1977, describing accessibility in 220 airport terminals around the world. Single copies are available from the Consumer Information Center, Pueblo, Colorado 81009; bulk copies from the Federal Aviation Administration, 800 Independence Avenue, S.W., Washington, D.C. 20591.
- *A Resource Guide to Literature on a Barrier Free Environment*, a bibliography, containing fifteen hundred annotated entries on research studies, surveys, books, standards, among others, relevant to creating a barrier-free environment, published in 1977.

- Annual reports listing activities conducted by the board and its available resources.
- Public awareness campaign materials, including posters, public service announcements for radio and television, and newpaper ads and "Access America," a film on awareness issues.

All materials, except *Access Travel: Airports*, can be obtained free of charge directly from the board. Multiple copies of some materials are available. Anyone who is interested in regularly receiving the board's publications can have his or her name placed on the mailing list.

The National Easter Seal Society
2023 West Ogden Avenue
Chicago, Illinois 60612
Telephone: (312) 243-8400

The National Easter Seal Society is the nation's largest and oldest voluntary health agency providing direct rehabilitation serves to disabled persons. The society has been involved in architectural accessibility issues since 1945 when it established an ongoing liaison with the American Institute of Architects. At that time, an advisory committee of architects was formed to guide the development of programs that would help World War II disabled veterans gain full access to the community. The society later funded a project, conducted by the University of Illinois, that resulted in the first nationally approved standards for accessibility. It currently serves as one of a three-member secretariat to the American National Standards Institute for the development and periodic review of design standards for accessibility. The society continues to be actively involved in accessibility issues, actively participating on advisory committees and task forces dealing with accessibility concerns.

The society's information center disseminates materials on barrier-free design, as well as information related to the medical, social, and economic aspects of rehabilitation. Among its publications on architectural barriers is a resource list, published annually, *Current Materials on Barrier-Free Design*, that identifies relevant resources and provides specific information on how to obtain them. The center reprints many of the items on the list and distributes them at no cost or a minimum charge. Other items can be obtained by writing to the sources listed. The center also publishes a catalog describing materials it makes available in other areas. The information center also develops conferences and seminars, independently or cooperatively with other organizations, sponsors and encourages the development of other organizations working to eliminate architectural barriers, and makes referrals to other organizations and individuals involved in barrier-free design. In

1978, it initiated the National Architectural Barriers Awareness Week that received presidential proclamation.

National Center for a Barrier Free Environment (NCBFE)
1140 Connecticut Avenue, N.W., Suite 1006
Washington, D.C. 20036
Telephone or TTY: (202) 466-6896

The National Center for a Barrier Free Environment was incorporated in 1974 as the result of a national conference on barrier-free design sponsored by the National Easter Seal Society, the American Institute of Architects, and the President's Committee on Employment of the Handicapped. The conference formed an ad hoc committee that developed a national policy on a barrier-free environment that was subsequently endorsed by more than a hundred organizations. In addition, the conference recommended that a national organization be established to act as a central coordinating, information collecting, and disseminating service in support of the barrier-free environment movement. The National Center was formed as a result of that recommendation. It was founded by ten organizations concerned with accessibility issues, including national organizations serving handicapped people, design professionals, and consumer groups.

The center serves as a coordinating link for its affiliated members, disseminates publications on accessibility issues, and operates an information clearinghouse, which responds to technical inquiries relating to accessibility issues. It collects and disseminates technical information developed by member groups on the removal of architectural barriers. Resource files include information on relevant standards, codes, projects, programs, equipment, new products, and other relevant technical information. Materials available from the center include: (1) reprints of relevant articles, (2) technical assistance materials developed by the center and member organizations, (3) resource packets dealing with specific architectural problem areas, such as housing design and home kitchen checklists, (4) an indexed resource file on all aspects of barrier-free design. The resources file includes sixty-six separate subject headings, which may be cross-referenced for specific information retrieval.

Available publications include:

- An eight-page, bimonthly awareness newsletter on new publications, conference activities, and new developments. Individual copies are available free of charge; an annual subscription to individuals is $10.00.
- *Opening Doors*, a thirty-two-page technical assistance manual that provides a review of generally accepted design criteria for facility accessibility with particular reference to modifying existing structure (1977).
- *Tools for Accessibility*, an eight-page booklet listing selected barrier-free design resources (1979). Single copies are provided free.

In addition the center provides customized information searches in response to inquiries and refers users to other relevant organizations, individuals, and information sources. It will also provide speakers for interested groups.

Any lay or professional person may request information from the National Center. Requests should indicate information needs specifically—the more specific the request, the more tailored the response. Inquiries may be made by telephone or by mail. Allow three days plus mailing time for return (additional time may be needed for more detailed information retrieval). No charge is made for most one-time requests, although services are directed primarily to the center membership. In order to receive a subscription to the bimonthly newsletter and other regular mailings, one must become a member of NCBFE.

Paralyzed Veterans of America (PVA)
4350 East West Highway, Suite 900
Washington, D.C. 20014
Telephone: (301) 652-2135

Paralyzed Veterans of America is a national organization of paralyzed veterans established to support improved programs of medicine, rehabilitation, and social integration for all spinal-cord-injured individuals. PVA has developed three information booklets related to the removal of architectural barriers, each of which is available for $2.50 from the PVA:

- *Home in a Wheelchair* is a thirty–two-page illustrated booklet that addresses the many questions disabled persons should ask when purchasing a home. The booklet presents many ideas that disabled persons may adapt to their particular home needs. Among the varied topics covered are ramps, doors, and floors. Three model-demonstration houses are diagramed and discussed.
- *Wheelchair Bathrooms*, a twenty-page illustrated booklet discussing the various devices available for the wheelchair user in the bathroom. Suggestions are given for all components ranging from the sink to the lighting. A brief bibliography is also included.
- *The Wheelchair in the Kitchen*, a thirty–two-page manual that presents many plans used in making kitchens accessible to individuals in wheelchairs. These plans range from adaptations of equipment such as sinks and ovens to gadgets that can be used as kitchen helpers. Several sources of information are also listed.

BIBLIOGRAPHY

Barrier Free Environments, Inc. *Accessible Housing.* Raleigh, North Carolina: Office of the Handicapped, 1980.

California Office of the State Architect. *Regulations for the Accommodation of Physically Handicapped Persons.* Sacramento: California State Printing Office, 1980.

Carver, V., and M. Rodda. *Disability and the Environment.* London: Shocken, 1978.

Federal Programs Information and Assistance Project. *Housing Development Programs.* Draft Document. Washington, D.C.: Federal Programs Information and Assistance Project, May 12, 1978.

"Fiscal 1983 Budget." *Congressional Quarterly Weekly,* Vol 40, No. 7, February 13, 1982, p. 277.

Frieden, Lex. *Independent Living Arrangements for Severely Physically Disabled Persons.* Paper Given at the First National Conference on Independent Living, 1975, Texas Institute for Rehabilitation and Research, Houston.

Gerensky, Samuel. "Architectural Barriers to the Partially Sighted—and Solutions." *Architectural Record,* May 1980, pp. 65-67.

Howard, Dick. *California Housing for the Disabled.* Lexington, Kentucky: Council of State Governments, 1980.

Laurie, G. *Housing and Home Services for the Disabled.* New York: Harper and Row, 1977.

Loomis, Donald. "Federal Departments and Public Groups Consolidate Rules to Guide Barrier-Free Design for the Handicapped." *Architectural Record,* April 1980, p. 36.

Steinfeld, Edward. "Designing the Site to Meet Barrier-Free Goals." *Architectural Record,* May 1979, pp. 69-71.

Thompson, Marie McGuire. *Housing for the Handicapped and Disabled.* Washington, D.C.: The National Association of Housing and Redevelopment Officials, March 1977.

U.S. Department of Health, Education, and Welfare. *A Guide to Federal Housing Programs for the Mentally Disabled.* Public Health Service, Alcohol, Drug Abuse, and Mental Health Administration, National Institute of Mental Health. DHEW Publication No. (ADM) 78-674. Washington, D.C.: Government Printing Office, 1978.

3 | FINANCIAL AIDS FOR THE DISABLED

When used in relation to services for the disabled, the term "financial aids" is often considered to be synonymous with "income maintenance" or even more restrictively, with national Social Security programs. This is a narrow definition that shrinks the focus and permits lesser known resources to go by unseen and unnoticed. Massive public programs of economic support, vital though they are, comprise only one element. The more precise definition of the term is the broader one, describing a wide spectrum, ranging from basic public financial support to assistance in budgeting and money management. In between are included many other sources of financial assistance, such as provision for minor personal needs and even places to turn to when drastic financial emergencies occur.

Although it may seem contradictory, society's shift in attitude toward the disabled and the shift in the way disabled people have begun to think about themselves have actually increased their dependence. The quest for more freedom, greater self-reliance, and approximations of normalcy carries a price tag of greater financial dependency. The consumers of services are the handicapped children and adults who have communicative, orthopedic, mental, sensory, or multiple deficits. The disabled are generally poorer, less educated, and employed less than the non-handicapped population. Release from the closet of home confinement and from isolation in institutions has increased the demand for economic security. This economic security is translated into the financial ability to purchase the amenities of life and to buy professional medical and social services in order to more fully enjoy daily living. Money permits the disabled to participate more actively in the mainstream of community life.

The past, by contemporary standards, has been neglectful in providing for the economic needs of the disabled. Patterns of care throughout the western world emphasized institutional placement of the disabled rather than maintenance in the familiar neighborhood. Some financial benefits were available, commonly in the form of meager doles from local government. Not until the 1970s did there emerge in the United States any national program of guaranteed income for the disabled population. This federal program, known as Supplemental Security Income, at least disburses funds on a predictable calendar schedule, even though the paltry amount of money allocated an individual is inadequate to meet any but survival needs. What continues to be missing is a systematic arrangement for providing for financial needs not only on a scheduled basis, but in a timely fashion commensurate with an individual's changing financial requirements and in an amount sufficient to meet these needs.

Historical efforts to develop an organized system of financial care seem to have been thwarted by a national fear of "welfarism" along with a deeply rooted faith in rugged individualism. Vast changes occurred as the nation changed from a predominantly agricultural to a highly mechanized and interdependent society. Hard work, personal initiative, and thrift were insufficient to meet the threats of economic insecurity. During the twentieth century, a veritable mountain of financial service programs were developed for many separate groups of needy persons. Yet repressive features of structure and administration often seemed to deter the very people the programs were designed to help. Services, too often, were located piecemeal in a complicated assortment of governmental and private agencies that taxed the ingenuity, patience, and stamina of all but the most persistent and determined claimant.

National public social policies have undergone some major alterations in the past few years. A new basic income program for the disabled has emerged, and legions of social and personal assistance policies have had some unification. Regardless of inadequacies, for the first time standardization has been injected into financial aid programs and created at least the semblance of a guaranteed income-maintenance system for the disabled.

Yet the future of all government-sponsored programs of financial maintenance and assistance is, in 1982, questionable and uncertain. The impact of federal reduction in social-program funding and staffing, resulting from a political climate that advocates private philanthropic and voluntary assistance in lieu of governmental aid, affects public service programs at all levels of government. State programs are especially vulnerable to these damages. The Omnibus Budget Reconciliation Act, signed into law by President Reagan on August 13, 1981, consolidated many specific programs for handicapped persons into large block grants at lowered funding levels. Additional refinancing proposals, if approved by Congress for the 1983 federal budget, will drastically reduce the magnitude of America's most popular and successful public support programs: those conducted under the Social Security Act. These proposed changes constitute, in a report by the Chairman of the House of Representatives' Select Committee on Aging, "the most fundamental assault on the Social Security system since its inception 46 years ago."

This chapter is about programs of financial aid, singly and as individual components in a system of financial service. Some are of great benefit to the disabled, while others are of less utility. Seven categories of aid will be discussed: (1) basic public income-maintenance programs, (2) public programs for special groups, (3) public unemployment programs, (4) public special service programs, (5) private income-maintenance programs, (6) private unemployment programs, and (7) community financial services and resources.

Basic income-maintenance programs are of primary importance. These will receive careful attention because they are a government-guaranteed platform of aid available to the majority of the disabled. Of equal value, but applicable to fewer people, are public programs designed for special groups. Also there are country-wide insurance programs aimed at reducing income loss during sickness or unemployment. Other national services have been established to meet special needs of housing and food.

Tax-supported public programs are the most valuable resources for the greatest number of people. Yet private enterprise, through insurance plans, can be of help in income maintenance and earnings loss while a person is unemployed because of sickness or disability. However, these individually purchased insurance coverages are primarily designed to supplement what is available from the public sector.

Every community has organizations and businesses, both nonprofit and commercial, that offer specialized assistance. Some services are expected and have become well known; others are more arcane and must be sought out. The range of direct aid can include emergency cash grants from a social service agency or loans at the neighborhood bank. Supportive aid can range from receiving help in budgeting from a voluntary agency to instruction from a legal aid society in filing for bankruptcy. The size of these potential resources makes comprehensive description impossible, so only those services with a national scope and availability will be covered. Suggestions for investigating this rich field are given under the heading of "Community Financial Services and Resources."

Names and sources of financial assistance will be given, along with a description of the benefits and conditions of eligibility. Directions for obtaining these services will often contain information that answers possible questions. Occasionally there will be tips about how to cut red tape to receive these financial services speedily and effectively. "Useful information" comments will be given from time to time in order to share the experience of people who have been there before. Finally, this survey is designed mainly for the disabled with a prognosis of long-term duration, but in many instances, it will be equally applicable to individuals with short-term disabilities.

DEFINITIONS

Basic needs are food, clothing, and shelter.

Benefits are the amount of money paid or services provided.

Earned income is the payment received as salaries or wages on a job or through self-employment. *Unearned income* consists of money, gifts, or goods the individual receives that is not in return for work.

Financial aids consist of (1) cash income, (2) any type of benefit that could be converted to cash, or (3) assistance in the management of finances.

Income includes all amounts of money or items of value that an individual regularly receives and expects to continue to receive. Under the interpretations of some agencies, income also means money that is received unexpectedly or comes only irregularly.

In-kind income means anything given to an individual that has a cash value, something that could be sold for cash, or under some interpretations, an item or service that otherwise would have to be purchased.

Income maintenance is the systematic provision of money in predictable frequency, amount, and sequence for an individual's basic life support.

Insurance can be defined as "protection by written contract against the hazards (in whole or in part) of future events" or, more simply, an agreement indemnifying or guaranteeing an individual against loss.

Supplemental benefits include cash or services intended to augment basic needs. Examples are health and transportation services.

GOALS OF FINANCIAL AID SERVICES

FUNCTIONAL GOALS

Immediate and long-range goals for the disabled are related to continuous growth toward personal and social independence and the strengthening of physical and mental skills that lead to maximum self-functioning. Both limited and long-term disabilities involve dynamic changing processes; similarly, needs vary in time and from individual to individual. The ability of a disabled person to exist at a certain economic level is a false criterion of financial need. Rather, the criterion is the cost of those goods and services that must be provided if the individual's functioning level is to *progress*. The nature of financial services required to promote the functioning level must be reflective of the individual's changing needs. Financial aids should include cash benefits in conjunction with a spectrum of health, personal, and social services in a variety of settings, including institutions, the community, and different combinations.

SOCIAL GOALS

Other considerations, more subjective and experienced by each of us, also apply. Aside from the clothes we wear, the food we eat, and the place we live, there are extra joys and pleasures that a surplus of dollars at the end of the month can buy. These are not only enhancements to routines of daily monotony; they also supply a zest to life that is essential to emotional health and social growth. The assurance of a platform of economic security is a springboard of motivation to increased physical, social, and mental development. Thus the social goals of financial aid are the development, provision, and utilization of cash and service benefits that will enable the disabled to attain maximum independence and well-being.

BASIC PUBLIC INCOME-MAINTENANCE PROGRAMS

For the handicapped, as for all members of society, the assurance of an adequate income base supplied at predictable intervals is vital. It is not only a mechanism for satisfying daily living needs, but also serves to elevate feelings of self-esteem and self-worth. A variety of public subsidies and benefits are available to the disabled as part of a system of income maintenance. "Social Security" popularly refers to the national social insurance program—Old-Age, Survivors, Disability, and Health Insurance. Commonly known as OASDHI, this is the nation's basic method of assuring a continuing income when family earnings are reduced or stop because of retirement, disability, or death. A broader interpretation of social security is frequently found in other countries, where it includes all types of social insurance, social assistance, and related programs such as mother's and children's allowances. In these countries the social security program also provides a wide variety of health and social services, which are included in the cash benefits. In the United States, these services are treated as supportive and are administered separately.

Social Security in the United States is a combination of public and private programs. It includes not only OASDHI, but also Supplemental Security Income (SSI), programs for special groups such as railroad workers and coal miners, retirement for government employees, and veterans' compensation. There are also state unemployment insurance and temporary disability insurance and workers' compensation programs. And, to round out the picture of organized income-maintenance provisions, public assistance, private retirement and disability plans, and health and hospitalization insurance are available from the federal government and private sources. Here, Social Security means only those public insurance and welfare programs offered by the national and national-state governments under provisions of the federal Social Security Act.

PRINCIPLES OF THE SOCIAL SECURITY ACT

In the years that the Social Security Act has been in effect, the program has undergone many alterations—generally in expanding coverage. The basic thrust has been at providing for the material needs of individuals and families and protecting aged and disabled persons. Programs were designed to prevent destitution and poverty rather than to relieve these conditions after they occur. In addition to the broad altruistic purpose, the OASDHI program was developed with certain basic democratic and fiscal principles in mind. Familiarity with these principles is essential to fully understand the program.

INSURANCE

Two interpretations of the word "insurance" were part of the original social security concept. In one, insurance is the mechanism of funding. The intent of Congress was to make the program self-supporting by having workers make regular contributions, just like payments to an insurance company. These payroll contributions or deductions were expected to constitute an unending source of money from which to pay benefits as new workers entered the labor market and older ones left. As Winston Churchill declared, the magic of the masses would finance the needs of the few. In recent years, many flaws have been found in this pay-as-you-go theory, and recent congressional amendments have greatly changed the benefit and revenue structure.

In the second interpretation, benefits under Social Security are not viewed as being guaranteed income; rather, they are an addition to, and not a substitute for, other financial resources. Since the benefits are payable as a matter of right, the individual is encouraged to supplement these benefits and build up additional protection through "his own initiative, thrift, and personal effort." Under this "social insurance theory," social security was conceived as an inducement to have people obtain steady employment and to improve their work skills, so that they would get better and better jobs. Since the level of cash benefits varies according to past wages and employment, there is added stimulus to obtain regular employment at increasingly higher earnings.

WORK-RELATED BENEFITS

Also underlying the program is the principle that security for the worker and his family grows out of his own work. A worker's entitlement to benefits is based on past employment; the amount of cash benefits is related to earnings in covered work. Generally, the more the worker earns, the greater his protection.

NO MEANS TEST

Benefits are an earned right and do not depend on other means of income. They are paid regardless of income from savings, pensions, private insurance, or other income.

CONTRIBUTORY BASIS

The concept of an earned right is reinforced by the fact that workers make contributions to help finance current benefits. Theoretically, the contributory nature of the program encourages a responsible attitude toward the program by the worker, promotes his personal interest and his stake in the soundness of the program.

COMPULSORY COVERAGE

Coverage, with minor exceptions, is compulsory. This principle was established with the fear and expectation that if it were not compulsory, the program's financial soundness would be undermined, and its effectiveness in preventing dependency diminished. Moreover, those who might logically be expected to participate in an optional program would be those who could expect to profit most by choosing to be covered. This factor would force costs rapidly upward.

RIGHTS CLEARLY DEFINED IN LAW

An individual's rights to Social Security benefits—how much he gets and under what conditions—are clearly defined in the law and are related to facts that can be objectively determined. This principle was intended to limit any caprice of administrative interpretation. Conditions for eligibility and benefits are clearly defined in law. If a claimant disagrees with the decision in his case, appeal can be made to the courts.

Many programs are operated under the Social Security Act. Some have taken on an identity of their own, removed from Social Security because of their close tie with state government; but they are part of the Social Security Act. Aims of the present administration are to substantially alter federal participation in these programs through legislative changes, reduced funding, or by administrative regulations. Only those basic programs will be reviewed that have special importance for the disabled and were operational in 1982.

OLD-AGE, SURVIVORS, AND DISABILITY INSURANCE

DESCRIPTION

Three monthly cash-benefit programs — Old-age, Survivors, and Disability Insurance — are what is generally meant when one refers to Social Security. They are the nation's basic sources of financial aid to the disabled. Actually, five insurance programs are operated by the Social Security Administration, and they appear on payroll check deductions as OASDHI. The two others combine with the first three to make the official title, "Old-Age, Survivors, Disability, and Health Insurance." Since the medical insurances are not a form of direct financial maintenance, they are discussed in Chapter 1. To further complicate the picture, the three worker's insurance plans have been combined under a newly popular two-part name: (1) "Retirement and Survivors Insurance" (RSI) (rather than Old-Age and Survivors) and (2) "Disability Insurance" (DI).

The three insurance programs are separate programs, but they are so intricately linked through structure, eligibility, funding, and administration that they are nearly indistinguishable from each other. They were created by the Social Security Act, or amendments to it, and are administered by the Social Security Administration, which is part of the U.S. Department of Health and Human Services. Together, these programs comprise the largest, nearly the oldest, and certainly the most important of the social insurance programs in the country. The system started in 1935 as a means of income protection for retired workers only, but it broadened rapidly to encompass the entire family unit. No serious attempt was made to include disability insurance as part of the original Social Security blueprint. Income replacement for disabled workers was recognized as a need, but this consideration was overriden by uncertainty about the cost of such a program. In contrast to Retirement and Survivors Insurance, eligibility for Disability Insurance is complicated to assess, and the number of disabled applicants qualifying is difficult to predict. Support for inclusion of disability coverage expanded during the 1940s. In 1956 the DI program was added to Social Security and became operational the following year. Now protection in both insurance plans extends not only to the worker but to the worker's dependents and survivors.

There is a significant difference in the administration of the two programs. The Retirement and Survivors Insurance program is administered on a completely federal level, whereas the Disability Insurance program involves both the federal and state governments. This distinctive feature will be illustrated later. Despite dissimilarity in the two names, each program has importance for the disabled. Under RSI, retired workers, their disabled dependents, and the disabled survivors of deceased workers classify as beneficiaries, as the title implies. Disabled workers and their disabled dependent children qualify for entitlements under the Disability Insurance Program.

The following examples will help to explain how the programs work. Under RSI, if a retired worker has a disabled child, monthly benefits are paid to the child for the rest of his life. Likewise, a disabled child whose parent has died is eligible under Survivors Insurance if the deceased parent was covered by Social Security while working. Disabled children qualify under Disability Insurance if, first, their parent was a worker who became disabled. The intricate relationship between the programs can be illustrated in the situation where a worker becomes disabled. In this event the worker will receive monthly disability insurance checks until he reaches the age of 65. Then the insurance program is shifted over to the retirement program. Benefits will remain the same.

Actually, the system is neither that restrictive—nor that simple. Disabled grandchildren may be considered eligible for benefits as well as disabled spouses or divorced spouses who are disabled. In a commendable effort to keep up with the times, Congress has also taken a liberal view in defining who a dependent disabled child is as well as who a spouse is.

Before a worker or a family member can obtain monthly cash disability benefits, the worker must have credit for a certain number of years of work covered by Social Security. Having enough credit means only that the worker and his family, or a disabled family member, can receive benefits. The amount of Disability Insurance benefit is based on "years of credit." This, in turn, is computed on three factors: the worker's earnings over a period of years, age of disability onset, and recency of work. (This latter is sometimes called the "timeliness requirement.") In general, the older a person is at the time of disability, the greater the number of years of credit which must have been earned and the more recently the work must have occurred. At present, no more than ten years of work credit are required.

When applied solely to earnings, "years of credit" refers to wages earned during a three-month period or quarter. In 1982, a worker received credit for one-fourth year of coverage for each $340 in earnings up to a maximum of a full year's credit of $1,360 or more. The amount of earnings required for these credits has gradually increased each year. Some examples will illustrate how work credit is calculated:

1.   If disability occurs before age 24, a worker needs credit for one-and-one-half

years of work in the three-year period immediately before the onset of disability.

2. If disability occurs between ages 24 and 31, a worker needs credit for having worked half the time between 21 and when the disability started.

3. If disability occurs at age 31 or older, the worker must have earned at least five years of the requirement in the ten years preceding the onset of disability.

Workers who are disabled because of blindness are exempt from the recent work requirement. For them, the minimum required work credit of one-and-one-half years must have been accumulated between 1950 (or the year the worker reached 21, if later than 1950) and the year when blindness occurred.

For disabled dependents of the worker, the essential condition for benefit eligibility is that the worker was part of the Social Security Insurance program. An unmarried child of a worker, age 18 or over, who became disabled before age 22 can receive disability benefits for life if retirement, survivors, or disability benefits are payable on the worker's account. Disabled children are placed under any one of the three programs, depending upon whether their parent is retired, deceased, or disabled. When application is made for children's benefits, the local Social Security office will request a copy of the worker's Social Security earnings record from the headquarters office in Baltimore, Maryland. This record will show whether the worker to whom the claim, as a disabled dependent, is linked worked long enough to make the dependent eligible.

ELIGIBILITY REQUIREMENTS

Efforts by the present administration to cut costs could have an impact on these programs. However, at the time of writing, the eligibility requirements for most people who apply for Social Security benefits are as follows:

RETIREMENT (OR OLD-AGE) INSURANCE

1. Worker

   —Age 62 or over

2. Wife (of worker getting retirement benefits)

   —Age 62 or over
   —Any age with disabled child under 18 in her care

3. Child (of worker getting retirement benefits)

   —Under age 18

—Age 18-22 and attending school full-time
—Age 18 or over with a disability that began before age 22

4. Husband (of worker getting retirement benefits)

   —Age 62 or over
   —Any age with disabled child under 18 in his care

SURVIVORS INSURANCE

1. Widow

   —Age 60 or over
   —Age 50-59 and disabled
   —Any age with disabled child under 18 in her care

2. Child

   —Under age 18
   —Age 18-22 and attending school full-time
   —Age 18 or over with a disability that began before age 22

3. Widower

   —Age 60 and over
   —Age 50-59 and disabled
   —Any age with disabled child under 18 in his care

4. Divorced wife

   —Age 50 and over and disabled

DISABILITY INSURANCE

1. Worker
2. Wife

   —Age 62 and over
   —Any age with disabled child under 18 in her care

3. Child

   —Under age 18
   —Age 18-22 and attending school full-time
   —Age 18 or over with a disability that began before age 22

4. Husband

— Age 62 and over
— Any age with disabled child under 18 in his care

DISABILITY ELIGIBILITY

Three specific and basic conditions for eligibility must be met. The individual must be (1) unable to engage in any substantial gainful activity because of (2) medically determinable physical or mental impairment that (3) has lasted or is expected to last at least twelve months or to result in death. (Items incorporated in the administration's 1983 budget proposals would require disability prognosis of twenty-four months instead of the present twelve months.) The impairment must be so severe that the individual is unable to engage in any work that exists in the national economy. This is regardless of whether such work exists in the immediate area in which he lives, whether a specific job vacancy exists for him, or whether he would be hired if he applied for work. A less strict rule applies to workers who become blinded. The worker is considered disabled if he is unable, because of blindness, to engage in work requiring skills or ability comparable to those required in his past occupations. The three fundamental criteria will be examined further:

(1) Physical or mental impairments must be the primary reason the individual is unable to engage in *substantial gainful activity*. Lack of work opportunities, work layoffs, and the like are not sufficient reason.

(2) To be *medically determinable*, the condition must be one that can be demonstrated by medically acceptable clinical or laboratory diagnostic techniques. Proof is required; the applicant's word is not enough. A report signed by a doctor or a copy of a medical record from a hospital, clinic, institution, or public or private medical agency must be used as supporting documentation. The individual applying for disability benefits is responsible for paying the charges involved in obtaining these records or medical examinations. The actual checking of these data is conducted by a state disability determination service agency, usually the state vocational rehabilitation agency. Here, nonmedical disability examiners, working with physicians, obtain the medical evidence necessary to support a disability decision. Very likely, the state disability evaluation team will be able to make its decision based on the medical reports. If more information is needed, the team will, at government expense, require further examinations or tests.

(3) The *duration of impairment* refers to that period of time during which an individual is continuously unable to engage in "substantial gainful activity" because of a physical or mental condition. Duration starts from the date of onset of disability to the time the impairment no longer prevents return to work.

BENEFITS

Once the three criteria for eligibility are met, there is still a waiting period before monthly benefits are paid. Benefits begin after the worker has been totally disabled for five full calendar months. In other words, an individual *becomes eligible* for disability checks *at the beginning of the sixth month.* Benefit checks are issued after the first month of eligibility; so the first payment will come early in the *seventh month.* Certainly the waiting-period requirement can cause financial difficulties for disabled workers and their families. The Social Security Administration is aware of this hardship, but the waiting-period requirement was included in the law when social disability benefits were first created in order to limit the cost of the program. The original waiting-period was longer than that required now. It was reduced by one month in 1972. An additional proposal for the 1983 federal budget, described by the administration as a "minor change in the disability program," would restore the original six month's waiting-period.

The amount of monthly benefits is based on average earnings under Social Security over a specified period of years. The formula for calculating benefits is infinitely complicated, occasionally changes, and requires actuarial wizards to figure out. Confidence must be placed in the reliability of the Social Security people. What can be said is that the maximum amount paid to an individual disabled worker in 1982 was around $720 a month and to a disabled worker and his family, $1,100. The figure depends on the number of years the worker was "covered," or employed, and on his age at retirement, death, or disability. A worker receiving the maximum amount to which he is entitled is said to have "full benefits." Any amount less than this amount is known as a "reduced benefit." Full and reduced benefits are determined this way:

RETIREMENT (OLD–AGE) INSURANCE

1. Worker

   —Age 65: full benefits
   —Age 62-64: reduced benefits

2. Wife (of worker getting retirement benefits)

   —Age 65: full benefits
   —Age 62-64: reduced benefits
   —Any age with disabled child under 18 in her care: full benefits

3. Child (of worker getting retirement benefits)

—Under age 18: reduced benefits
—Age 18-22 and attending school full-time: reduced benefits
—Age 18 or over and disabled before 22: reduced benefits

4. Husband (of worker getting retirement benefits)

—Age 65: full benefits
—Age 62-64: reduced benefits
—Any age with entitled child in his care: full benefits

SURVIVORS INSURANCE

1. Widow

—Age 65: full benefits
—Age 60-64: reduced benefits
—Age 50-59 and disabled: reduced benefits
—Any age with disabled child under 18 in her care: full benefits

2. Child

—Under age 18: reduced benefits
—Age 18-22 and attending school full-time: reduced benefits
—Age 18 or over and disabled before 22: reduced benefits

3. Widower

—Age 65: full benefits
—Age 60-64: reduced benefits
—Age 50-59 and disabled: reduced benefits
—Any age with disabled child under 18 in his care: full benefits

DISABILITY INSURANCE

1. Worker: full benefits
2. Wife

—Age 65: full benefits
—Age 62-64: reduced benefits
—Any age with disabled child under 18 in her care: full benefits

3. Child

—Under age 18: reduced benefits
—Age 18-22 and attending school full-time: full benefits
—Age 18 or over and disabled before 22: reduced benefits

USEFUL INFORMATION

An indication of the importance of Social Security Insurance as an income source can be drawn from some statistics. Coverage is nearly universal in this country, with nine out of ten workers subscribing to the program. The number of all persons receiving monthly cash-benefit checks was 35.8 million during early 1982, or about one out of seven people in the United States, and monthly benefits totaled $12 billion. The approximate number of beneficiaries in the three major categories were:

(1)	Retired Workers and Dependents	22,900,000
(2)	Survivors of Deceased Workers	8,200,000
(3)	Disabled Workers and Dependents	4,700,000

The Social Security Administration operates the largest record-keeping system in the world. Until the creation of the Supplemental Security Program (SSI), which is discussed next, this office had one of the most enviable records among government agencies for quick, efficient, accurate, and dignified service in administering the nation's basic entitlement programs. Since then, burdened with the massive SSI welfare program, it has seen some tarnish on this reputation. Nevertheless, most observers agree that the staff in these offices try valiantly to handle claims and inquiries with efficiency, interest, dispatch and concern. Waiting in line by number is increasingly becoming a way of life, and the situation is no different at the Social Security Office. The time can be spent profitably reading the pamphlets that are available and are periodically updated to reflect pertinent changes in the law. Some of the most helpful are "How Recent Changes in Social Security Affect You," "Your Social Security," "If You Become Disabled," and "Your Disability Claim."

ESTIMATION OF ONE'S BENEFITS

Although the Social Security Administration has booklets designed ostensibly to help an individual estimate the benefits that may be received when retiring or disabled, not too much trust can be placed in the reliability of these guides. Changes in the law, effective January 1979, make current prediction of benefits extremely difficult. Prior to that time, Social Security checks were based on average earnings over a period of years; and this method will continue to be used for workers who reached 62 or became disabled before January 1979, and for survivors of those who died before that time.

An alternate method of calculating benefits, which went into effect in January 1979, affects workers or the survivors of workers who reached 62, became disabled, or died after December 1978. This new method was authorized by Congress to compensate for the effects of inflation. Actual earnings for past years are adjusted to take account of changes in average wages since 1951. This new method is intended to ensure that benefits will reflect changes in wage levels over the years the worker was employed, and that the benefits will have a constant relationship to pre-retirement or pre-disability earnings.

To avoid "unfairly disadvantaging" people who had planned for their retirement on the expectation of Social Security income under the original benefit structure, the new law guarantees that benefits will be figured in two ways — under the old method using benefit rates that were in effect until December 31, 1978, and under the new method. The benefit rate paid is the higher of the two calculations. Both methods will be used until December 1983 when the transition period ends.

For the past several years, Social Security benefits have increased automatically as the cost-of-living rises. Budget proposals, introduced by the administration in 1982, would curtail this provision. Presently, benefits reflect annual cost-of-living increases when the Consumer Price Index rises by 3 percent or more. The annual raise is determined by the price levels during the first three months of the year compared with the same period a year earlier. Social Security benefits increased by 7.4 percent in July 1982.

RIGHT TO INFORMATION

There is a regulation, the "Freedom of Information" regulation, that says the public has a right to see and copy any Social Security Administration material pertaining to the policies and procedures used in the program it administers. If you are having trouble seeing any policies or procedures at the district office, speak to the manager of the office. If you still have a problem, contact legal services and/or the director of district office operations in Social Security's regional office. The manager should provide the address and phone number.

DISSATISFACTION AND APPEALS

The rules of the Social Security Administration are determined by Congress and thus are part of federal law. This fact not only makes them less susceptible to discriminatory or prejudicial handling, but also assures that any decision can be tested in court. If you feel a decision made on your claim is incorrect, you may ask the Social Security Administration to reconsider it. If, after this reconsideration, you still disagree with the decision, you may ask for a hearing by an administrative law judge of the Bureau of Hearings and Appeals, which is part of the Social Security Administration. If you are not satisfied with the hearing decision, a request for review may be made to the Appeals Council. A final appeal may be made to the federal courts. No charge may be made for any of the administrative appeals. You may, however, choose to be represented by a person of your choice, and he may charge you a fee. The amount that can be charged is limited and must be approved by the Social Security Administration.

Personnel in any Social Security office are well versed in the appeal procedures and are instructed to courteously and willingly explain how appeals are made. They will help you to get your claim reconsidered or to request a hearing. Generally, when you apply to *any* agency and do not receive the benefits or services to which you feel entitled, pursue the route of appeals. Appeals do pay off. *Twenty-nine percent of the initial determinations are reversed at the reconsideration level*, the first step. *Fifty percent of reconsideration determinations are reversed at the hearing level.* The reconsideration may be a duplication of the initial decision, but a larger rate of reversal at the hearing level is because the claimant is afforded face-to-face contact with the decision maker. Obviously, the longer you pursue an appeal, the greater the chances of making an impact and proving your point. In 1981, over one-quarter million Social Security claimants requested appeal hearings.

Benefits under Social Security are an earned right, paid for in payroll deductions either by you or by the worker on whom you are dependent. These are not welfare programs but insurance programs. To underscore this fact, benefits are called "entitlements." Approach your application for claims or questions about claims in a businesslike manner without any feeling that you are asking for favors or charity.

WHERE TO GET SERVICES?

Over 4,000 Social Security offices are scattered throughout the nation. The main ones are the district and branch offices that operate full-time. The others, contact and resident stations, provide part-time service for residents of communities where work loads are too small to justify a full-time facility. Thus, Social Security's coverage ranks a little below that of the Postal Service and probably slightly above the number of Internal Revenue Service offices. So it is one of the most accessible agencies in the nation.

SUPPLEMENTAL SECURITY INCOME

DESCRIPTION

Supplemental Security Income—better known by the initials SSI—is the first and only national assistance program for aged, blind, and disabled people. It took effect in January 1974 after being enacted by Congress two years earlier as Title, or Division, XVI of the Social Security Act. Under this law many state welfare programs, including Old-Age Assistance, Aid to the Blind, and Aid to the Permanently and Totally Disabled, were eliminated and replaced.

SSI represents part of a comprehensive strategy to help the aged, blind, and disabled through a new kind of federal-state partnership. With the turning over to the federal government the primary responsibility for administering financial aid, the way was paved for enabling states to concentrate their resources on improving social and rehabilitation services for the aged, blind, and disabled. The idea is that each level of government — federal and state — should be responsible for those functions it is best able to perform. The word "supplemental," in the term "Supplemental Security Income," is used because payments from this program supplement whatever income may be available to the claimant. Even those Social Security benefits that fall below the SSI minimum payments are supplemented. In some cases, full payments are made because the claimant has no income at all.

Even though the Social Security Administration is responsible for its operation, SSI is completely different from the Social Security Insurance programs. For instance, one can obtain benefits under both programs at the same time, but Social Security benefits are counted as income that is deducted from SSI benefits. Regular Social Security checks are green. SSI checks are gold. Also, Social Security benefits are paid primarily from SSA's own trust funds, while SSI is financed entirely by general revenue from the United States Treasury. Most significantly, Social Security benefits are an insurance program; SSI is a welfare benefit. SSI differs from Social Security in another important way. The amount of a Social Security check is based on work and earnings when the work was done and how much was earned. The SSI basic payment amount is the same for every individual, but the total amount of an SSI check varies according to the amount of other income (earned or unearned) an eligible person receives. At the beginning of 1982, SSI benefits were being paid to 4,027,072 persons. Among all states, benefits were paid to 1,686,502 aged people, 78,596 blind, and 2,261,974 disabled persons. California had the largest number of beneficiaries, 696,212, and Wyoming the least, 1,762.

ELIGIBILITY REQUIREMENTS

PHYSICAL

Any aged, blind, or disabled individual with limited income and resources may be eligible for monthly payments. There is no minimum age. Children, including infants, may be found disabled if the basic income and resources test is met. To get SSI benefits, a person or couple must (1) be aged, blind, or disabled, (2) require money for the basic needs of food, clothing, and shelter, and (3) have a limited amount of resources.

The three criteria of aged, blind, and disabled are not as simple as they appear on the face:

(1) *Proof of age.* To be eligible for SSI on the basis of age, an individual must be at least 65 years old. The Social Security Administration requires proof of age in addition to an individual's word; there must be some written evidence establishing the individual's age as 65 or over. The law requires the district office to help the individual, or "claimant," get this proof if he does not already have it and cannot easily get it. If there is any cost in obtaining evidence of age, Social Security must pay the cost.

(2) *Proof of blindness.* Certain individuals will be automatically considered blind under the SSI program. This consideration applies to those individuals who were receiving aid under the old state welfare programs for the blind in December 1973. These programs were either the Aid to the Blind (AB) or the Aid to the Aged, Blind and Disabled (AABD). To be eligible for SSI, an individual who was not on the state welfare rolls in December 1973 as a blind person must meet the medical definition of blindness that is required by law under SSI. Under this definition, one of two requirements must be met: (a) Vision in the better eye can be no better than 20/200 with glasses, or (b) "tunnel vision" in the better eye cannot be greater than 20 degrees. This is a medical definition of blindness, which must be assessed by either a medical doctor or an optometrist. Since the SSI definition of blindness is easier to meet than the OASDHI (Social Security) definition, people may more easily qualify for benefits under SSI.

(3) *Proof of disability.* The definition of disability for the SSI program considers two different groups of people. One group consists of individuals who were receiving Aid to the Disabled (AD) or Aid to the Aged, Blind and Disabled (AABD) in 1973. The other group, new claimants since 1973, must meet the definition of disability given by SSI. As with the regular Social Security program, a new claimant must prove that (a) there is a medically determinable impairment, (b) the disability is expected to result in death or has lasted or is expected to last at least 12 months, and (c) the disability makes the claimant unable to engage in substantial gainful activity. The key question in deciding whether an individual is disabled is whether the impairment prevents the claimant from working, or makes him "unable to engage in substantial gainful activity." "To engage in substantial gainful activity" means to be able to do productive work (a) that requires physical or mental skills and (b) for which the individual is or could be paid. A part-time as well as full-time job could be considered substantial gainful employment. The president's budget for 1983 would change the definition of disability to require a twenty-four-month, rather than a twelve-month, prognosis.

DISABLED CHILDREN AND SSI.

A child of any age, even an infant, can receive aid as a disabled person if certain requirements are met. For children under the age of 18, it is not necessary to prove that they cannot engage in "substantial gainful activity" as a result of their impairment, since most children, even those without disability, do not have any work history. SSI has a special test to determine if a child's impairment meets this part of the definition of disability. What is looked for is how the impairment affects the child's growth and development. For a child's impairment to be considered a disability, its effects must be of "comparable severity" to the effects of a disability in an adult. That is, the child's impairment must prevent his growth and development to a degree that is equal to the impact of an adult's impairment or the adult's ability to work.

An adult and a child could have exactly the same type of impairment but with different results. The impairment could prevent a child from reaching normal physical or mental development, whereas the adult may have already reached normal development before becoming impaired. Thus, an impairment that is not considered disabling in the adult may be considered disabling in a child. The important factor is not just the type of impairment, but the impact of the impairment on the child's future mental and physical development. This developmentally-based concept of impairment would be eliminated under the President's budget for 1983. To limit the number of SSI recipients, the scope of disability would be greatly diminished. The definition of disability would be based on a preponderance of medical factors only.

For both children and adults who claim benefits because of disability or blindness, the Social Security office will send the application to the state agency responsible for making these medical decisions. In most instances, as with regular Social Security, this will be the state agency that gives vocational rehabilitation. Some states have special agencies that will make the determination for the mentally retarded and developmentally disabled. If medical tests or examinations are necessary, these will all be paid by the government.

ELIGIBILITY OF RETARDED CHILDREN.

In determining that a retarded child is disabled, it must be shown that: (1) IQ is 59 or less, (2) IQ is 60 through 69 with marked dependence, in relation to age, upon others for meeting basic personal needs and a physical or other mental impairment that restricts function and development, or (3) achievement of developmental milestones is no greater than that generally expected of a child half the applicant's age.

ELIGIBILITY OF RETARDED ADULTS.

One of three conditions must be met for a retarded adult to be considered disabled: (a) IQ is 49 or less, (2) IQ is 50 through 69 with an inability to perform routine, repetitive tasks and a physical or other mental impairment resulting in restriction of function, or (3) there is severe mental and social incapacity that creates a marked dependence on others for meeting personal needs, characterized by inability to understand the spoken word, inability to avoid physical danger or follow simple directions, and inability to read, write, and perform simple calculations.

FINANCIAL

SSI benefits are paid to aged, blind, or disabled people who have a limited amount of income. In other words, SSI is a welfare program for people who are "needy." It is not an insurance plan entitling an individual to benefits. The SSI benefits are paid to meet a person's basic needs for food, clothing, and shelter.

The Social Security office, which administers the SSI program, decides whether a person is financially needy by looking at the individual's income and resources to see if they fall below a set standard. There are very specific rules about what income and resources are to be counted. Income may be in the form of cash or in-kind items, such as food, clothing, or shelter. Resources are any type of property owned by a person, including cash and items that can be converted into cash. One of the 1982 requirements for a person or couple to receive SSI is that the value of resources owned not exceed $1,500 for one person or $2,250 for a couple. Other resources that the claimant may have without jeopardizing eligibility are: (1) life insurance policies with a face value is $1,500 or less per person, (2) an automobile valued up to $4,500 or up to its full sale price if needed for a medical or work reason or if specifically equipped for a handicapped person, (3) household goods and personal effects with a value up to $2,000, (4) property needed for self-support, such as work tools and equipment, (5) resources specifically designed in a plan for self-support for a blind or disabled person, and (6) certain funds and property held by American Indians and Alaskan natives. The value of a house, if a claimant lives in and owns it, is not considered. If the value of cash or "countable" resources exceeds the $1,500 or $2,250 limit, a person or couple must dispose of the excess over a period of time, usually three to six months. An agreement to dispose or "spend down" is required, in this situation, by the Social Security office.

People can have some money coming in and still get Supplemental Security Income payments. The first $20 a month of income is not, as a general rule, counted. Income above the first $20 (apart from earnings) generally reduces the amount of the SSI payments. This income includes Social Security checks, Veterans Pension, Workers' Compensation, and gifts. If adopted by Congress, the president's budget of 1983 would stop SSI from disregarding the first $20 of income in setting benefit levels for new recipients coming on the rolls after January 1, 1983.

Some wages can also be received. SSI regulations during 1982 permit an individual to receive $65 a month earned income without any reduction in the government payment. For example, a disabled person working part-time or attending a workshop can earn this amount without having his SSI payment reduced. When work income exceeds $65 a month, the payment is reduced $1 for each $2 in earnings.

An individual's eligibility for SSI can also be affected by whether or not he lives in a public or private institution. For SSI purposes, a "private institution" is defined as a facility that provides food, shelter, and medical services to six or more people who are not related to the owner. A "public institution" is one that is operated by the federal, state, or local government or financed by government funds. When an SSI claimant or recipient is in any institution, public or private, that receives more than 50 percent of its funding from the federal government's Medicaid program, SSI continues to pay in 1982 only $25 a month. This $25 is for the individual's personal and incidental (P & I) expenses.

BENEFITS

SSI is a floor of income for the aged, the blind, and the disabled throughout the nation. It provides monthly checks to make certain that the recipients have a basic cash income. For one person, the maximum amount in 1982 is $284.30 a month; for a married couple, $426.40 (if not in an institution or another person's household). *Even the highest amount of SSI possible was not intended to constitute more than a basic income level.* Nor will the income floor be the same for every recipient, since not every eligible person gets the same amount. Some people get less because they already have other cash income or are getting help that SSI considers to be the same as cash. In some states cash-benefit levels are also affected by a "State Supplementation Program," whereby the state adds money to the federal payment. In California, these additional funds are known as the "SSP" portion of SSI.

DETERMINING INCOME AND BENEFITS

To be eligible for SSI, an aged, blind or disabled person's countable income must be below the benefit-level standard that applies to him. In other words, the person must have an income lower than that which Congress thinks a person needs to live on. Generally, income includes almost all amounts of money or items of value that the individual may receive. Income is divided into countable and uncountable. Countable income is subtracted from the person's benefit level to determine his eligibility and the amount of payment. Whether or not income is countable depends on the kind of income it is, and how and why the individual received it. A person may sometimes be considered to have income that is not really his but belongs to someone with whom he lives. The question of countable income is a tricky issue with SSI. When applying for benefits, you should bring: (1) your latest tax bill or assessment notice if you own a house or other real estate, (2) your latest rent receipt if you pay rent, (3) your bank books, insurance policies, and other papers that show what resources you have, (4) motor vehicle registration if you own a car, and (5) pay slips or other papers that show your income.

Payment standards, or benefit levels, differ depending on whether the individual is single, married, or living alone. The payment is the difference between a person's countable income and the payment or benefit level that applies to him. Three-fifths of the states, throughout 1982, augmented federal SSI by State Supplemental Programs (SSP). In 26 states and the District of Columbia, the SSP portion is included in the federally-issued SSI check; in the remainder, the program is state-administered and separate SSP checks are sent to recipients. Table 2 sets out the benefit-payment levels for eligible individuals and couples living in a variety of situations with basic SSI income. The increase in benefits when one state, California, supplements the basic SSI, is dramatically illustrated in Table 3. Recipients of SSI are not required to pay income taxes on this welfare income.

Table 2
Federal Monthly Amounts of Basic SSI Effective July 1982

	Own Household	Nonmedical Board and Care	Independent without Cooking Facilities	Another's Household
Individual:				
Aged or disabled	$284.30	$284.30	$284.30	$189.54
Blind	$284.30	$284.30	$284.30	$189.54
Disabled child				
under 18	$284.30	—	—	$176.47
Couples:				
Aged-aged				
Aged-disabled				
Disabled-disabled	$426.40	$426.40	$426.40	$284.27
Blind-aged				
Blind-disabled	$426.40	$426.40	$426.40	$284.27
Blind-blind	$426.40	$426.40	$426.40	$284.27

Major changes in eligibility and benefit standards, already discussed, have been recommended in the president's 1983 budget. Others, more subtle but nevertheless significant for poor people who must count every penny, are also proposed: (1) prorate the first month's SSI application for new aged recipients from the date of application or the date of eligibility; and (2) round off the SSI payment standard to the next lower dollar, thus eliminating all cents in the actual payment amount.

Table 3
State of California
Combined Monthly Amounts of SSI/SSP* Effective July 1982

	Own Household	Nonmedical Board and Care	Independent without Cooking Facilities	Another's Household
Individual:				
Aged or disabled	$451.00	$510.00	$499.00	$336.24
Blind	$506.00	$510.00	$499.00	$391.24
Disabled child under 18	$348.00	—	—	$259.77
Couples:				
Aged-aged				
Aged-disabled				
Disabled-disabled	$838.00	$1020.00	$935.00	$682.67
Blind-aged				
Blind-disabled				
	$929.00	$1020.00	$985.00	$771.67
Blind-blind	$985.00	$1020.00	$985.00	$825.67

*Supplemental Security Income/State Supplemental Program

CASH ADVANCES

A person may receive an immediate payment for help with emergencies of up to $100 ($200 for a couple) at the time he applies for benefits and while he waits in the Social Security office. In most cases the agency will not require any proof of this emergency other than a statement of facts. The payment is an advance from, not an addition to, the monthly benefits the individual may become entitled to under the program. The total amount of the emergency advance payment is subtracted from the first month's SSI check if the applicant is found to be eligible. If the individual is given the emergency advance and is later found not to be eligible, Social Security may try to get it back. About half the time Social Security forgets it. To receive an emergency advance, there must be a "financial emergency." A financial emergency is when: (1) there is an immediate threat to a person's life, health, or safety such as a need for food, clothing, shelter, or medical care, (2) there is an urgent need for funds to meet the emergency situation, and (3) the claimant will not have the income or resources needed to meet the emergency before he receives the first SSI checks.

RESTAURANT ALLOWANCE

For aged, blind, and disabled people who do not have a kitchen or a place to prepare food in their dwelling, SSI payments may provide an additional $47 each month. This "restaurant allowance" was available, during 1982, as part of the State Supplemental Program only in California, Massachusetts and Wisconsin.

Interim assistance may also be given as part of the SSI benefit. This assistance is also an advance check. However, the interim assistance check is issued by the county welfare office to help with the person's basic living expenses while he is awaiting his first SSI check. Through an arrangement between the county and SSI office, the first SSI check will be sent directly to the county welfare office. When the check arrives, the welfare office will subtract the amount of money it paid and send the rest to the person within ten days. Subsequent checks will come directly from SSI.

USEFUL INFORMATION

For 95 percent of people who have a disability or handicap, the SSI program is their largest, most reliable, and most permanent source of income. Every disabled person should apply for benefits. If parents give birth to a disabled infant or have a child who is handicapped, they have the right to apply on behalf of their child. Applications for eligibility may be made by the disabled person himself, his parents, guardian, or other responsible person at any Social Security office.

The enormous size of the SSI program, with its millions of claims and complicated regulations, has affected the efficiency of the operation. Delays in checks frequently occur, and mixups in the amounts of the check are legendary. This inefficiency results in no checks, in late checks, and in windfall amounts paid at one time followed by reductions in subsequent checks because of this overpayment. Too, changes in the person's disability status or living arrangements inevitably cause problems in amounts of checks and the time when they are sent. SSI personnel invariably explain these failures as being the fault of the mammoth SSI computer in Maryland. Patience is not necessarily the answer. As with most problems, persistence is usually the best way of getting it solved. If problems occur, be sure either you or someone else gets in touch with the Social Security office by telephone or by visit. Starting in June 1982, a new accounting procedure called Retrospective Monthly Accounting (RMA) was to be instituted. This new system represents a radical change in the method of computing Supplemental Security Income payments; it is designed to promote payment accuracy and to shorten the period of time required to adjust an overpayment.

If an applicant has questions about the amount of his benefit or if his claim is denied, there is a definite and forthright system of appeals. This information will be supplied openly and candidly by someone in the Social Security office. As a permanent aid, a special pamphlet has been prepared, and the SSI recipient should keep it as a handy and useful reference. It is published by the Social Security Administration and called "Your Right to Question the Decision Made on Your SSI Claim." The appeals system was built into the SSI law and is there to be used.

Just because a person is once "determined" eligible does not mean he or she always will be. After the person starts to receive SSI checks, the Social Security Administration periodically reviews his eligibility and the amount he is paid. This review process, called "redetermination," usually occurs at least once each year. The redeterminations are made to assure that payment is made only to an eligible person and that the past, current, and prospective amount of the SSI payment and any state supplement is correct. The annual redetermination evaluates one's marital status, residence and living arrangement, resources, earned and unearned income. This information may be obtained in person, by telephone, or by mail. To keep on the safe side, which means protecting as much as possible the regularity of the check's arrival, the person should promptly report to the SSA office any changes in living arrangements or income.

There is a glaring contradiction in the SSI program's payment level. Base payment rates are considerably lower than the government's own definition of poverty. In July 1982, for example, the estimated income level used by the federal government as an official poverty guideline was $390.00 per month for an aged individual. SSI recipients were guaranteed an income level of $284.30 per month. True, state supplementation, if available, may help make up the difference. Nevertheless, the inconsistency is striking. The Social Security Administration itself has taken note of this inequity and requested congressional correction.

PUBLIC PROGRAMS FOR SPECIAL GROUPS

Numerous governmental financial aid programs have arisen to meet the needs of special groups. This development has occurred more or less parallel to OASDHI. In lieu of an expansion of basic Social Security coverage and eligibility, new programs were created to cover special population groups then outside the Social Security umbrella. The enactment of SSI consolidated many of these aid programs. Several still remain either separate from or conjoint with Social Security. The programs under the Veterans Administration (VA) encompass a range of financial and service benefits so complete as to constitute a comprehensive social and health system. The VA system occupies one end of this spectrum; the other is occupied by the county public assistance programs that, with their meager benefits, are intended to give bare financial aid to people in the direst of straits, who have not yet become enrolled in any other income-maintenance program. Falling in between is the Railroad Retirement Program in which benefits are combined with Social Security insurance. Nearly all of these programs face alteration and possibly extinction, if the Reagan administration's budget proposals are adopted by Congress. As of this writing, the only prediction that can be made is that their future direction and intactness remains uncertain and unsure.

VETERANS BENEFITS

DESCRIPTION

Persons who served in the military forces during wartime are eligible, as are their families, for an astonishing number of benefits and services. All of these are provided by the federal government, primarily through the Veterans Administration. A narrower range of benefits is available to persons who served during peacetime. Veterans' benefits most frequently take the form of cash payments as compensation for service-connected disabilities, pensions for nonservice-connected disabilities, and compensations and pensions for survivors.

ELIGIBILITY REQUIREMENTS

In general, veterans of service in the U.S. armed forces are eligible for benefits if they were honorably discharged or discharged under conditions other than dishonorable. Benefits are related to service-connected disabilities and nonservice-connected disabilities:

(a) COMPENSATION FOR SERVICE-CONNECTED DISABILITIES

Veterans who were disabled by injury or disease incurred in or aggravated by active service in line of duty, during either wartime or peacetime service, are entitled to monthly payments.

(b) PENSIONS FOR NONSERVICE-CONNECTED DISABILITIES

Veterans of recent wars who are permanently and totally disabled from conditions not connected with military service may receive pensions based upon economic need. Annual income and assets are considered in determining the veteran's eligibility and the amount of benefits or benefit base.

(c) PAYMENTS TO DISABLED DEPENDENTS

Disabled dependents of veterans and dependent survivors of deceased veterans are eligible for monthly cash grants and some other services depending upon how much income they already receive.

BENEFITS

More than forty different benefits and services are provided for disabled veterans. Many may be available to their dependents, disabled or nondisabled, and their survivors.

Cash payment compensation is made to veterans for service-connected disabilities, pensions for nonservice-connected disabilities, and compensation and pensions for survivors. Other tangible benefits and services include (1) payment for automobiles equipped with adaptive equipment, (2) money to acquire suitable housing with special fixtures and facilities, such as paraplegic housing, (3) education assistance, well known as the GI Bill, (4) educational help for dependents, and (5) personal and social adjustment programs for blinded veterans or blind dependents.

A major vocational rehabilitation program is also available for disabled veterans. Up to four years of training is provided in an attempt to restore the employability of veterans with service-connected disabilities. Tuition, books, fees, and other equipment are supplied. During training and for two months following rehabilitation, a veteran is paid a subsistence allowance in addition to disability compensation. Again, the continuation of all these programs, including veterans' pensions and disability benefits, is threatened by severe reductions. President Reagan, desiring to reduce expenditures for domestic social programs, has proposed that Congress make substantial changes in the VA benefit structure.

USEFUL INFORMATION

The VA conducts one of the most comprehensive and extensive benefit programs in the world. Although most veterans are well aware of the VA's range of services, their dependents may not be. Disabled dependents of veterans should investigate. The best source of information is a brochure: "Federal Benefits for Veterans and Dependents," Veterans Administration IS-1 Fact Sheet, available for $4.00 and worth much more. Order from Superintendent of Documents, Government Printing Office, Washington, D.C. 20402.

Other more specialized literature may also be helpful. Some of the more useful are: "Service-disabled Veterans Insurance," VA pamphlet 29-9A; "Summary of Benefits for Veterans with Military Service before February 1, 1955 and Their Dependents," VA pamphlet 20-72-2; "Benefits for Veterans and Service Personnel with Service Since January 31, 1955 and Their Dependents," VA pamphlet 20-67-1; "Tutorial Assistance for Veterans, Dependents and Service Personnel under the GI Bill," VA pamphlet 22-75-3; "Veterans Benefits — Inside . . . Outside," VA pamphlet 27-79-1; "Veterans Benefits for Older Americans," VA pamphlet 27-80-2; "Veteran-Student Work-Study Programs," VA pamphlet 27-80-3, and "Questions and Answers on Guaranteed and Direct Loans for Veterans," VA pamphlet 26-4. These can be obtained from the Veterans Administration or from the Government Printing Office, Washington, D.C. 20402.

RAILROAD WORKERS SOCIAL INSURANCE

DESCRIPTION

Disabled persons may be eligible for financial aid under a special program designed only for railroad employees and their families. The legislation that mandates this coverage is the Railroad Retirement Act, a law that has been in effect on an on-again-off-again basis since 1934. Twice, during its infancy, the law was declared unconstitutional and invalid by the courts, but that has long since been settled. In 1982, the future of the Railroad Retirement Act is again clouded since proposals in the president's budget call for abolishing the agency.

Insurance provisions for the disabled are a combination of both the railroad program and OASDHI. This marriage is a long one, as both programs evolved during the same era. To show how they are interwoven: A railroad employee who works less than ten years before becoming disabled is covered solely by the Disability Insurance plan of the Social Security Act. Conversely, if the individual were employed longer than ten years, he would be covered under the railroad plan. If a deceased worker had been employed in the industry less than ten years, benefits to survivors would be paid under the Survivors portion of the Social Security Act. Similar transfer of jurisdiction would occur if the worker retired before completing the ten-year requirement. In these instances, benefits due are paid either by the Social Security Administration or the Railroad Retirement Board. The magical ten-year figure separates the agency having responsibility for benefit payment.

With the exception of SSI, which developed as a drastic overhaul of a patch-work quilt of payment programs, most governmental social insurance plans have developed some interdependency with Social Security. Very often the program was created as an island of special legislation to meet critical social needs of separate groups of people, but as demonstrated in the railroad plan, attempts have been made in recent years to combine them into one financial aid system.

ELIGIBILITY REQUIREMENTS

Eligibility is, in general, the same as for Social Security. Broadly, the requirements for coverage are:

RETIREMENT

1. Worker

    — Age 60 and over

2.   Spouse (of worker getting retirement benefits)

   —Age 60 and over
   —Any age if caring for a child disabled before age 22

3.   Child (of worker getting retirement benefits)

   —Under age 18
   —Age 18–22 and attending school full-time
   —Age 18 or over and disabled before age 22

SURVIVORS OF DECEASED EMPLOYEES

1.   Spouse

   —Age 60 or over
   —Age 50–59 if permanently disabled and unable to work
   —Any age if caring for a child disabled before age 22

2.   Child

   —Under age 18
   —Age 18–22 and attending school full-time
   —Age 18 or over if permanently disabled before age 22
   —Grandchild under age 18 if dependent upon worker
   —Grandchild over 18 if permanently disabled before age 22, but both parents
     must be deceased or disabled

BENEFITS

As might be expected, benefits are derived from a tortuous formula, which involves unraveling a complicated payroll structure for the worker. In Railroad Retirement Board language, benefits are called "annuities." Worker's earnings that go toward annuities are split into two parts, Tier I and Tier II. On Tier I earnings, payroll taxes are collected for both OASDHI and railroad retirement. Only railroad insurance premiums are paid out of the second tier. This combination means that an employee or his beneficiaries will always receive a higher payment than under Social Security alone. If Congress accepts the president's proposal to abolish the agency, Tier I benefits would be administered by the Social Security Administration. A private insurance or quasi-government agency, similar to Amtrak or the Postal Service, would be created to administer Tier II benefits.

The average monthly annuity awarded in 1982 to employees age 60 and over who retired directly from railroad service was $579. Disability annuities averaged $525. Monthly annuities for disabled and aged widows ranged from $331 to $401. Benefits follow the customary pattern of ranging from full to reduced. The full amount is the maximum that the insured worker or his family would receive under the most generous terms of the coverage. Payment of full or partial annuities is determined as follows:

RETIREMENT

1. Worker

   —Age 65: full annuity
   —Age 60-64 after 30 years of work: full annuity

2. Spouse

   —Age 60 and over: full annuity
   —Any age if caring for a disabled child: full annuity

3. Child

   —Under age 18: reduced annuity
   —Age 18-22 and attending school full-time: reduced annuity
   —Age 18 or over and disabled: reduced annuity

SURVIVORS OF DECEASED EMPLOYEES

1. Spouse

   —Age 60 or over: full annuity
   —Age 50-59 if permanently disabled: full annuity
   —Any age if caring for a disabled child: full annuity

2. Other Survivors

   —Child under age 18: reduced annuity
   —Age 18 or over and disabled: reduced annuity
   —Grandchild under age 18: reduced annuity
   —Grandchild over 18 and disabled: reduced annuity

DISABILITY

1. Worker: full annuity
2. Spouse

   —Age 60 or over: reduced annuity
   —Age 50-59 if permanently disabled: reduced annuity

—Any age if caring for a disabled child: full annuity

3.   Child

—Under age 18: reduced annuity
—Age 18 or over and disabled: reduced annuity
—Grandchild over 18 and disabled: reduced annuity

USEFUL INFORMATION

Although an industry-linked coverage, the railroad insurance system is an invaluable source of financial aid to several hundred thousand workers and members of their families. A disabled person may be eligible for these benefits if he was once a railroad employee or if he is dependent upon someone who once was.

Whether disabled dependents are better off under this program than they would be under SSI depends upon whether the state in which they live enlarges the basic SSI grant, by adding the state supplement, and how much additional personal income from other sources may be received. Based on past experience of SSI in setting payment rates, it is likely that the railroad program will be more liberal. As with SSI, railroad annuities are not subject to federal or state income taxes. However, this tax free status would be changed if Administration proposals are instituted.

Like all provisions that come about as the result of legislation, this insurance program is a contractual right and not a welfare service. Premiums were paid throughout the working career of the employee to guarantee that benefits would be available when needed. Questions and disagreements can be resolved through a carefully laid out appeals procedure, similar to that of Social Security. District offices of the U.S. Railroad Retirement Board (RRB) are the best place to obtain answers about retirement or disability eligibility and annuities, and to initiate an appeal. Or, written inquiries can be mailed to the U.S. Railroad Retirement Board, 844 Rush Street, Chicago, Illinois 60611. It is essential, when making a claims inquiry, to cite the RRB claim number and, additionally, the process can be expedited by presenting a record of the annuity claim. The U.S. Railroad Retirement Board has 76 district offices located in chief cities.

BLACK LUNG BENEFITS

DESCRIPTION

Two unique occupation and disease-specific programs have been established by the federal government which, in combination, are popularly known as the Black Lung Program. One, formed by the Federal Coal Mine

Health and Safety legislation in 1969 is directed toward coal miners who have become disabled due to pneumoconiosis (black lung disease or other chronic lung disease) and their dependents or survivors. It is identified separately as the Specific Benefits for Disabled Coal Miners program and, officially, as the Black Lung Benefits Act, a later revision in 1972.

Related legislation, the Federal Mine Safety and Health Act of 1977, was enacted to extend coverage to a larger number of workers in the coal industry and to provide compensation for total disability incurred because of employment. The two components of the Black Lung Program differ in the range of coal workers covered and, to a lesser degree, in the scope of disability required for eligibility. Both operate in unison, and the Black Lung Program is another one in which the Social Security Administration shares responsibility with another governmental agency, in this case the Department of Labor. The point of public contact is, again, the local Social Security office. The Black Lung Program pays monthly cash benefits to coal miners and other coal workers disabled due to chronic lung disease. Financing for this insurance is by the employer, sometimes jointly with employee participation.

ELIGIBILITY REQUIREMENTS

Benefit eligibility under both parts of the Black Lung Program has a dual focus. Requirements apply, first, to the mine worker who is totally incapacitated due to pneumoconiosis; second, to relatives of the worker. To be considered eligible an applicant must be: (1) an underground coal miner or a surface worker involved in coal transportation in and around mines or in coal mine construction, (2) partially or totally disabled by pneumoconiosis or another chronic lung disease (3) affected as a result of employment in or directly associated with the nation's coal mines. An unusual feature of this combined program is the range of family members who are eligible for benefits if a miner or coal worker (1) was entitled to black lung benefits when he died, (2) was totally disabled by the disease or, (3) died because of the condition. In descending order they are the wife or widow, children, parents, and brothers and sisters. Eligibility also requires proof of employment and of disability due to black lung or similar chronic lung conditions arising from coal mine employment. Disabled coal workers who might be eligible for the coal mine workers' compensation portion of coverage are required to undergo rigorous medical tests that include extensive pulmonary function studies and blood gas tests. Nevertheless, applicants may be able to work in nonmining industries and still be eligible for benefits.

BENEFITS

When viewed as a single insurance system, the benefit schedule is less elaborate than that for other governmental social insurance programs. Basic benefits are on a progressively rising annual scale that is established by Congress. A miner's benefit multiplies according to the number of relatives who are dependent upon him. The average family benefit in 1979 was $334 per month, $364 in 1980 and, in 1981, $420. The average family benefit allowed during 1982 is $559.50 and, throughout that year, 367,000 miners, widows and dependents were expected to receive monthly cash benefits under the Special Benefits for Disabled Coal Miners portion of the program. Also during 1982, over 233,000 claimants for Coal Mine Workers' Compensation were expected to receive a total of $726,470,000 in benefits.

Since black lung benefits are tied indirectly to federal employee salary scales, increases are payable automatically when federal salaries are increased. If a miner or his widow is getting workers' compensation, unemployment compensation, or disability insurance benefits under state law, the benefits are offset by the amount being paid under these programs.

Although the larger segment of the disabled population is ineligible for this program, it is of enormous value in meeting some of the critical needs of workers and their families who historically have been exempt from coverage. Taking into account the hazards surrounding the coal-mining industry, the program's benefits are not as bountiful as might be expected. In some instances, benefits may be received along with OASDHI payments. Very few changes, other than in restricting annual cost-of-living adjustments, have been proposed in the president's 1983 federal budget.

USEFUL INFORMATION

Entry into this system is through the Social Security agency. Social Security offices provide information and assistance to claimants in the filing and processing of their claims. Prompt application for benefits is vital, since the law explicitly states that "a timely application for benefits" must be made. In the case of a disabled miner, benefits cannot be paid until an application is filed. When a worker dies, claims by family members are required within six months of the worker's death. A more liberal view of a coal miner's disability is taken under this program than under OASDHI. The same basic criterion of inability to engage "in substantial and gainful employment" is widened to "comparable and gainful work." The law carefully states that this means work in the immediate vicinity of the miner's residence.

AID TO FAMILIES WITH DEPENDENT CHILDREN

DESCRIPTION

AFDC, or Aid to Families with Dependent Children, is a state-conducted program financed by the federal government and operating in all states. It was created to aid children who have become financially needy because of the total or partial absence of their parents or because of the unemployment of the parent who is the primary wage earner. The primary wage earner is defined as the parent with the most earnings during the immediate past 24 months. AFDC is a cash-benefit welfare program and is part of the Social Security Act. As with most other entitlement and welfare programs, its future is in jeopardy. If the administration's 1983 budget proposal to shift the financing of the program to the individual states is accepted by Congress, the organization, operation and benefit structure of AFDC will undergo major changes. Some changes, already instituted by administrative regulations, have affected eligibility criteria and deductible income allowances for beneficiaries.

ELIGIBILITY REQUIREMENTS

An applicant must be (1) deprived of support by reason of the parent's death, continued absence from the home, or physical or mental incapacity, or (2) deprived of support or care because of the primary wage earner's unemployment, and (3) either under the age of eighteen or attending a high school, vocational or training program that must be completed before reaching the age of nineteen. An applicant may be disabled. Although there is some variance, most states permit claimants to have land or a house with an assessed value no greater than $5,000, a car worth no more than $1,500, and other personal property not exceeding $1,000. Personal property is cash, savings bonds, checking accounts, or property that can be converted into cash, such as insurance policies, and burial crypts and plans.

BENEFITS

Benefits are provided by either semi-monthly or monthly checks. They are exempt from federal and state income taxes. AFDC is a joint federal-state venture, and, within general rules set by the federal government, each state administers its own program and decides its own level of public assistance. The benefits vary from state to state with the range extending, in 1982, from a low of $96 in Mississippi to a high of $514 in Alaska for one adult parent with two children. Employable recipients are presently required to register for work and training projects under the work-incentive program (WIN); however, this program may be discontinued since the president's 1982 budget minimizes its importance. Conversely, sweeping changes in the AFDC program created by the Omnibus Budget Reconciliation Act of 1981 that took effect in October of that year tightened eligibility requirements and strengthened work requirements for beneficiaries and applicants. If the 1983 budget is accepted by Congress, a job search would be mandatory for all AFDC applicants, and all states would be required to have community work-experience programs. AFDC's Emergency Assistance program would also be eliminated; and the financial payments made to poor people under the federal government's Low Income Energy Assistance program would be considered as income to AFDC recipients.

A person eligible for AFDC is now automatically eligible for government health services, under Medicaid, and may be entitled to food stamps. Food stamp entitlement, however, is ambiguous. Since 1981, states are permitted to count as income the value of food stamp coupons to the extent that they duplicate the AFDC food allowances in the state's payment standard.

USEFUL INFORMATION

A single disabled child, under 18, who is eligible for AFDC would be eligible for SSI and should generally select the latter. Why? Because benefits for an individual are higher. There may, however, be instances when the entire family would receive more income under AFDC. The choice is up to the disabled person or his representative; a child cannot receive both Supplemental Security Income and AFDC.

There are practical advantages in choosing SSI over AFDC because enrollees in the latter have to complete a great deal of paperwork and more forms. Eligibility determinations for SSI are held once a year, but for AFDC they are held at least semi-annually, sometimes more often; and monthly reporting by the recipient is required by the states through the county department of welfare or social service. Inquiries should be made there. Welfare departments go by different names in many places. To track down this program, look in the white pages of the telephone directory under the name of the county where the disabled applicant lives. Then, below the county name, look for "Welfare Department," "Social Welfare," "Public Social Services," or "Social Services."

PUBLIC EMPLOYEE PROGRAMS

DESCRIPTION

Contrary to a widely held misconception, the federal civilian workforce decreased slightly between 1970 and 1981, from 2.23 million to about 2.12 million employees. Upward adjustments in salary scales and annual cost-of-living raises have, however, steadily increased government pensions for income-maintenance. These financial security programs are provided by the federal government, all states, and nearly all county and city governments. They consist of retirement, disability, and survivor benefits for some or all of the government employees. Frequently, they include medical care benefits and compensation for injury or illness on or off the job. Because of their great variety, no single pattern of coverage or benefits can be given. Employees may be covered under a specific program, such as a public employees' retirement program, federal civil service retirement (CSR), the Social Security Administration's OASDHI parasol or a combination of either the public or civil service system and Social Security. In many instances, government employees have the option of participating under alternative programs as well.

About one-half million federal employees were covered under Social Security in 1981, despite the fact that the entire federal work force was excluded from coverage when the Social Security Act became law in 1935. The "Feds" were exempted because the Civil Service Retirement System was already well established at that time and there seemed to be no need for dual coverage. In 1950, amendments to the Social Security Act brought coverage to all civilian federal employees who were not part of a federal retirement system. In 1957, civilian employees of the Armed Forces also began paying into Social Security. This coverage was in addition to their non-contributory pension program. In 1981, 28 percent of SSA-covered civilian employees worked for the Department of Defense and 23 percent, the next highest proportion, with the Postal Service.

State and local governments participate in Social Security on an elective, or voluntary, basis. About ten million of the approximately 13.5 million eligible employees are covered. Similarly with federal workers, employees at other levels of government were not covered by the original Social Security legislation. Commencing in 1950, SSA amendments provided a way for state and local governments to obtain coverage for their employees through voluntary agreements with the federal government; each year an average of 25,000 nonfederal civil service employees elect to enter the Social Security system. There is not, however, any consistent trend to enrollment. Between 1959 and 1982, 795 state and local government entities, representing some 150,000 employees, terminated Social Security coverage.

ELIGIBILITY REQUIREMENTS

Civilian employees of both the federal government and state and local governments are covered. These plans are called retirement plans, but they always include a disability feature. Under the Federal Civil Service Retirement System, cash annuities are payable to disabled employees at any age if they have had five years of service under the system. The majority of state or local governments have similar provisions.

BENEFITS

For federal employees, the amount of disability annuity depends on their past earnings and length of service. There is, however, a guaranteed minimum.

This minimum is based on a percentage of the highest salary received over a number of years and provides for automatic increases to accommodate upward changes in the annual cost-of-living. New proposals, advanced by the president for the 1983 national budget, would make the Civil Service Retirement System more comparable to Social Security. Specific recommendations include raising the employment retirement age, increasing disability contribution rates, and lowering both retirement and disability benefits. Limiting federal compensation costs for civilian employees and decreasing retirement and disability benefits, the Office of Management and Budget has stated, "could yield significant budgetary savings."

USEFUL INFORMATION

The adequacy of protection for disability provided by any retirement plan should not be left to faith and the expectation that "everything will fall into place." As a brochure from the United Cerebral Palsy Associations so aptly states, "tomorrow is today." The formula for the computation of benefits under all governmental retirement systems is formidable and is particularly complicated in determining disability benefits. The best advice is to ask the plan's representative what the provisions are should you become disabled or die, from what sources benefits could be drawn, and what monthly cash income you or your dependents would receive.

Disabled children of any age whose parent has died or retired from government service because of disability will more often than not be eligible for benefits. If benefits are already being received, monitor their accuracy. Do this by checking once a year at the plan's office. Laws and regulations administering these annuity systems change, often on an annual basis, and reliance upon the retirement system's computer accurately and regularly to pass on the correct benefits is hazardous.

GENERAL ASSISTANCE

This form of public assistance, usually known as general assistance, is aid furnished by counties to needy individuals who do not qualify for help under, or who are not enrolled in, any of the Social Security programs. Not being federally mandated and having no federal financial participation, it varies greatly throughout the states and even from county to county. This type of aid, typically referred to as county welfare, often is the only resource for many disabled persons unable to work and who are not yet linked to a dependable long-term income program such as SSI, or whose critical financial needs are not met by any other public income-maintenance program. At the beginning of 1982, slightly over 1 million citizens were receiving this assistance. The number of recipients was expected to surge dramatically during the year because of more stringent AFDC eligibility requirements and unless the current recession was curbed and unemployment rates reversed.

Assistance is usually limited in duration and in both the type and amount of aid given. Some programs provide only emergency or short-term help; in others, aid is restricted to a special situation. Most counties have fluctuating limitations, depending on available funds. Method of payment takes three forms: (1) direct money payments to recipients, or cash grants, (2) purchase of services from vendors, or (3) a combination of both. Some states, such as Texas, have no general relief programs.

ELIGIBILITY REQUIREMENTS

Disabled individuals who are not receiving OASHDI, SSI, or other cash-grant benefits usually are eligible. Age may be a factor. Some localities restrict benefits to people between the ages of 18 and 65. Most counties require that an applicant register for work, search for work or, if a recipient, "work off" the grant by assignment to a county work project.

BENEFITS

The range of benefits varies by the county's funding resources and prevailing social attitudes. Assistance may be "a tank of gas to get to the next county," or grocery vouchers and lodging, or enrollment in an established general assistance cash-grant program. In December 1981, cash assistance in most states hovered around $130 monthly with the lowest amount, $12.59, being paid in Mississippi and the highest paid in Hawaii, $175.63. Cash grants in Los Angeles during 1982 averaged $196.50 monthly for each recipient. Redetermination of eligibility is usually conducted every six months for unemployable recipients and often more frequently for those deemed employable.

USEFUL INFORMATION

Public or general assistance, while not a substitute for a stable and fixed income plan, is an important source of temporary funds, which should not be overlooked. An inquiry into this program may also provide leads to other peripheral services, usually nonfinancial. A person applies for assistance at a local public welfare office. This agency will conduct an investigation of need and will institute plans for a permanent income-maintenance program. While these welfare benefits are nontaxable, most counties will place liens on a recipient's real property or valuable personal possessions until the grant is repaid. As with any government-operated program, anyone whose claim for aid is denied or delayed, or whose grant is to be reduced or discontinued, may request and is guaranteed a fair hearing.

PUBLIC UNEMPLOYMENT PROGRAMS

Massive work layoffs and rampant unemployment during the Great Depression of the 1930s led the federal government to take preventive steps against the prospect that this social catastrophe should ever be repeated. A primary measure, Unemployment Insurance, was one of the first parts of the Social Security Act. This continues to be the only federally mandated nationwide program of its kind. Other forms of protection against income loss are regularly found throughout the individual states, but there is no common pattern of benefits and coverage.

In addition to insurance for temporary unemployment, other types of programs are designed to protect against income loss because of illness or accident. These may be mandated by state legislation, but if so, the direction and extent of coverage is widely permissive. Programs may be conducted through a publicly supported agency or, optionally, by employers, through private commercial insurance companies.

Disabled people will find any type of public unemployment program to have pluses and minuses. The value depends upon whether an individual has (1) been a member of the work force, (2) become disabled or sick while working, and (3) is physically and mentally capable of holding down a job. Amendments to the Federal Rehabilitation Act have, finally, made the statutory unemployment program more responsive to the needs of the disabled. Yet recent cutbacks in federal appropriations to Social Security programs have diminished unemployment agency activities. Section 504, created in the spring of 1977, requires that all employers seek out disabled and handicapped individuals as prospective employees. This long overdue regulation, already operating in some European countries, was further delayed until 1980 when administrative procedures for implementation were completed. National focus since then has been more concerned with budget decreases imposed by the current administration on basic support programs for the disabled, rather than on actively pursuing the intent of this section. At present, the employment potential of the disabled continues to be presented as a pious axiom rather than as a vigorously sought reality.

UNEMPLOYMENT INSURANCE

DESCRIPTION

Unemployment insurance programs are designed to provide cash benefits to regularly employed members of the labor force who are able and willing to accept suitable jobs. Income is partially replaced for a limited period to persons who become unemployed. Although we tend to think of this as solely a state program, it is a state-conducted federal program and is Title III of the original Social Security Act. The *Social Security Bulletin*, capsulizing the accomplishments of 1937 singled out Unemployment Insurance as "the outstanding event" of the year when full operation of unemployment compensation started in 21 states and the District of Columbia. Each state has the direct responsibility for establishing and operating its own unemployment insurance system, while the federal government finances the costs of administration. State unemployment insurance tax collections are used only for the payment of benefits; federal unemployment insurance taxes are used to pay for the administration of the state's program. Every state, territory, and the District of Columbia has an unemployment program.

This program has limited significance for the disabled. If a disabled worker is temporarily out of work, it does help with immediate cash-flow problems. For those disabled persons who cannot work or whose previous work was on jobs not covered by the insurance programs, there are some services that may still be of value. The name Unemployment Insurance Program is somewhat misleading, since these offices provide, in addition to the cash benefits, a public employment roster listing jobs available in the community, some assistance in obtaining work, and occasionally training programs.

ELIGIBILITY REQUIREMENTS

The federal law contains few requirements concerning eligibility and disqualification provisions. Each state establishes its own requirements which an unemployed worker must meet to receive unemployment insurance. All states require that an individual must have earned a specified amount of wages or must have worked for a certain length of time, or both, within a time frame known as a "base period," to qualify for benefits. Nearly one-fourth of the states require applicants to have worked for a definite number of weeks with at least a specific weekly wage. Florida, Michigan, Minnesota, Montana, New Jersey, New York, Ohio, Rhode Island, and Vermont count only weeks in which the claimant earned the required amount of wages. Hawaii requires fourteen weeks of employment in addition to wages of thirty times the individual's weekly benefit amount. Wisconsin requires fifteen weeks. In all states the base period is used for determination of qualifying wages or employment, weekly benefit amount, and duration of benefits.

All except eleven states—Alaska, Connecticut, Delaware, Iowa, Kentucky, Maine, Maryland, Michigan, Nevada, New Hampshire and Wisconsin— require a waiting period of one week of total unemployment before benefits are payable. The waiting period may be waived in Georgia if the unemployment is not the fault of the claimant. In New York and Rhode Island the waiting-period requirement may be suspended when unemployment results directly from a disaster and the Governor declares the existence of a state of emergency.

Similarly, other requirements for obtaining unemployment insurance benefits vary from state to state but they generally follow this pattern:

1. The worker must register for work at a public employment office and file his claim for benefits.

2. He must have worked previously on a job covered by the state law. Jobs in factories, offices, or other places of private industry and commerce are generally covered.

3. He must have a prescribed amount of employment or earnings in a covered job during a specified base period, generally a year, prior to the time benefits are claimed.

4. He must be able to work. Usually, unemployment insurance benefits are not payable to workers who are sick or unable to work for any other reason, although a few states continue to pay benefits for workers who become ill after they have established their claims.

5. He must be available for work and must be ready and willing to take a suitable job if one is offered to him.

6. He must not have:

    a. Quit his job voluntarily without good cause.

    b. Been discharged for misconduct in connection with his work.

    c. Refused or failed, without good cause, to apply for or accept an offer of suitable work. (What is "suitable" work is generally decided by the state and thus varies throughout the nation.)

Any individual is eligible for services other than cash benefits. The only eligibility requirements relate to the individual's desire to find work, undergo training for a job, and willingness to work.

BENEFITS

Under all state laws the weekly benefit amount is in proportion to the worker's past wages. There is wide variation in the formulas used by the various states in computing these benefits. In most, the formula is designed to compensate for a fraction of the full-time weekly wage. Several states provide additional allowance for dependents. The most commonly followed practice is to use a formula that bases benefits on wages in that quarter of the base period, generally a year, in which wages were the highest. Benefits are payable only for a set number of weeks and, in some instances, benefits are paid retroactively for the waiting period if unemployment lasts a certain length of time. During 1981, the average weekly benefit was $105.98. Benefits ranged from a low of $72.92 in Mississippi to Illinois' high of $130.81. A few states have extended-benefit programs to aid workers who have exhausted their entitlement to regular benefits during periods of high unemployment. In contrast to other entitlement and insurance programs, unemployment insurance is subject to federal income taxes depending upon the amount of the beneficiary's adjusted gross income during the yearly period.

Although recent reductions in federal support of unemployment programs have drastically changed the volume and scope of available services, titular recognition is still given to services that disabled people may find helpful. For the disabled person who is ineligible for unemployment benefits, this assistance may be: (1) testing and assessment of job skills and abilities, (2) job placement, (3) labor market information, (4) job restructuring, and (5) consultation with employers and prospective employees. Services that were always limited but now are nearly nonexistent include: (1) job and vocational counseling, (2) referral to educational and training programs, and (3) assistance in obtaining transportation to job or training.

USEFUL INFORMATION

Services for the disabled traditionally have tended to be a low-priority item with the Unemployment Insurance Program. The state's vocational rehabilitation office has been thought to have the major responsibility in this area. To find out what the program offers that may be of help to you, get in touch with the unemployment office. Offices are found in most towns and in all cities. The program is listed under any number of names, but can be located in the white pages of a telephone directory under the name of the state. Frequently, the State Departments of Unemployment and Rehabilitation work closely together, so it is entirely possible that an inquiry to the unemployment office will result in a referral to the rehabilitation agency.

WORKERS' COMPENSATION

DESCRIPTION

Workers' Compensation or industrial accident insurance programs are designed to provide cash benefits, medical care, and rehabilitation services for persons who experience job-related injuries and diseases. Workers' Compensation, occasionally referred to as Workmen's Compensation, was, incidentally, the first form of social insurance to develop widely in the United States. The first programs were enacted by state governments around the time of World War I to overcome legal injustices and financial hardship incurred by workers who became injured or ill because of job-related factors. The cost of industrial injury and disease was viewed as a proper charge against the expense of business, thus costs of the program are financed entirely by the employer. Because each state operates its own compensation program, the levels of protection for workers differ considerably among jurisdictions. There are five basic types of benefits: (1) temporary total disability, (2) permanent total disability, (3) permanent partial disability, (4) medical benefits, and (5) death benefits. Eighty million workers were covered by Workers' Compensation programs during 1981 and benefits paid during that year totaled over $12 billion.

ELIGIBILITY REQUIREMENTS

There are over fifty Workers' Compensation programs in operation, each differing from the other in terms of eligibility and in types and amounts of coverages. To generalize, the usual condition for benefits is that the worker became disabled "out of and in the course of employment," in other words, while on the job. Most programs exclude injuries due to the employee's intoxication, willful misconduct, or gross negligence. An increasing number of states are including certain occupationally induced diseases under benefit coverage. Not all workers are covered under the program. States differ widely in defining which workers are protected for work-connected injuries. In some states, nearly 95 percent of all workers are covered, in others, as few as 60 percent.

BENEFITS

The benefits provided under Workers' Compensation laws include periodic cash payments, lump-sum payments, and medical/rehabilitative services to the worker during the period of disability, as well as death and funeral benefits for the worker's survivors. In many states, the benefits take into account the worker's marital status and the number of dependent children. All the laws require a waiting period, ranging from two days to a week, before benefits are paid. In some instances, when the worker's disability lasts beyond a specified time, there will be retroactive payment for this waiting period. In 1981, maximum weekly temporary total disability compensation ranged from $119 in Tennessee to $650 in Alaska.

Under practically all laws, compensation is payable to the survivors of workers who die from injury. Weekly or monthly cash benefits are usually available to the deceased worker's children of any age if they are disabled. Each compensation act requires that medical aid be furnished to injured workers without delay. This includes first-aid treatment, services of a physician, surgical and hospital services as needed, nursing, and all necessary medical drugs and supplies, appliances, and prosthetic devices. In most states, medical aid is furnished as long as needed and regardless of cost. Rehabilitation is available under most of the compensation acts. It may be directly provided by a special program for injured workers or by the State Office of Vocational Rehabilitation. Service is usually in the form of medical examination, medical and vocational diagnosis, retraining, education, counseling and guidance in selecting a suitable job, and placement on the right job.

USEFUL INFORMATION

It is the claimant's responsibility to prove his disability and his eligibility, not the state's or the employer's. Benefits under Workers' Compensation are not given in addition to regular earned income. They are insurance benefits to replace lost wages. They are tax-free cash payments.

The appeals procedure is a prominent part of all states' programs. If an employer disputes a worker's claim, the employee can file an appeal with, what most states call, the State Workers' Compensation Appeals Board. After that, an unsatisfied employee can file a petition for reconsideration to the main appeals board. The next recourse is through the courts.

With over fifty Workers' Compensation programs in operation, variations in the name are also likely to occur. To locate services, consult the white pages of the telephone book under the name of the state; under that designation, search for "Workers' Compensation," "Workmen's Compensation," "Industrial Accidents," or "Industrial Relations." If that fails, call the state employment or unemployment office for information in tracking down the program.

TEMPORARY DISABILITY INSURANCE

DESCRIPTION

Temporary disability insurance (TDI) is also known as "cash sickness insurance." It differs from Workers' Compensation in that the disability need not be work-related. In a scattering of states and in one territory, it is compulsory; in most, it is not. Rhode Island passed the first law in 1942, California followed in 1946; New Jersey in 1948, New York in 1949, Puerto Rico in 1968, and Hawaii in 1969. A seventh program, established by Congress for the railroad industry is solely a federal program. Over 32 million employees were enrolled in temporary disability insurance plans during 1981.

ELIGIBILITY REQUIREMENTS

In general, each law defines disability in terms of the inability of an individual to perform the regular or customary work because of the individual's physical or mental condition. Most commercial and industrial workers in private employment are covered in the few states that require employers to provide this coverage.

The principal occupational groups not included are domestic workers, family workers, government employees, and the self-employed. However, no clear picture can be drawn. Agricultural workers, for example, are covered in varying degrees in California, Hawaii, and Puerto Rico. State and local government employees are included in Hawaii, and hospital employees in Rhode Island. Self-employed individuals may be covered voluntarily under the California law. California also includes individuals suspected of being infected with a communicable disease and acute alcoholics undergoing treatment.

Women employees who become pregnant qualify as being disabled. Two of the state systems and the railroad program have had this provision for several years. Coverage has become more universal with the enactment of the Pregnancy Discrimination Act in the fall of 1978. The law, which was attached as an amendment to the Civil Rights Act of 1964, became effective early in 1979. The terms of the statute extend not only to disability insurance but to medical and other coverages as well. It directs that pregnancy be considered as any other disability is in any employee benefit plans offered by an employer.

In both Hawaii and New York, workers who become disabled while unemployed are covered. In other states, benefit payments for the disabled unemployed are made from the regular State Unemployment Department. To qualify for benefits under the TDI program, as under any other, a worker must fulfill certain requirements regarding past earnings or employment and must be "disabled" as defined in the specific law of the program. Two broad requirements are looked at before a disabled worker is considered eligible for cash benefits:

1. EARNINGS OR EMPLOYMENT REQUIREMENTS

An individual must have a prescribed amount of past employment or earnings to qualify for benefits. This is usually in the neighborhood of fifteen weeks of employment preceding the onset of disability; however, in some states it is considerably lower.

2. DISABILITY REQUIREMENTS

The laws generally define the disability as "inability to perform regular or customary work owing to a physical or mental condition" that was not caused by the work performed. In other words, it must be a non-occupational disorder. And it must be temporary in duration. Most of the laws also deny payments for periods of disability due to "willfully self-inflicted injuries or to injuries sustained in the performance of illegal acts." Generally, disabilities caused by automobile accidents are not covered, the reason being that other coverages will probably apply.

BENEFITS

In temporary disability insurance programs, as with unemployment insurance, weekly cash-benefit amounts are related to previous earnings.

Generally, the benefit is intended to replace at least half of the weekly wage loss during a limited time. All laws, however, put absolute limits on the minimum and maximum amounts payable for a week. All systems, too, set a maximum duration for the length of benefits, ranging from four to nine weeks. Depending upon the state or the type of private program the employer has, there may be hospital benefits. In addition to the regular cash benefits, California provides hospitalized claimants with a set dollar amount of benefits for a limited number of days in any one period of disability. In Puerto Rico, a death benefit is payable in case of accident. The average weekly benefit in 1980 was $92. New York paid the highest, $116, and Rhode Island and Puerto Rico the lowest, $75 and $65, respectively.

USEFUL INFORMATION

Prior to the present administration and its restructuring of national priorities, attention had been given to developing income-maintenance programs for protection of workers. Yet one major gap has received little if any federal attention—cash sickness benefits for short-term non-work-connected disability. At most, the present programs are only a partial and generally unsatisfactory solution to loss of wages caused by off-the-job illness or accident. Five states, Puerto Rico, and the railroad industry have statutory programs providing insurance benefits to workers when they become sick or injured. In all other states, workers have this type of protection only by private purchase or when the employer voluntarily provides it. Despite the limitations of any temporary disability program, it is a source of short-term financial assistance that can be used while other avenues of help are explored. When seeking employment, one should inquire if this is a part of the employee-benefit package.

VERIFICATION OF DISABILITY

One crucial eligibility element for those seeking TDI benefits is verification of disability. In those states where the program is mandatory, the claimant must be under the care of a physician or a Christian Science practitioner. Supporting evidence includes a physician's certification, with diagnosis, dates of treatment, opinion as to whether the illness or injury prevents customary work, and an estimate of the date when work can be resumed. Fees for this are paid by the person seeking benefits. If additional verification is required, the agency administering the program is responsible for costs.

The claims and supporting medical statements are reviewed by nonmedical examiners, but usually under medical supervision. When the examiner feels that further medical opinion is needed, the agency will most likely designate a physician. The physicians who give these medical examinations are generally not employees of the government. They are selected from a panel of physicians in private practice who have indicated their willingness, for a set fee, to perform examinations and submit reports.

CLAIMS INVESTIGATION

Most of the programs provide for unscheduled visits to claimants' homes. These visits, made by claims investigators, verify whether a claimant's appearance and activities at the time of the visit are consistent with the medical reports.

APPEALS PROCEDURES

An individual whose claim for benefits is denied has the right to appeal the determination up through the state courts. This right applies whether the claim was denied in whole or only partly.

WHERE TO GET SERVICES.

First, only a few states have laws requiring that workers be insured for temporary disability or sickness. In the others it is a voluntary program for employers or employees. Where mandatory, both the benefits and the administrative agency go by various names. In California, New Jersey, Puerto Rico, and Rhode Island, the TDI program is administered by the state unemployment agency. Hawaii's program is operated separately from unemployment insurance by the Temporary Disability Insurance Division of the Department of Labor and Industrial Relations; and the New York law is administered by the Workmen's Compensation Board. Benefits in California are called unemployment compensation disability benefits; in Hawaii, New Jersey and Rhode Island, temporary disability benefits; and in New York and Puerto Rico, disability benefits.

PUBLIC SPECIAL SERVICE PROGRAMS

Government cash-grant and insurance programs are a fairly new method of responding to the needs of people who are incapable of earning a livelihood and caring for themselves. The traditional way, practiced in both this and many European countries, was to give the basic services directly to the people who needed them. Traces of this ancient pattern can be seen in some government programs that provide purchasing assistance for individuals who cannot meet marketplace costs on their own. Two major programs were established by Congress to help low-income people with food and housing.

FOOD STAMP PROGRAM

DESCRIPTION

Food stamps were devised as a means of improving the diets of low-income individuals and households by supplementing their food purchasing ability. Because the average income of most disabled people falls far short of the nondisabled, this program has special significance. Since 1964, when the Food Stamp Act was legislated, there have been over two dozen revisions and amendments. Original procedures have been completely overhauled and recent changes, largely in decreasing the scope of the program and reflecting the Omnibus Budget Act of 1981, have already been implemented and others are scheduled to be. The Food Stamp Program remains as a highly controversial item in the administration's proposed 1983 budget. The program is federally administered by the U.S. Department of Agriculture, and locally through county departments of welfare or social service. During 1981–1982, twenty-two million persons, nearly one-tenth of the population, received food stamps at a cost to the government of $11.3 billion.

Under the original provisions, eligible applicants purchased food stamps by paying a sum of money based on their family size and net monthly income. They then received food stamps worth more than the amount paid. On January 1, 1979 this system changed, and a new one started.

Localities may vary the new procedures within limits established by the federal government. Generally, four steps are involved: (1) determination of financial eligibility, usually assessed by an eligibility worker in the local, or county, department of social services, (2) determination of the benefit level, or value of stamps to which the applicant is entitled, by the eligibility worker, (3) issuance of an identification card to the prospective beneficiary and, in many areas, (4) issuance of an Authorization to Participate (ATP) card usually within a week or two after eligibility has been established. The ATP cards are then exchanged by the recipient for food stamps at banks, savings and loan institutions, post offices, or other business organizations that have bid successfully for a government contract as a stamp distribution center. (One state, Connecticut, requires banks to provide this service as a condition of their charter to operate.) In some regions, ATP cards are not issued; rather, coupons are mailed directly to the recipient. The stamps, or coupons, can be spent like money at authorized food stores. If a recipient is unable to personally obtain food stamps or to shop for food, because of age or disability, the program permits an authorized representative to do this.

ELIGIBILITY REQUIREMENTS

Requirements for participation are the same throughout the nation; however, shifting of the Food Stamp Program responsibility to each state, as advocated by the Reagan administration, would alter this uniformity. Currently, need is based upon income level. Absence of income is usually sufficient evidence of eligibility; in large cities nearly two-thirds of all food stamp recipients are also receiving public assistance or general welfare. Low-income persons are individuals who have no jobs, who may have part-time work but do not earn much money, who are on public welfare, or who live on Social Security benefits, SSI, or small pensions.

Somewhat surprisingly, the program recognizes what modern society refers to as "alternative living arrangements." Rather than defining a family in the classical sense, a "household and economic unit" concept is used. Under this definition a household is a group of people that (1) shares common cooking facilities, (2) usually buys food together, and (3) lives together as an economic unit. It can also be an individual living alone who purchases food for home consumption, an individual who is a resident of a narcotic or alcoholic treatment and rehabilitation program, or a resident of a shelter for battered women, and receives meals through the program. Elderly and handicapped persons unable to prepare their own meals are eligible to use food coupons for authorized meal delivery, or meals on wheels, services; or when they live in a setting that provides communal dining arrangements. Strikers are ineligible unless they would have been eligible the day before they went on strike. Nor can children living with their parents and earning a salary be considered part of a household dependent upon food stamps. Out-of-job recipients are usually required to register with the state unemployment office, but this requirement, in 1982, is not rigorously enforced. Congress has been alerted, however, that the Reagan administration seeks more stringent compliance.

Depending upon their living situation, many SSI recipients are eligible automatically, particularly if they live alone or with a similar group of friends in an independent living arrangement. In California, Massachusetts, and Wisconsin, they are not eligible because the large state SSI supplementation raises the total SSI payment to an amount that exceeds the maximum income permitted by the Food Stamp Program.

Since the inception of the program, determination of financial eligibility has been a complicated process, and increasingly so since 1981. Eligibility is based on a measurement known as level of income. Some counties verify an applicant's income; most rely on the honor system. Gross income is established by comparing an individual's or house and economic unit's total income to a nationwide poverty level designated by the President's Office of Management and Budget (OMB) which, in turn, is based on a national consumer price index. The income of eligible applicants may exceed the poverty level by 30 percent only. This basic screening limit is known as "130 percent of the poverty threshhold" or the gross income limitation. It can be illustrated by the OMB's poverty level of $704.62 for a household of four people with total income of $916. The household is considered eligible for food stamps because its gross income falls within the 30 percent excess permitted. In his 1983 budget the president would make eligibility more strenuous. Similar to proposals affecting AFDC eligibility, Energy Assistance payments granted poor people to help pay the high costs of home heating would be counted as income, thus restricting food stamp eligibility to fewer people. Also, as the administration proposes for SSI, fractions of dollars would be rounded down to the next lower full dollar amount.

Limitations are also placed on the value of certain cash-convertible possessions of an applicant. A $1,500 resource limit means that the cash value of items such as insurance policies cannot exceed this amount. Owned dwellings are excluded. Automobiles, when used for work-related purposes, are exempt from the resource limitation. The program limits the gross and equity value of other vehicles to $4,500.

BENEFITS

Benefit level is the amount of food stamps to which an eligible person or unit is entitled. It is based on net income. This latter figure is determined by subtracting specified standard allowances for living expenses and an earned income disregard of 18 percent from the gross income. (Originally the amount of income disregarded was 20 percent but was reduced by the president's 1982 budget.) Benefit level is, however, a misleading term since after the net income is computed, a further reduction of 30 percent is made. This is known as the benefit-reduction factor. The amount of food stamps is based on the reduced income level that is always straddling, and most often below, the government's own defined level of poverty. The president proposed, in 1982, that Congress further reduce this amount by 5 percent. Individuals and household and economic units with a net income of over $608 monthly are ineligible for food stamps. A three-person household with no net income received, in 1982, $183 worth of food stamps each month, with a monthly net income of $100, food coupons valued at $153; and with $200 net income, a monthly allowance of $123 in stamps. A family of four can receive no more than $233 in monthly benefits. The President's Office of Management and Budget states that "benefit amounts are determined by the 'thrifty food plan,' designed to reflect a minimum nutritionally adequate family."

Food stamps amount to assistance in buying more food than income would allow ordinarily. They can be used to buy almost any food or to buy seeds and plants for growing food. The Agricultural Department envisioned food stamps as a way of enabling poor people to buy more and a greater variety of food to improve their diets. What the stamps cannot be used for is strictly pointed out. They cannot be used to buy pet food, liquor, beer, cigarettes, most other nonfood items, and quite inexplicably, soap. In certain remote areas of Alaska, recipients may use the coupons to purchase hunting and fishing equipment to obtain food; however, the purchase of firearms, ammunition, and other explosives is prohibited.

USEFUL INFORMATION

VARIATIONS IN THE PROGRAM

Rules and regulations govern the procurement and use of food stamps, just as they apply to any other type of cash grant or welfare service. These specifications change with amazing frequency, often from month to month and certainly from year to year. Even if once denied food stamps, a person should make periodic reapplications. This can also be said for all other programs involving cash payments, in-kind or other supplementary services.

The reasons for this variation in eligibility and benefit come from many sources: court rulings, cash appropriations by Congress, and the administrative structure of the program. Administration involves three levels of government — federal, state, and county. The proliferation of regulations piled one upon the other by successive layers of government frequently distorts programs so that they are virtually unrecognizable from their original intent. However, the single greatest contributor to fluctuation in this program's eligibility policy lies in changes in the consumer price index. The index determines what the federal government considers to be a poverty standard. Financial eligibility in the Food Stamp Program depends upon maximum monthly income standards. The cost of food stamps is based upon these income standards, and the figures change semiannually.

With the rigid linkage of this program to income, changes in a recipient's income must be reported to the food stamp agency — the welfare department. Redetermination of eligibility always occurs if the gross monthly income changes by more than a few dollars, usually about $25, for either an individual or a household. A condition of food stamp eligibility is the individual's promise to report these financial changes.

Insistence upon personal initiative is a prominent feature of the Food Stamp Program. Applicants as well as long-term participants have definite responsibilities to prove economic need, recertify for the program at least annually and sometimes more often; and report any changes in income, extent of disability, employability, household status, and residence. Monthly reporting by all recipients will be required beginning October 1983.

EFFECT ON SSI PAYMENTS

Generally, an individual whose income does not exceed SSI eligibility criteria would be eligible for food stamps. However, it is very likely that acceptance of food stamps would be considered as "in-kind income" by SSI with the unfortunate results that the payment might be reduced. The actual benefit of the stamps must then be judged against the possible amount of SSI reduction. To avoid an SSI reduction, an SSI recipient should check with the Social Security office before applying for stamps. The likelihood of payment reduction applies as well to individuals receiving any type of welfare payment. More often than not, the amount of the food stamp benefit will be deducted from the welfare payment.

EFFECT OF LIVING ARRANGEMENTS

An individual's living arrangements are also an important factor, both in determining eligibility and in deciding whether the benefits are worth any alteration in residence circumstances. The "household and economic unit concept" takes in a broad span: from an individual living alone to a group of people who live together as an economic unit. In order for a group to be considered a household, it must also be an economic unit. This means that everyone must share all the income, resources, and expenses. It is entirely possible that a group of disabled individuals live in separate apartments and may or may not share in a communal kitchen and dining program. In this event, those people who take care of their own personal expenses or who buy and cook their own food could be a separate household. Here the program's regulations become somewhat more complicated.

RIGHT OF APPEAL

Differences or grievances are resolved under a clearly defined "fair hearing" procedure. Any applicant, participating household, or anyone who has been turned down has the right to seek review by a higher authority when benefits have been denied. The appeals procedure must be described to every applicant. The household or a person acting for it, such as a friend, relative, or legal representative, can make a request for a hearing either orally or in writing. The welfare office is required to assist the appellant in making out the request and in preparing his case. The welfare agency sets the time, date, and place of a hearing. The law requires that a final decision must be reached within sixty days from the date the fair hearing request is first filed.

STOPPAGE OF BENEFITS.

Except for reasons of the most flagrant abuse, recipients must be given ten-days advance notice of any action to reduce or stop benefits. Requests for a fair hearing may be made when the benefit is stopped by the county agency or when a recipient or prospective recipient challenges the eligibility determination or the computation of Food Stamp benefits. People who are already receiving coupons will continue to do so until the question is resolved by the fair hearing. This is known as aid paid pending. When the action taken by the agency is to comply with a legislative or legal change in the Food Stamp Program, aid paid pending is not permitted.

WHERE TO GET SERVICES

The county or, as the case may be, city department of welfare or social services is the agency responsible for the Food Stamp Program. For individuals who are receiving SSI, it is wise to consult with the Social Security office prior to making food stamp application in order to avoid any offset against the SSI payment.

HOUSING FOR THE HANDICAPPED

DESCRIPTION

For the disabled who seek their highest level of independence, few barriers loom larger and more stubbornly than that of finding a satisfactory place to live. Affordability, even more than architectural design, is the major problem. Numerous pieces of legislation have been enacted since the 1930s, but only in the past decade has decisive Congressional impetus been given. Two laws, known as Section 202 and Section 8, give the U.S. Department of Housing and Urban Development (HUD) authority and money to provide housing and make it available at a marginal cost. Under Section 202, government loans can be made to private nonprofit corporations and consumer cooperatives to construct or rehabilitate apartments for the elderly and handicapped. Of greater importance to the disabled is the Housing Assistance Payments Program for Lower Income Families, which is abbreviated as Section 8. Financial grants are given to public housing agencies in order to subsidize the rent that low-income tenants must pay.

ELIGIBILITY REQUIREMENTS

Specific criteria are established by local housing agencies or housing authorities, as they are frequently called. The principal requirements for participation in Section 8 are that individuals must be physically or developmentally disabled, mentally disordered, or at least 62 years of age and must be within certain income limits. No flat amount of income is stipulated; rather, the prospective tenant's income is compared to the average income received by families or individuals in the area where the housing is located. There is little deviation from these conditions since, even though the programs are locally administered, they are based on federal law.

BENEFITS

Financial assistance covers the difference between what the tenant can pay and the fair market rental price of the property. The agency administering the housing program determines how much rent a person can afford — usually 20 to 30 percent of his gross income — and then makes up the difference.

USEFUL INFORMATION

The rental subsidy grants administered by HUD are not widely known; local housing programs that exist are sparse and scattered; and those that are in operation do not seem to be known by the people who most need this help. Why? In the past the main reason appeared to be that the Department of Housing and Urban Development was less than aggressive in advertising its housing program. Also, a community agency was required to operate Section 8 housing programs. Until the past two years the cloud of mystery and ignorance appeared to be dissipating, as an increasing number of cities and counties were forming housing authorities to develop Section 8 housing. Reduced funding by the current administration has impaired this program for the forseeable future. The legislation has been adopted by Congress, however, and it exists to be used. Disabled people, individually and in groups, should be assertive in making their housing needs known to their elected local and national representatives. Nor can individual action and initiative be relaxed even when communities have such programs. Ordinarily the housing council maintains a list of landlords and rental units; yet this is often a meager list. It is usually up to the would-be tenant to locate the actual apartment or house and then apply for a rent subsidy.

Procurement of housing in itself is a major benefit, but there is additional advantage in that the rent subsidy cannot be taken into account by most other government insurance welfare programs. Social Security, Supplemental Security Income, and Public Assistance programs are prohibited by law from deducting the amount of Section 8 rental subsidies from monthly cash allotments.

Since no single name is used to identify these programs, the best way to start locating programs is to inquire at the welfare department or, in larger cities, to look in the yellow pages of the telephone book under the "housing projects" classification.

PRIVATE INCOME-MAINTENANCE PROGRAMS

Income maintenance is available under private auspices, chiefly from the commercial banking and insurance markets. There are two main types: (1) retirement, including so-called annuity plans, and (2) estate trusts, arrangements where capital and income from capital are earmarked for some particular use, most often to provide long-term income for another person.

RETIREMENT INSURANCE

DESCRIPTION

The purpose of private pension or retirement plans is to give income coverage to workers who retire from their job after attaining a specified age. Income security for early retirement, which includes disability, is a secondary purpose, and a far distant consideration is that of benefits for disabled family members. However, some plans are good sources of income to disabled people if the benefits include income to (1) workers who become disabled while still in the work force or (2) to disabled children of workers who have stopped working or died. Disability retirement occurs when a worker is retired prematurely because of total and permanent disability. Most plans, particularly those that are union-negotiated, provide coverage for such retirement. Coverage is less common among nonnegotiated plans. Rarer still are those plans that guarantee any long-range income to disabled children of enrolled workers. Usually the plans will include a lump-sum death or life insurance benefit, which will go to any person whom the worker has designated. Once this payment is made, the insurance carrier is discharged from further obligations. It is assumed that disabled dependents will then come under the retirement, survivors, and disability coverages of Social Security.

Nevertheless, for those covered workers who have become disabled or have elected to retire, the private pension movement is a strong source of long-term income. Nearly 40 million workers are so enrolled, and the plans have become increasingly more equitable and extensive in their benefits. Reform legislation, enacted as the Employee Retirement Income Security Act (ERISA) in 1974, required all plans to conform to minimum standards, but there is no requirement that plans be offered by every employer.

ELIGIBILITY

The only uniformity among the hundreds of retirement plans is that they must meet the minimum standards specified by the ERISA legislation. In terms of eligibility, the law stipulates that if an employer has a plan in operation or is starting one, it must be offered to *all* employees who are over age twenty-five.

The federal act does not require that plans include a disability feature. Paradoxically, however, the greatest uniformity among them is in disability coverage. Ordinarily in the past, an employee had to work a specified period of time before qualifying for retirement for disability with benefits. Sometimes, too, there has been a minimum age requirement. The trend is rapidly changing, and most present plans disregard both age and length of service requirements if the employee's disability is total and permanent.

The elimination of age and years of service as requirements is of trivial significance and reflects only a slight expansion of coverage, since the age when a worker incurs a disability determines how much the payment of benefits will cost the insurer. The benefit plan invariably sets a maximum dollar amount for monthly benefits; the insurance company computes what will be paid by Social Security and other public disability insurances and pays only the remainder.

BENEFITS

There is no single benefit formula. Disability benefits are, in most plans, payable after a six-month waiting period. Financial loss during this time is expected to be filled by either Workers' Compensation or Temporary Disability Insurance. If the disability is total and permanent, the Disability Insurance of Social Security takes over. Union plans usually require that the employer's disability insurance continue until the worker reaches age 65. Then the worker becomes eligible for the Retirement Insurance of Social Security and the employer's obligations have ceased.

Retirement plans that do not involve union-negotiated contracts show great variation. The disability benefits may be: (1) calculated in relation to the worker's earnings and length of credited services, (2) calculated in relation to the years of work only, (3) a uniform or flat benefit for all workers who fulfill specified service requirements, or (4) a flat dollar amount based on the employee's level of highest salary and years of service.

USEFUL INFORMATION

The marketplace abounds with any number of retirement programs, and the generosity of coverage is restricted only by the amount that the purchaser wishes to pay. The purchaser may be the employer, an individual, or jointly; often an individual purchases this insurance privately as a supplement to that provided at work.

As part of the Economic Recovery Act of 1981, a new option opened allowing working people to build a tax-deferred retirement system of their own. Previously, they were not permitted to do so unless self-employed, not covered under a company pension plan, or under other special work circumstances. The expanded legislation established Individual Retirement Accounts or, popularly, IRAs. The new law that became effective on January 1, 1982 allows workers to put aside money for retirement and thus to shave their tax bills. Up to $2,000 a year or 100 percent of income, whichever is less, may be placed into interest-bearing accounts. This money and the interest it earns are exempt from all federal, state, and local taxes until the time it is withdrawn. Generally, IRAs are recommended only if an individual won't need the money before retirement. If the money is withdrawn before retirement age, 59½, there are tax penalties. Many banks, savings and loan organizations, and insurance companies require that six months' interest be forfeited. The Internal Revenue Service levies a 10 percent tax-penalty on the amount withdrawn; in addition, the income must be declared and prevalent federal, state and local income taxes paid on the amount. There are definite financial advantages if funds from an IRA account are not withdrawn until retirement. For example, if an individual deposited $2,000 a year into an IRA for twenty years, earning 12 percent interest on the funds invested, $160,000 would be accumulated. It should always be remembered, however, that IRA accounts are tax-deferred, not tax exempt. IRA income is taxed as ordinary income at the time of withdrawal. Some of the presumed tax benefit of the tax-deferred feature is that the participant will be in a lower tax bracket when retiring. Savings and loan institutions, commercial banks, brokerage firms, insurance companies, credit unions, mutual funds, and other financial agencies offer IRAs. The interest rates paid vary, as do other aspects of the accounts.

Disability retirement provisions of retirement plans are of utmost importance yet seem to be one of the least understood—or least considered—features of future benefits. Few plans, if any, give any benefit to a worker's disabled children. By their very nature, the plans are otherwise directed—toward meeting the worker's anticipated needs of income during natural retirement or when disabled.

ESTATE TRUSTS

DESCRIPTION

A trust is a legal arrangement that permits financial interests held by one person to be designated for the benefit of another. The interests are cash, property, investments, or the anticipated cash benefits from a life insurance policy. The basis of a trust is the distribution of these assets, the income derived from them, or both. In the simplest form, three individuals are involved: the trustor, often one or both parents of a disabled child, who establishes the trust; the trustee who administers the trust, either a corporate entity, such as a bank, or an individual who might be an attorney, a relative, or an esteemed friend; and the beneficiary, in this example the disabled child. Trusts may be created by more than one person, as in the case of parents. There may be cotrustees and any number of beneficiaries. Three general categories are found under the broad heading of estate trusts: fiduciary, testamentary, and life insurance.

A *fiduciary* trust is established and operates while the parent, or trustor, is still living. Capital and/or proceeds from the capital that are set aside by the trustor go to the person or persons named as beneficiary.

Testamentary trusts, as the name implies, originate under a last will and testament. The testamentary trust is the customary form of estate trust. Here the trust becomes effective upon the death of the donor and is administered by a probate court. Property that is designated to remain "in trust" will be distributed to the beneficiary over a period of time. Most likely, and particularly if the assets are extensive, the capital will be invested, and the income it generates will go to the beneficiary. All trusts contain a provision about the final disposition of the original capital assets.

Life Insurance trusts, the third major alternative, are generally considered the simplest to develop and the easiest to afford. They typically involve less assets than do the fiduciary and testamentary forms. This kind of trust is not to be confused with ordinary life insurance policies, where a designated beneficiary receives the death benefits directly. Rather, under the life insurance trust the death cash benefit becomes part of an estate created in the last will of the parent or trustor. Under a "declaration of trust" clause in the will, the parent appoints a trustee to collect the proceeds of a life insurance policy, invest them, and disburse the money in the manner desired by the parent. In most states the court will scrutinize the trustee's performance.

In all forms of trust, the parent has a choice of trustee, ranging from a large corporate trust company or bank to a relative or friend willing to assume this responsibility. A joint arrangement, combining the fiscal skill and financial management capabilities of the corporate trustee with the personal interest of an individual who serves as cotrustee, can also be worked out. Trustees are paid a fee for their duties.

One application of the life insurance trust, although once fairly widespread, has met with only lukewarm endorsement and has shown but mediocre effectiveness. Known as "Parents Trusts" or "Living Trusts," this variation grew out of parents' concern for the future care of their retarded sons and daughters. The plans were developed during the 1950s and 1960s, almost simultaneously on both sides of the continent. Parents of retarded children organized nonprofit corporations solely for the purpose of being trustees of life insurance policies. The retarded children were the beneficiaries. The organization was the trustee. The purpose was to provide systematic, perpetual, and constant attentiveness to the needs of these retarded people as long as they lived. Unfortunately, the idea never quite got off the ground. Cost of the insurance policies, reluctance of parents to surrender family responsibilities to a surrogate, and the inflexibility of state laws all helped to dampen the spread of this innovation. Because the trusts had only modest assets, it was often impossible to obtain enough money to finance the operating costs of the corporation. The final blow to the parents' surrogate trust movement occurred with the enactment of SSI; the SSI benefit of the disabled children was reduced by income they received from the trust. However, some of these programs still exist as vestiges of this creative adaptation among affiliates of the Association for Retarded Citizens.

ELIGIBILITY

Anyone who can afford to establish a trust is eligible to do so. From any angle, trusts are expensive, both in the legal fees for setting them up and in the amount of assets needed to make them worthwhile.

BENEFITS

Benefits are the only reason any estate trust is formed. The parent, or trustor, can specify what amount of income or capital is to be expended for the beneficiary, over what duration of years, and for what purpose. Specific duties of the trustee can be stipulated. Obviously, this must be agreed upon before the trustee accepts the appointment.

USEFUL INFORMATION

Considerable discussion and dispute has arisen around estate trusts. The issues are adequacy of assets and realism of desire. A trust is as rich a resource for income maintenance as the amount of money that created it. There is a common belief that a trust possesses magical qualities that will guarantee complete lifetime income for a disabled person from a minimal outlay of funds. This is an illusion; it ignores the devastating effects of inflation, projections of the beneficiary's life expectancy, and the costs of administration. The expectation that a sizable income can be bought by most parents is, sadly, based on fantasy. Nearly two decades ago, research was conducted on the utility of trusts. Even then, the study concluded, anyone with a moderate income who envisioned forming a trust was fantasizing that "insurance companies were either magicians or philanthropists." For most people such trusts are just not feasible.

The most realistic type is the life insurance trust. Although insurance premiums do cost money, the assets of the life insurance trust can be accumulated in a relatively painless way through the payment of monthly or annual premiums. Although obtaining a trustee might be difficult, because of the duties involved, there is the likelihood that a relative, friend, or citizen advocate would be willing to tackle the job of compassionate trustee, even if the assets were modest. Of course, the costs of operation should be considered.

The possibility of a reduction in the disabled person's SSI benefits must also be weighed. Unless the size of the trust fund is so great that the beneficiary will receive more than SSI provides, there is no reason to consider a trust. If the income from a trust falls below the SSI maximum, it is sure to be deducted from the SSI payment.

PRIVATE UNEMPLOYMENT PROGRAMS

Privately purchased unemployment programs actually mean insurance for disability rather than coverage for being out of work because of termination from a job or the inability to find work. More specifically, it means financial protection from income loss because of nonoccupational disability. The protection plans are offered by private insurance companies and purchased by the employer, the employee, or jointly with contributions from both. They may be bought by individuals for themselves as self-insurance or through group insurance plans. Group plans are a popular form offered to members of groups such as professional organizations, unions, clubs, lodges, credit unions, churches, and other voluntary associations. The coverage may be either for temporary, or short-term, disability or for long-term. This insurance is elective and not mandated by state law.

TEMPORARY DISABILITY INSURANCE

DESCRIPTION

Short-term disability is defined as any illness or injury lasting less than six months that was not caused by work-related illness or accident. Insurance policies are available from most of the nation's major insurance carriers. Including those few states where coverage is mandatory, over thirty-two million workers have some form of temporary disability insurance.

ELIGIBILITY

Terms of all policies include distinct eligibility criteria. *The sickness or injury must not have occurred because of conditions on the job.* Otherwise, financial benefits would be available from public programs such as Workers' Compensation, Temporary Disability Insurance offered by the employer, or in some instances, federal-state Unemployment Insurance. Plans typically require a waiting period before coverage goes into effect. Ordinarily this is from three to seven days or until job sick-leave benefits are exhausted.

BENEFITS

Each insurance policy has its own set of benefits, and as might be expected, there is much variation. What can be said is that the size of benefits is in direct proportion to what one wishes to pay for premiums. Most plans, similar to those TDI programs that are required by state statute, give one-half to two-thirds wage replacement. Some provide a flat amount. Duration of benefits may vary according to the length of time one has been on the job, or they may be limited to a fixed period, usually from thirteen to twenty-six weeks.

LONG-TERM DISABILITY INSURANCE

DESCRIPTION

Long-term disability insurance is coverage for an extensive period of time. It is designed for the individual who has an impairment that is expected to last a number of years, even a lifetime, and will probably prevent future employment. In 1981, about twenty million people had long-term disability insurance policies.

ELIGIBILITY

The basic eligibility provision is that the nature and cause of disability cannot qualify the individual for any type of public insurance coverage such as Workers' Compensation. The definition of "long-term disability" may also be an issue, and the differences among insurance companies on this score are great. Six months is usually the cut-off period for distinguishing between short-term and long-term disability. Occasionally, long-term disability is defined as a limitation in the kind or amount of work, including housework, that one can do caused by a chronic health condition lasting over three months.

Severity of the disability may also be questioned. Some policies differentiate between inability to perform *any* kind of work and limited ability to do *some* types of work. In the language of insurance policies, this limited ability is known as "secondary limitations of work capacity." The picture becomes even hazier in trying to describe what is meant by secondary work limitations. Some policies, for example, explain that although a person is disabled he may be "able to work full time, regularly, and at the same work, but with limitations in the kind or amount of work that can be performed."

BENEFITS

The amount of cash income is usually stipulated in the policy. Sometimes it is in relation to what the employee was earning before becoming disabled, or it may be a flat dollar amount. Some policies have an offset against the Disability Insurance of OASDHI, or an "OASDHI linkage." In that case, any benefits coming from Social Security would be deducted from the maximum cash amount stated in the policy. An OASDHI linkage should be stated in the LTD policy and, it may be hoped, understood by the policyholder.

USEFUL INFORMATION

Benefits and eligibility qualifications of both temporary and long-term disability insurances differ as much as the companies that write the policies. So do the costs of premiums. Both forms of insurance are designed only for the worker who becomes disabled. It is very unusual to find plans that cover disabled dependents or dependents who become disabled.

Rarely do the benefits reach the salary level that the disabled person had when working. Unless the plan has the OASDHI linkage, this difference may be made up by payments from Social Security. The most valuable plans are those that do not offset benefits against any payments received from public insurances.

COMMUNITY FINANCIAL SERVICES
AND RESOURCES

Many sources of financial aid are not structured programs containing specific conditions of eligibility or a precise set of benefits. These are a miscellany of often overlooked facets of financial aid that are found formally or informally in most communities. Sometimes they are of a casual nature, known and accepted as matter of fact by the nondisabled population, which has always been familiar with money matters and the management of personal finances.

The consumer and civil rights movements were instrumental in bringing disab' d people into society's mainstream. The vigor of these social movements, particularly during the early 1970s, brought about a wide range of new services that have become as closely identified with financial aids as is a guaranteed income-maintenance program. These services fall into two major categories: (1) financial management and (2) procurement of money or financial resources. These services are provided by many agencies; each agency has its own rules for determining who is eligible; and the benefits apply to anyone who needs a particular kind of help and obtains it.

FINANCIAL MANAGEMENT

Financial management is assistance in handling money, or in learning how to get the most benefit possible from the money available. Financial management can be broken down into several components. The most common needs are instruction and assistance in budgeting, debt counseling, establishing credit, referral to other services or sources of money, training in purchasing and shopping, insuring for future needs, and linkage to suppliers of goods.

BUDGETING

Budgeting is a thought-out plan for coordinating resources and expenditures. It involves estimates of expenditures, assigning amounts of money to particular purposes for specific periods of time, and developing priorities of need.

Extension programs of high schools and colleges regularly have courses in budgeting, although they are often at night. Voluntary agencies, such as the United Cerebral Palsy Associations, the National Easter Seal Society or other organizations set up to help the handicapped, may provide help, as well as the YMCA and YWCA and the Catholic and Jewish family service agencies. As a rule, the well-known voluntary agencies and lesser-known, newer self-help organizations will be highly responsive to setting up new programs if the need is presented to them. More and more, banks and savings and loan associations are sponsoring budget training as a service to their customers and as a lure to the general public. Commercial institutions, such as banks, are beginning to exhibit more responsiveness to the needs of disabled people.

DEBT COUNSELING

Debt counseling is usually needed because a budget was not established or followed or because unanticipated emergencies have occurred. Debt counseling will include instruction in setting up a budget and a plan for paying off debts. It will also help the person learn to discuss his financial plight with his debtors and present them with a plan of action, and it will include instruction in the use of bankruptcy laws.

There are professional money management experts who, for a fee, will sell their skills and abilities to individuals. Equally competent assistance, often from the same experts, may be provided by the nonprofit or commercial organizations that offer training and help in budgeting.

CREDIT

Credit refers to a system whereby money is advanced to an individual to make purchases that he will pay for at an agreed upon later date. The money is not advanced in cash; purchases of goods or services are charged to the individual's credit account. If credit is once established with a business firm, it is usually easy to get from others. However, many disabled people, particularly if they have never worked or have had only nominal employment, may have trouble establishing credit initially. Credit is useful in purchasing major items whose cost exceeds the individual's or family's cash supplies. The management of credit purchases is always part of budgeting.

The easiest way to establish credit is to have a bank account, either checking or savings, and then apply through the bank for a VISA or MasterCard account. Both of these are national credit systems and accepted by most merchants, but most large retail stores also have their own credit system and listing a bank account on the store's credit application is the surest way to obtain a credit account there. Small amounts of cash can also be borrowed against either VISA or MasterCard, but restraint must be exercised. These borrowed sums accumulate rapidly, must be systematically and promptly repaid, and interest rates are high. If repayments are delayed, a card holder runs the risk of having the card privilege cancelled and credit revoked.

Obtaining credit may not be at all simple. Although the Office of Consumer Affairs, established by Presidential Executive Order in 1971 and expanded in subsequent amendments, originally did undertake a strenuous educational program to assure that credit would be extended to more people, old prejudices about the financial risk of disabled people still abound. If problems are encountered, the local legal aid society is a good source of assistance. Suggestions and techniques for obtaining credit should also be part of any training given in money management and budgeting.

REFERRALS

The sharing of information is what is meant by referral. Knowledge about alternate sources for services frequently comes by word of mouth from other disabled people. Disabled people traditionally have had the disadvantage of being excluded—or protected—from dealing with financial matters. The best source of practical education and quick information comes from self-help organizations or other groups of disabled people whose members can share their experiences and give realistic suggestions.

Local information and referral agencies are another resource, but the information will be presented in a more formal manner, and it may lack the value of firsthand experience. These agencies will be listed in the yellow pages of the telephone directory under "Social Service and Welfare Organizations." One can also call the county welfare department, since public welfare agencies are required by law to maintain an information and referral service.

PURCHASING AND SHOPPING

Intelligent purchasing and shopping are learned skills, which one develops from experience. One needs, for instance, to have a knowledge of quality, the comparability of prices, and seasonal variations in the cost of goods.

There are few programs to teach shopping skills, but that does not mean that they could not be created. The best form of help is found in such consumer organizations as consumer cooperatives. Inclusion of this training in the counseling and training programs of social service organizations seems so natural that its absence is surprising. If enough people make the demand, the agencies will respond.

INSURANCE

Buying an insurance policy is a way of taking precautions against future needs or hazards. Policies can be bought, for instance, to insure against the risks of fire, personal accident, or death or to meet the income requirements of old age.

Instruction in this complicated and confusing topic requires an expert's hand. Insurance agents may seem to be the most logical sources of information, but they may not be, since they are in the business of selling insurance. The best way to obtain an unbiased and clear picture is to consult an objective instructor. Requests for help in understanding elementary insurance should be made to local high schools and community colleges. These institutions have the obligation of giving many kinds of training if enough people desire it. They should always be a first resource for any type of training or instruction.

Social service agencies, both public and private, should also be asked to provide this service. Consumer cooperatives will probably be the most responsive. A call to an information and referral center will tell you if there are any in your locality.

LINKAGE TO SUPPLIERS OF GOODS

Linkage to suppliers of goods means learning where to buy what one needs at the best price. Other than organized consumer groups, the best source of information is from friends. Despite the need, even agencies serving the handicapped have given scant attention to this service. Here and there, some organizations have compiled lists of markets and merchants who recognize the income limitations that most disabled people have. Requests for such information should be made to all appropriate local agencies, such as Goodwill Industries.

FINANCIAL RESOURCES

As disabled people move toward fuller participation in community life, new sets of problems arise for them. No one, disabled and nondisabled alike, is exempt from financial problems, and they always appear critical and troublesome. For those disabled people who are unfamiliar with a community's business operations and financial institutions, ordinary problems of emergency cash needs may loom as overwhelming and insoluble. Disabled individuals who are competing in the community may find they have difficulty in obtaining certain financial services, because of still-prevailing attitudes of fear, ignorance, and paternalism. Their service needs tend to revolve around obtaining emergency cash assistance, either through loans or through cash grants, and obtaining insurance coverage.

LOANS

Loans are the usual and time-honored way of obtaining cash to meet immediate cash requirements. Obtaining a loan means borrowing money for temporary use, on the condition that it be returned and that a certain amount of interest be paid for borrowing the money. Interest is nearly always computed as a percentage of the amount borrowed. Loans always include an agreement between the lender and the borrower regarding the terms for repayment.

Banks are the most common source for loans. Loans may be granted for a relatively short period of time, or they may extend over a period of years. Typically, they are made to help the person meet specific cash flow problems or to make a major purchase. Banks have been accused of being generally resistive toward meeting the needs of most disabled people. Even the consumerism movement, begun in 1962 with President Kennedy's declaration of "The Consumer Bill of Rights," has yet to alter this picture significantly. In fairness to the banking industry, it is reasonable that lending institutions need some evidence of the loan applicant's salary, other income amounts and sources, and credit history.

Smaller banks, particularly privately owned banks and those getting started, often appear to be more receptive to the needs of minorities. Occasionally, too, interest rates on loans are slightly lower than those offered by massive and multi-branch corporations. Savings and loan associations loan money primarily for the purchase of property. Unless one's purpose is to buy property and he has a lengthy employment history or can show substantial income, they are not the answer for critical cash needs.

Credit unions are another resource, but only for members. These financial organizations are formed and owned by people who share some common bond. Fellow employees, for instance, frequently form a credit union, as a cooperative, with the purpose of making small loans to members at low interest rates. Groups of disabled people have expressed a desire to develop their own credit unions, but action seems to have been thwarted by legal requirements, inadequate interest on the part of potential participants, and lack of leadership.

Private social service agencies may make temporary loans of small amounts, usually with no interest payment, but they are far more prone to give cash grants. For short-term loans of small amounts, usually no more than $50, one of the world's most ancient business institutions should not be overlooked — the pawnshop. These private businesses loan money on personal property, which is secured in their keeping. There are hazards, however. Interest will be as high as the law allows, and, if the article is not redeemed by the time repayment is due, it will be sold. If the item being pawned is of considerable value, the pawnbroker will require the individual seeking the loan to verify that it was not obtained by theft.

CASH GRANT

A cash grant is money that need not be repaid. Frequently, cash grants are given for a particular purpose such as the payment of rent or the purchase of food. They usually are made in amounts of less than $100, and they may be paid directly to a vendor rather than to the applicant.

Only a limited number of organizations and agencies provide this service, particularly those with a decidedly local focus. Those most likely to give cash assistance are fraternal societies, such as local lodges of the Elks (BPOE), Knights of Columbus, and the Masonic Order. Others include civic organizations like Rotary and Soroptomist clubs, local labor unions, ethnic associations; and veterans and military associations, such as the Jewish War Veterans and American Legion. Membership is rarely a requirement for assistance. In general, health, welfare, and social service agencies that are community-based without any affiliation to a large national organization are more receptive to cash grant requests. An even better record is found in local voluntary organizations that were formed to provide services to people with a specific type of disability and whose programs have an emphasis on rehabilitation. However, the affiliates of some national associations, such as the Easter Seal Society, do, in some localities, give individual cash grants for specific purposes.

The next best resources are welfare organizations operated under religious sponsorship. More often than not, however, commodities such as food and clothing will be given rather than a flat amount of cash for undesignated purposes. Community action groups and family social service agencies also have a sporadic history of providing cash assistance.

Requesting cash assistance from an agency may appear to be demeaning and humiliating, but it should be remembered that under the laws of every state and by their own charters, these nonprofit agencies exist, with tax exemptions provided by the Internal Revenue Service, to provide personal and community services. Such agencies occasionally need to be reminded of their own commitments to service.

INSURANCE COVERAGE

Insurance coverage for disabled people is a vexing and discouraging social issue throughout the nation. Commonly, life, health, and disability insurances are either denied to disabled people or sold at higher premium rates. There is statistical evidence that disabled people have a greater incidence of health problems than the nondisabled, but justification of prevalent practices is questionable when it comes to the reluctance of insurance companies in making life and disability policies available at all and when formulated, often provided at inequitable rates. Responsibility for this situation does not fall on individual representatives of the insurance industry but rather on corporate policy. The solution is to seek legislative correction.

There are two steps that can be taken as interim measures. Disabled people who seek insurance coverage should continue making applications. If turned down or presented with inordinately high premiums, they should complain vigorously to the insurance commissioner of the state.

CONCLUSION

People with a physical, mental, or emotional impairment have as an ultimate goal their full participation in society. Many barriers stand between an individual and the attainment of this goal. Yet none seems so formidable as the need for a rich resource of financial aids, including a reliable source of personal income.

Only during the last half century has there been any large-scale governmental effort to initiate a primitive policy of income maintenance. Even the early efforts, part of an emerging national social security policy, were directed less toward the disabled than toward other segments of society. As the social and technological structure of the nation changed, a patchwork quilt of piecemeal income-assistance programs developed. Each piece contained some fragmented aspect of economic help for the disabled. Finally, in the 1970s, reform legislation ushered in a new lifeline of economic support for the aged, blind, and disabled. Now, ten years after the cohesive SSI legislation was enacted, all public support programs are in jeopardy. The Administration's demonstrated attitude toward the nation's social programs clearly places them in an inferior position to what are perceived as more important national priorities. Fifty years of national progress toward assuring all citizens security and sustenance is now in peril of being swept away.

All legislated and governmental programs carry disappointments and inadequacies. Experience with SSI and each program of the Social Security Act makes it clear that an equitable program of guaranteed income is difficult to create and even harder to administer. The problem is that the coverage must be designed for the millions, but attention must be given to the individual.

Every important problem is imbedded in a much larger set of problems. Similarly, there is more to economic security than merely the provision of income, imperative as that is. Supplying money to an individual without concomitant instruction in its management is both a waste of money and a disservice to the individual. Financial management, like other human behaviors, is a learned skill.

BIBLIOGRAPHY

Commerce Clearing House, Inc. *1981 Economic Recovery Tax Act Highlights.* Chicago: Commerce Clearing House, Inc., 1981.

Gilbert, Neil and Harry Specht, eds. *Handbook of the Social Services.* Englewood Cliffs, New Jersey: Prentice-Hall Inc., 1981.

Howards, Irving; Henry P. Brehm and Saad Z. Nagi. *Disability. From Social Problem to Federal Program.* New York: Praeger Publishers, 1980.

Lee, A. James. *Employment, Unemployment, and Health Insurance: Behavioral and Descriptive Analysis of Health Insurance Loss Due to Unemployment.* Cambridge, Massachusetts: Abt Books, 1979.

Meyer, Charles W. *Social Security Disability Insurance.* Washington, D.C.: American Enterprise Institute for Public Policy Research, 1979.

Schechter, Evan S. "Commitment to Work and the Self-Perception of Disability." *Social Security Bulletin,* Vol. 44, No. 6, Social Security Administration Publication No. 13-11700. Washington, D.C.: Government Printing Office, June 1981, pp. 22–30.

Stein, Bruno. *Social Security and Pensions in Transition: Understanding the American Retirement System.* New York: Free Press, 1980.

U.S. Congress. *Reducing the Federal Deficit: Strategies and Options. A Report to the Senate and House Committees on the Budget — Part III.* Congressional Budget Office Publication No. 89-377. Washington, D.C.: Government Printing Office, February 1982.

U.S. Department of Education. *Pocket Guide to Federal Help for the Disabled Person.* Office of Information and Resources for the Handicapped, DE Publication No. E-80-22002. Washington, D.C.: Government Printing Office, October 1980.

U.S. Department of Health and Human Services. *A Message From Social Security about the Special Medical Examination Needed for Your Disability Claim.* Social Security Administration, SSA Publication No. 05-10087. Washington, D.C.: Government Printing Office, September 1981.

_____. *Claims Representative Basic Course: Program Introduction, Student Workbook.* Social Security Administration, Office of Management, Budget and Personnel, SSA Publication No. 23-123. Washington, D.C.: Government Printing Office, May 1980.

_____. *History of Social Security.* Social Security Administration, SSA Publication No. 05-10011. Washington, D.C.: Government Printing Office, October 1981.

_____. *How Recent Changes in Social Security May Affect You.* Social Security Administration, SSA Publication No. 05-10314. Washington, D.C.: Government Printing Office, January 1982.

_____. *How Work Affects Your Social Security Checks.* Social Security Administration, SSA Publication No. 05-10069. Washington, D.C.: Government Printing Office, March 1981.

_____. *If You Become Disabled.* Social Security Administration, SSA Publication No. 05-10029. Washington, D.C.: Government Printing Office, September 1981.

_____. *Oasis.* Social Security Administration (Monthly Publication for Employees and Retired Personnel of the Social Security Administration). Washington, D.C.: Government Printing Office.

_____. *Rulings. Social Security Rulings on Federal Old-Age, Survivors, Disability, Supplemental Security Income; and Black Lung Benefits. Cumula-*

tive Edition 1980. Social Security Administration, Office of Operational Policy and Procedure, SSA Publication No. 65-002. Washington, D.C.: Government Printing Office, April 1980.

_____. *SSA Training, SSI: RMA (Retrospective Monthly Accounting) Initial Lessons.* Social Security Administration, Office of Management, Budget and Personnel, SSA Training Publication No. 81-09. Washington, D.C.: Government Printing Office, December 1981.

_____. *Social Security Bulletin, Annual Statistical Supplement, 1980.* Social Security Administration, Office of Research and Statistics, Office of Policy, SSA Publication No. 13-11700. Washington, D.C.: Government Printing Office, 1981.

_____. *The Supplemental Security Income Program for the Aged, Blind, and Disabled.* Social Security Administration, Office of Research and Statistics, Office of Policy, SSA Publication No. 13-11975. Washington, D.C.: Government Printing Office, April 1980.

_____. *What You Have to Know About SSI.* Social Security Administration, SSA Publication No. 05-11011. Washington, D.C.: Government Printing Office, June 1981.

_____. *Your Disability Claim.* Social Security Administration, SSA Publication No. 05-10052. Washington, D.C.: Government Printing Office, August 1981.

_____. *Your Right to Question the Decision Made on Your Social Security Claim.* Social Security Administration, SSA Publication No. 05-10058. Washington, D.C.: Government Printing Office, August 1981.

_____. *Your Social Security.* Social Security Administration, SSA Publication No. 05-10035. Washington, D.C.: Government Printing Office, September 1981.

_____. *Your Social Security Rights and Responsibilities, Retirement and Survivors Benefits.* Social Security Administration, SSA Publication No. 05-10077. Washington, D.C.: Government Printing Office, January 1982.

U.S. Department of Health, Education, and Welfare. *Program Introduction: The Social Security Programs.* Social Security Administration, Office of Management and Administration, Office of Human Resources, Division of Personnel and Training Operation, OHR Training Manual Publication No. 025-2. Baltimore, Maryland: Social Security Administration, Office of Management and Administration, February 1978.

_____. *Ready Reference Guide; Resources for Disabled People.* Rehabilitation Services Administration, Stock No. 017-000-00201-5. Washington, D.C.: Government Printing Office, June 1977.

_____. *Social Security Handbook.* Social Security Administration, HEW Publication No. (SSA) 77-10135. Washington, D.C.: Government Printing Office, July 1978.

_____. "Social Security Program Charts. Chart Presentation for 1979 Advisory Council on Social Security." Washington, D.C.: U.S. Department of Health, Education, and Welfare; Social Security Administration, May 1978.

U.S. Executive Office of the President. *1981 Update to the Catalog of Federal Domestic Assistance.* Office of Management and Budget, Federal Program Information Branch. Washington, D.C.: Government Printing Office, 1982.

U.S. House of Representatives, Select Committee on Aging. *Impact of Administration's Social Security Proposal on Present and Future Beneficiaries.* A Report by the Chairman of Select Committee on Aging, House of Representatives, Ninety-Seventh Congress, Comm. Pub. No. 97-280. Washington, D.C.: Government Printing Office, July 1981.

U.S. Senate. *Comprehensive Community Based Noninstitutional Long-Term Care for the Elderly and Disabled.* Hearing Before the Sub-Committee on Health of the Committee on Finance, Ninety-sixth Congress, No. HG 96-98. Washington, D.C.: Government Printing Office, August 27, 1980.

U.S. Veterans Administration. *Benefits for Veterans and Service Personnel with Service Since January 31, 1955 and Their Dependents.* VA Pamphlet 20-67-1. Washington, D.C.: Government Printing Office.

_____. *Federal Benefits for Veterans and Dependents.* VA Fact Sheet IS-1. Washington, D.C.: Government Printing Office.

_____. *Questions and Answers on Guaranteed and Direct Loans for Veterans.* VA Pamphlet 26-4. Washington, D.C.: Government Printing Office.

_____. *Service-Disabled Veterans Insurance.* VA Pamphlet 29-9A. Washington, D.C.: Government Printing Office.

_____. *Summary of Benefits for Veterans with Military Service before February 1, 1955 and Their Dependents.* VA Pamphlet 20-72-2. Washington, D.C.: Government Printing Office.

_____. *Tutorial Assistance for Veterans, Dependents and Service Personnel Under the GI Bill.* VA Pamphlet No. 22-75-3. Washington, D.C.: Government Printing Office.

_____. *Veterans Benefits for Older Americans.* VA Pamphlet 27-80-2. Washington, D.C.: Government Printing Office.

_____. *Veterans Benefits — Inside . . . Outside.* VA Pamphlet 27-79-2. Washington, D.C.: Government Printing Office.

_____. *Veteran-Student Work-Study Programs.* VA Pamphlet 27-80-3. Washington, D.C.: Government Printing Office.

4 | EMPLOYMENT AND VOCATIONAL REHABILITATION

Current labor statistics (1980) indicate that some 70 percent of the employable disabled in the United States are not working. Ninety percent of severely disabled people are unemployed. Because of economic conditions, prejudicial employer attitudes, and the general dearth of counseling, training, and specialized placement programs, the vast pool of human resources represented by disabled persons is utilized only minimally in our society.

However, there are disabled persons who are performing effectively in occupations ranging from the simplest to the most skilled. There are chemical engineers, diesel mechanics, and even physicians who are blind, computer programmers and machinists who are deaf, clerk typists and warehouse workers who are retarded, professors and electronic technicians who are paraplegic.

For most human beings, work is just as important to psychological and social functioning as it is to economic survival. The activities and social status associated with work are as vital as earnings in avoiding the destructive effects of being powerless. A sense of powerlessness has been cited as a causal factor in immensely varied kinds of human suffering, including depression, suicide, failure to recover from illness and trauma, and failure to rebuild a life after even the best medical and rehabilitative care has been offered. The individual in this society who is unable to work is deprived not only of the most effective survival tool that exists, but also of the major available path toward self-esteem and self-actualization. Typically, work occupies nearly half of one's waking life and considerably more than that for

Portions of this chapter draw on and are quoted, with permission, from "Vocational Rehabilitation," by Carolyn Vash, Ph.D., appearing in *Orthopedic Rehabilitation*, Vernon Nickel, M.D., editor.

some people. Many, if not most, people have important attachments to their work; it gives structure to their time, is a major determinant of their sense of identity, and frequently constitutes their primary raison d'etre—none of which can be relinquished lightly.

In a materialistically oriented society, to be without earnings is to be deprived of access to the vast array of material comforts and pleasures that one sees others enjoy. The barest necessities may be provided through a welfare system, but at enormous cost in terms of loss of privacy, loss of pride, and the devastating experience of what Erving Goffman has termed "the mortification process." Thus, almost everyone needs to work, and for a wide spectrum of psychological, social, and economic reasons. The advent of a permanent disability seldom changes any of those basic needs. What *does* change is the likelihood of being able to fulfill them. Ironically, the interference caused by the functional limitations of the disability itself may be minor compared to the additional and often unnecessary handicapping that is imposed by the external world.

This chapter will explore the realities of the world of work as confronted by the disabled, review the barriers to their successful entry into it, and outline the requirements and procedures of the chief public and private service programs that can facilitate that entry.

BARRIERS TO EMPLOYMENT FOR WORKERS WITH DISABILITIES

To begin, it is important to distinguish between the disability and any handicapping effects it may have. Residual anatomical, physiological, or psychological damage resulting from illness, injury, or birth defect is the *disability*. Paralysis is an example. Whether or not a paralyzed person is also *handicapped* depends on what he or she is trying to do. Even a severely paralyzed person may not be particularly handicapped in delivering a lecture before a group. However, if a fire drill were suddenly ordered, the person might be seriously handicapped indeed. The extent of handicapping in that situation would depend on such external factors as whether the lecturer had a wheelchair he could operate independently and whether the building was ramped and/or had fire emergency elevators. With these distinctions in mind, we'll look at the barriers to employment that exist for many workers with physical disabilities or limitations.

Many employment sites have architectural barriers that make it difficult or impossible for workers with disabilities, especially wheelchair users, to work there. Unramped staircases, absent elevators, inaccessible restrooms, narrow aisles, and cramped work stations are among the primary barriers to mobility within a workplace. In addition, even when a work site is reasonably accessible, workers who are too severely disabled to drive may not have access to public transportation to get to work.

Fortunately, legislation enacted in the past decade or so has brought about improvements in these problems. Section 16 (b) of the Urban Mass Transportation Act (P.L. 91-453) of 1964 was amended in 1970 to require eligible local jurisdictions to plan mass transportation facilities available to and usable by elderly and handicapped persons. In 1977, amendments to the Public Works Employment Act (P.L. 95-128) added the requirement that applicants for public works contracts give assurances to the Department of Commerce that their proposed projects comply with the Architectural Barriers Act of 1968. The Surface Transportation Assistance Act of 1978 (P.L. 95-599) authorized grants to local and national programs to improve mass transit, including special services for the elderly and disabled.

In addition, tax reform legislation (Tax Reform Act of 1976 (P.L. 94-455) and Tax Reduction and Simplification Act of 1977 (P.L. 95-300) provided tax incentives for employers and building owners who remove architectural barriers.

Attitudinal barriers must also be circumvented. Some employers have a prejudice against hiring workers who have disabilities. Many still believe that hiring the handicapped will cause their insurance rates to rise, although insurance companies in this country are leaders in rehabilitating and hiring the handicapped, and insurance rates do not rise when handicapped workers are hired.

However, employers are better educated than they were a decade ago as to the myths and realities concerning insurance risks. Their fears that workers with disabilities will somehow be unable to deliver a quality product or service on time have proved harder to dislodge, and many believe there is a higher injury rate among the handicapped than there is among the average nonhandicapped worker, although Department of Labor surveys have shown that "impaired persons" have fewer disabling injuries than the average worker exposed to the same work hazards.

Workers with a disability may also confront procedural barriers. These barriers include such diverse matters as labor contracts and job descriptions requiring job applicants to be able to perform certain tasks that in fact they will seldom or never be called on to do. Like mobility and attitudinal barriers, these procedural obstacles still persist to a significant degree, but they are slowly being combatted by legislation. Fortunately again, recent federal and state legislation relating to equal employment opportunity, affirmative action, and fair employment practices is also making the future outlook on this matter more favorable.

Finally, there is the barrier imposed by the disability itself—the loss of certain functions that would make job performance in certain areas possible or more feasible. This one is listed last because, in view of the richness of feasible work areas for people with even very severe disabilities, it may actually cause less handicapping than the others with respect to obtaining *some* kind of employment. It may, however, be a very significant barrier to getting and doing the specific type of job the individual has done in the past or wants to do in the future.

VOCATIONAL REHABILITATION

AVAILABLE PROGRAMS

The federal-state vocational rehabilitation program is the major resource for persons disabled by chronic or congenital illness or accident.

The federal-state vocational rehabilitation program originated in the National Civilian Rehabilitation Act of 1920, which established a system of State vocational rehabilitation agencies. Major revisions were made in 1954, when the Act was retitled the Vocational Rehabilitation Act. It was completely rewritten in 1973 (P.L. 93-112) to emphasize rehabilitation for the severely handicapped, and this emphasis was expanded by the Rehabilitation Comprehensive Services and Developmental Disabilities Amendments of 1978 (P.L. 95-602).

All U.S. states and territories have a service-delivery arm of this federal-state partnership, and they employ rehabilitation counselors as their primary service providers. As such, they directly provide the counseling and job placement services to clients and are responsible for procuring and coordinating all of the other specialized services that their clients may need. Some of the small states employ fewer than fifty counselors for this purpose, while California has more than seven hundred. Since the 1978 Rehabilitation Act Amendments the federal agency responsible for overseeing this program is the U.S. Department of Education. The department generates regulations that govern who can be served, toward what ends, and to what extent by the states agencies. The state agencies are usually designated "Division," "Bureau," or "Department" of "Rehabilitation" or of "Vocational Rehabilitation."

The Department of Education has also assumed the responsibility for developing rehabilitation facilities—in the private, nonprofit, and local government sections—that have the express purpose of vending the needed specialized services to the state agencies. These facilities employ the full range of vocational rehabilitation specialists. The Bureau of Education for the Handicapped provides grants to public or nonprofit institutions and to the state agencies for (1) the training of rehabilitation personnel, (2) construction of rehabilitation facilities, and (3) basic and applied research into new concepts of rehabilitation. It also provides funds to state agencies for vocational rehabilitation services to persons on Social Security Disability Insurance.

Vocational Rehabilitation for Disabled Veterans, a program of the Veterans Administration (VA), trains veterans with service-connected disabilities, in an attempt to restore their employability. Up to four years of training is available, including the entire cost of tuition, books, fees, and other training/schooling supplies. During training, and for two months following rehabilitation, a veteran is paid a subsistence allowance in addition to disability compensation.

Recently, significant numbers of vocational rehabilitation specialists, pursuant to Title VI of the Vocational Rehabilitation Act of 1973 that mandates rehabilitation for people who sustain industrial injuries, have moved into the private for-profit section. And increasing numbers of rehabilitation counselors, work evaluators, and others can be found there.

In the state-federal and private service-delivery systems, there are sources of funds available for people who cannot afford to pay for the often time-consuming and costly procedures involved. RSA programs are supported by public funds, and the third relies on insurance monies.

Section 503 of the nation's Vocational Rehabilitation Act of 1973 gave a substantial boost to job prospects for handicapped people during the 1970s. Section 503 requires that any company contracting more than $2,500 a year in business with the federal government have an affirmative action plan to hire and advance the handicapped. A conservative estimate by the U.S. Department of Labor in 1980 placed the number of handicapped Americans able to work at 7.2 million, with one million contractors doing over $2,500 worth of business with the federal government. Regulations issued by the Department of Labor in 1978 to implement Section 503 also require that government contractors undertake positive recruitment activities, including changing the attitudes toward handicapped employees by managers, supervisors, and all employees.

THE VOCATIONAL REHABILITATION PROCESS

In the federal-state system, the vocational rehabilitation process generally begins with a contact with the public agency's *rehabilitation counselor*, who is primarily an expert in vocational counseling. Rehabilitation counselors typically have a master's degree in rehabilitation counseling and may be certified by the Council on Rehabilitation Education. The counselor helps clients identify their interests and abilities and the skill resources that can be built upon to develop new or altered vocations. In doing so, the counselor also provides expert information on general occupational fields and specific labor markets to guide clients in making choices. If questions remain after initial counseling regarding what a client is able to do or would find satisfying on a relatively long-term basis, other vocational rehabilitation experts in the federal-state programs may be called upon. Such experts include *vocationally oriented psychologists*, who can administer and interpret standardized tests of interest, aptitudes, educational level, skills, and so forth, and *work evaluators*, who can test the client on real or simulated work samples to discern performance strengths and weaknesses. (Work evaluators, like rehabilitation counselors, are striving for professional growth and the standard of the master's degree.) Throughout these evaluative processes, the counselor and client use the information generated to move successively toward an appropriate vocational choice.

Once the client has made a tentative decision regarding his choice of work, the client will begin a *work preparation* program if such is needed. Some people who become disabled are fully able to continue their pre-disability training or work directions, either with or without adaptive equipment or services. Many more, however, must prepare to alter significantly their career plans or methods of functioning in training or work.

For those who have not had a great deal of work experience previously, or who must radically change their vocational directions, *work adjustment specialists* may be called upon to plan and conduct programs for work-habit training. Here, the client has an opportunity to experience realistic employer demands for punctuality, acceptance of supervision, and so forth, and to build up tolerance for a normal work day. Special settings, usually known as "sheltered workshops," may be used. However, these workshops actually attempt to minimize sheltering and maximize realistic work standards and expectations. When available, specially supervised work stations may be established in ordinary work settings for the same purposes.

Either simultaneously with or following the work adjustment process, actual job-skill training may take place. Just as the rehabilitation counselors coordinate the work evaluation and work adjustment services, they are also responsible for helping their clients secure vocational training so that they will have salable job skills to offer potential employers. The type of training will be selected on the basis of the evaluation results, the client's response to work adjustment, the length of training considered realistic given the client's needs and aptitudes, and costs. The program may range from as little as a few weeks of training in a circumscribed skill area to the seven or eight years required to obtain a graduate degree. If special equipment or services are needed for the person to succeed in training, these are potentially available through both public and insurance-funded programs. Specially equipped vans, motorized wheelchairs controllable with minute muscle action, and modified electric typewriters and tape recorders are among the more common devices used to help severely disabled students function in training. *Vocationally oriented rehabilitation engineers* may be called upon to develop unique solutions to equipment problems.

Whenever possible, ordinary resources for vocational education and training are used rather than programs designed solely for students with disabilities. This approach is advantageous because future workers who have disabilities, even severe ones, need to become integrated into the mainstream as early as possible to avoid a heightened "reentry trauma" later on. However, in some cases, specialized training programs have made it possible for severely disabled people to break gradually into the world of work. In these programs rich supports are provided at first and then reduced as independent means for solving day-to-day problems are found. Sometimes such training programs are located right on the grounds of a rehabilitation hospital.

After the job-skill training is completed, the next steps are job search and job placement. *Job placement specialists* may be called upon to tutor the client in the fine art of how to find and get a job. Methods for locating and understanding job market information are taught, as well as techniques for making a positive impression on potential employers. In addition to tutoring the client, the job placement specialist may personally assume responsibility for such activities as showing an employer how she or he could benefit by redividing the labor in a way that could create a "do-able" job for a severely disabled worker. Again, the rehabilitation engineer may be called upon to solve problems presented by the worker's physical limitations.

A distinction should be made between "sheltered" and "accommodated" employment for workers with disabilities. "Shelter" designates employment in which the worker is protected from the harsh necessity of meeting ordinary and usual performance expectations. Either the quantity or quality of production may be less than expected from the typical worker in an equivalent position without the usual sanctions being applied. "Accommodation," however, implies no such relaxation of standards. This term designates employment wherein needed adjustments and adaptations are made so that the disabled worker *can* meet ordinary and usual performance expectations. The accommodation may be physical, as in the installation of ramps or machine modifications, or procedural, as in allowing a flexible work-hour schedule or job duty trade offs with another worker. A major thrust within the entire vocational rehabilitation field is to maximize the degree of accommodation employers will offer disabled workers in order to minimize the degree of shelter those workers need.

The counselor continues service until the client is placed. After the client has landed a job and the initial problems have been solved, the rehabilitation counselor will continue to contact the person for a period of time (three months' minimum is required by the state-federal program) to help with problems that emerge with experience on the job. Post-employment follow-up services may include anything from psychological counseling regarding anxieties about "making it" to additional rehabilitation engineering inputs.

For many, this closes the vocational rehabilitation process. Having been counseled, evaluated, adjusted, trained, placed, and checked out, these clients are through with vocational rehabilitation forever (unless, of course, they enter the field themselves, as quite a number are inclined to do). Others, in these days of accelerating job obsolescence, will find it necessary to go through at least part of the process again. Job obsolescence is an important aspect of our society, and it touches everyone, including those with disabilities.

ELIGIBILITY

Two criteria are used by the vocational rehabilitation counselor and the state-federal agencies in judging whether an applicant is eligible and can be accepted for some kind of service: (1) the presence of a physical or mental disability that constitutes and results in a substantial handicap to the individual's employability and (2) a reasonable or feasible expectation that vocational rehabilitation service will enhance the individual's employability. These criteria may, of course, be variously interpreted by individual counselors and by the separate states. The "feasibility" of employment for a disabled person of sixty as compared with a twenty-five-year-old, may not be viewed as great enough to invest money in him. What constitutes a physical or mental handicap may be viewed differently in different states—pressures to add some diagnostic categories have resulted in conditions where some states accept and others reject those categories.

Eligibility requires documentation, through detailed evaluation of the individual's medical condition, through examinations and tests, provided at no cost to the applicant, and through psychological tests and evaluation of previous work and school histories. Evaluation is thorough, and for severely disabled persons, it can last up to eighteen months. Some services may be given during this time, prior to acceptance, to determine whether the applicant can benefit enough from them to return to work. Most determinations are made relatively quickly, within weeks or months, so that training programs can begin quickly.

SERVICES PROVIDED AND
WHERE TO LOCATE THEM

A generous range of services is available to the accepted client under the state-federal programs. They may be any, or all, of the following: (1) physical and mental restoration services, generally purchased for the client as needed, including surgery, psychological counseling, and the provision of appliances, prostheses, or special equipment, (2) general counseling and guidance during the whole process of rehabilitation, (3) vocational guidance and training services, including higher, technical, or remedial education, (4) maintenance costs to assist the client in becoming able to sustain and benefit from the rehabilitation program, (5) transportation services, with a similar aim, (6) telecommunications, sensory, and other technical aids, such as reader services, "talking books," Braille instruction, and mobility for the blind and interpreter services for the deaf, (7) assistance to the client's family in their effort to help the adjustment and rehabilitation of the client, (8) placement in suitable employment when the rehabilitation program is completed, (9) tools, equipment, licenses, and supplies for the self-employed or small business person when needed, (10) post-employment services, when necessary, to help the client maintain suitable employment, sometimes provided even after a case is technically "closed."

The vocational rehabilitation program operates throughout the country through a network of state and local agencies. Local offices exist in almost every major city. They are generally listed under "Vocational Rehabilitation" in telephone listings for city, county, or state services.

THE POLITICS OF VOCATIONAL REHABILITATION

Although work is important to all human beings, psychologically, socially, and economically, there are simply not enough jobs to go around. In recent years, 8-10 percent of the work force has been out of work at any given point in time. First the ethnic minorities, then women, and finally disabled and older workers coalesced in the 1960s and 1970s into special interest groups fighting to ensure that they would not be overrepresented among the unemployed. "The organized disabled" are now fighting hard and effectively to reassert and recapture their constitutional rights to equal protection under the law, and predictably, the central issue is jobs. Lobbyists from a long roster of national and local "consumer" organizations address Congress, state legislatures, county boards of supervisors, city councils, and other public officials daily, demanding that their disabled constituents' needs be heard and responded to when decisions are made regarding such things as job opportunity programs and welfare regulations, which, ironically, contain disincentives to gainful activity.

Although the program can be criticized in some ways, the sixty-year history of the federal-state vocational rehabilitation services is one of the brightest spots in public programs in the United States. The program has convincingly demonstrated that it is not a person's disabilities but the abilities that can be developed that are important. In 1979 alone, more than 289,000 individuals were rehabilitated under the program, and over 1.4 million were given some service. It is estimated that for every dollar the service spends to rehabilitate a client, at least $5 is returned to the government in taxes when the individual goes back to work.

As a result, ongoing job programs designed expressly for workers with disabilities have received some impetus. One of the best known is "Projects for Industry," (PWI) which originated under the 1973 Vocational Rehabilitation Act. PWI is characterized as a partnership between the state-federal vocational rehabilitation program and industry. Here, special recruiting, selection, prejob and on-job procedures are established by public financing for getting workers with significant disabilities into productive work through the cooperative efforts of local industries and vocational rehabilitation agencies. Because of the involvement of industry, the costs of rehabilitating individual participants in the program can be reduced considerably. Under the PWI program, some 2,000 disabled persons were recruited, trained and placed in 1976, in diverse industries, such as garment and furniture, cablesplicing, restaurant, and computers, in fifteen cities of the United States. Despite the initial promise and vitality of the concept of industry-government partnership in vocational rehabilitation, the PWI program has not been vigorously pursued, and in the present political climate its potentials are not likely to be further developed.

Another result of political pressure is mainstreaming in education, whereby youngsters with disabilities are being educated along with their nondisabled peers in mainstream schools. (See Chapter 6.) Once mainstreaming becomes familiar, it should contribute greatly to reducing the attitudinal barriers facing disabled adults. Contact with people who have disabilities from childhood on should significantly reduce the prejudices that develop because their differences are not accepted or understood. Through a combination of efforts such as those described above, plus the inclusion of workers with disabilities as a "protected population" under affirmative action, fair employment practice, and equal opportunity programs, the job picture for disabled workers is gradually improving.

WHERE TO OBTAIN INFORMATION

EMPLOYMENT AND REHABILITATION RESOURCES

For general information on programs to assist handicapped people in gaining employment and on the federal-state vocational rehabilitation program contact:

Bureau of Education for the Handicapped
400 Maryland Avenue, S.W.
Washington, D.C. 20202

Information requests from potential clients are referred to the appropriate state agency. Local offices can also be located in the telephone book under "Vocational Rehabilitation" in city, county, or state listings.

For general information on vocational rehabilitation for disabled veterans, contact:

Veterans Administration
Washington, D.C. 20420

Applications for the program (VA Form 22-1900) are available at any local Veterans Administration office.

For information on governmental employment services, contact:

United States Employment Services (USES)
Employment and Training Administration
Department of Labor
Washington, D.C. 20213.

USES and its affiliated state agencies operate over twenty-five hundred local offices to help place people in jobs. Preference is given to disadvantaged groups, including the handicapped. Applicants are tested, counseled, and referred for interviews with employers; sometimes referrals are first made to special training or support services, if these are needed to make the person employable. USES also counsels and aids employers in resolving their management problems and developing better management.

Office of Selective Placement
Office of Personnel Management
1900 E Street, N.W.
Washington, D.C. 20415

The Office of Personnel Management administers the federal government's personnel programs. The Selective Placement Program specifically aims at the hiring, placement, and advancement of handicapped individuals in the federal work force. Mentally and physically disabled persons may be given trial appointments to jobs in the federal government. Anyone becoming disabled while a federal employee has the possibility of job restructuring to accommodate the disability whenever feasible. CSC has local offices listed in the phone directory.

Interagency Committee on Handicapped Employees
Civil Service Commission
1900 E Street, N.W.
Room 6514
Washington, D.C. 20415

The Interagency Committee on Handicapped Employees, also a part of CSC, is mandated by law to look after the interests of disabled employees. The committee reviews the practices of executive branch agencies in regard to handicapped employees, and reports to Congress annually on the federal government's progress as an employer of the handicapped. It also tries to identify and relieve problems of hiring, job restructuring, and architectural/transportation barriers to employment.

There are numerous federal publications on employment, some of which are included in the bibliography at the end of the chapter.

PROGRAMS REGULATING EMPLOYMENT POLICIES
AND PRACTICES

Employment Standards Administration (ESA)
Department of Labor
200 Constitution Avenue, N.W.
Washington, D.C. 20210
The Employment Standards Administration conducts its programs through the following offices and divisions:

1. Office of Federal Contract Compliance Programs

This office sets policy, investigates complaints, and monitors compliance with Section 503 of the Rehabilitation Act of 1973, which requires contractors and subcontractors of the federal government to provide equal opportunity and affirmative action for handicapped persons seeking employment or already employed.

2. Wage and Hour Division

The Wage and Hour Division authorizes subminimum wages under the Fair Labor Standards Act, where necessary and for the shortest period necessary, to prevent curtailment of opportunities for employment of handicapped individuals who would not be able to command the minimum wage.

3. Division of Special Minimum Wages

The Division of Special Minimum Wages, which is within the Wage and Hour Division, is responsible for administering the regulations governing the employment of handicapped clients in sheltered workshops and the employment of patient workers in hospitals and institutions. It is also responsible for certifying sheltered workshops.

4. Office of Workers' Compensation Programs

This office administers three basic federal workers' compensation laws, including the Black Lung Benefits Act of 1972.

The Employment Standards Administration administers its programs through ten regional offices. Information and services are generally available locally rather than through the national office. See your local phone book under U.S. Government.

5. Office for Civil Rights (OCR)
Department of Health and Human Services
200 Independence Avenue, S.W.
Washington, D.C. 20201
The Office for Civil Rights enforces Section 504 of the Rehabilitation Act of 1973, which prohibits discrimination against physically or mentally handicapped individuals in federally assisted programs of any kind. OCR investigates and resolves complaints based on discrimination in employment and requires that federal-dollar recipients take affirmative action to ensure that handicapped employees are treated without regard to their handicap. OCR provides technical assistance to employers who obtain federal funds, helping

them to comply with Section 504, and has launched a national public awareness campaign to inform handicapped individuals and the general public of the rights of the disabled under the law.

BIBLIOGRAPHY

FEDERAL PUBLICATIONS ON EMPLOYMENT

About Jobs and Mentally Retarded People. President's Committee on Employment of the Handicapped and National Association for the Retarded Citizens, Arlington, Texas, 38 pp., 1974, free. Government Printing Office, Washington, D.C., 20402. Provides a guide to jobs, worker evaluation, job preparation, and vocational rehabilitation and gives tips on job hunting and state contracts for the retarded job seeker.

Affirmative Action to Employ Disabled Veterans of the Vietnam Era. President's Committee on Employment of the Handicapped, 1974, 18 pp., free. Government Printing Office, Washington, D.C. 20402. A pocket guide on affirmative action: what it is, who is covered, its legal basis, and how to handle a complaint about discrimination.

Affirmative Action to Employ Handicapped People: A Pocket Guide. President's Committee on Employment of the Handicapped, 1974, 11 p., free. Government Printing Office, Washington, D.C., 20402. A simplified explanation of Section 503 of the Rehabilitation Act of 1973, written for government contractors, labor unions, counselors, and disabled persons.

All You'll Ever Need to Know about Hiring People with Disabilities. President's Committee on Employment of the Handicapped, 1978, 8 pp., free. Government Printing Office, Washington, D.C. 20402. Written by a handicapped employer. Discusses why and how handicapped workers can be employed.

Careers for the Homebound. President's Committee on Employment of the Handicapped, pamphlet, free. Government Printing Office, Washington, D.C. 20402. Lists accredited schools for home study. Includes lists of information available to homebound persons.

A Chain of Cooperation. U.S. Civil Service Commission, October 1976, 14 pp., free. Government Printing Office, Washington, D.C., 20402. Indicates employment avenues in federal service for the severely physically handicapped.

Disabled Veterans: You Paid Your Dues, Now Collect. President's Committee on Employment of the Handicapped, 1978, 12 pp., free. Government Printing Office, Washington, D.C. 20402. Discusses veterans' benefits and rights of employment. Includes list of helpful resources.

Employment Assistance for the Handicapped. President's Committee on Employment of the Handicapped, 1979, 37 pp., free. Government Printing Office, Washington, D.C. 20402. Indicates where to go for guidance, how to find a job, and where to find help for small businesses, sheltered workshops, and farmers. Includes a directory of resources.

Employment of Blind Persons in Federal Service. U.S. Civil Service Commission, October 1975, 6 pp., free. Government Printing Office, Washington, D.C. 20402. Gives policy and procedures for obtaining employment in federal service.

Employment of Deaf Persons in Federal Service. U.S. Civil Service Commission, free. Government Printing Office, Washington, D.C. 20402. Gives policy and procedures for obtaining employment in federal service.

Employment of Epileptics in the Federal Service. U.S. Civil Service Commission, free. Government Printing Office, Washington, D.C. 20402. Gives policy and procedures for obtaining employment in federal service.

Employment of Mentally Restored Persons in Federal Service. U.S. Civil Service Commission, free. Government Printing Office, Washington, D.C. 20402. Gives policy and procedures for obtaining employment in federal service.

Employment of Mentally Retarded Persons in the Federal Service. U.S. Civil Service Commission, free. Government Printing Office, Washington, D.C. 20402. Gives policy and procedures for obtaining employment in federal service.

Employment of Physically Handicapped Persons in Federal Service. U.S. Civil Service Commission, Government Printing Office, Washington, D.C. 20402. Gives policy and procedures for obtaining employment in the federal service.

Guidelines for General Rehabilitation Counselors Serving the Deaf. U.S. Civil Service Commission, Government Printing Office, Washington, D.C. 20402. Policy for counselors serving the deaf.

Guide to Job Placement of Mentally Retarded Workers. William Fraenkel. President's Committee on Employment of the Handicapped, 1973, 20 pp., free. Government Printing Office, Washington, D.C. 20402. Includes resources for finding a retarded person to employ. For employers.

Handbook of Selective Placement in Federal Service of Handicapped People. U.S. Civil Service Commission, April 1975, 51 pp., free. Government Printing Office, Washington, D.C. 20402. A reference manual on ways to place handicapped people in federal jobs.

The Heart Patient at Work: The Road Back. President's Committee on Employment of the Handicapped, the American Heart Association, and the National Fraternal Order of Eagles, February 1975, 8 pp., free. Government Printing Office, Washington, D.C. 20402. Report of a seminar. Includes a list of agencies to contact for health and rehabilitation services and a roster of each state Governor's Committee on Employment of the Handicapped.

He's Back: Business Backs the Disabled Veterans. President's Committee on Employment of the Handicapped, 1975, 11 pp., free. Government Printing Office, Washington, D.C. 20402. Reports responses of leading industries to hiring handicapped Vietnam veterans.

Hiring the Handicapped: Facts and Myths. President's Committee on Employment of the Handicapped, 1978, leaflet, free. Government Printing Office, Washington, D.C. 20402. Findings of an eight-month study conducted by DuPont, Nemours, Inc., of 1,452 employees with physical handicaps.

Hiring Persons with Hearing Impairments. President's Committee on Employment of the Handicapped, 1979, 12 pp., free. Government Printing Office, Washington, D.C., 20402. A guide for prospective employees and employers on how to find each other.

How to Accommodate Workers in Wheelchairs. Janet and Jules Asher. President's Committee on Employment of the Handicapped, September 1976, 7 pp., free. Government Printing Office, Washington, D.C. 20402.

How to Get a Job: A Handy Guide for Job Seekers. William Fraenkel. President's Committee on Employment of the Handicapped, 1972, 22 pp., free. Government Printing Office, Washington, D.C. 20402. Includes a list of more than 100 kinds of jobs. Is tops on where and how to find employment. Accompanied by a *Teacher's Manual* written by John D. Webster.

If You're an Employer in the Recreation, Parks, Leisure or Cultural Services, Then There Are Some Facts You Should Know about Hiring the Handicapped. President's Committee on Employment of the Handicapped, 1979, 6 pp., free. Government Printing Office, Washington, D.C. 20402. Provides profiles of successfully employed handicapped persons in a variety of work situations.

Opportunity for the Blind and Visually Impaired through Vocational Rehabilitation. Social and Rehabilitation Service, 1973 reprint, 1969, 20 pp., free. Government Printing Office, Washington, D.C. 20402. Discusses vocational rehabilitation elements — employment, counseling, medical services, and others — for the blind.

People at Work. National Multiple Sclerosis Society. President's Committee on Employment of the Handicapped, 1975, 16 pp., free. Government Printing Office, Washington, D.C. 20402. Provides fifty profiles of working men and women with multiple sclerosis.

Preparing for Work. William Fraenkel. President's Committee on Employment of the Handicapped, 1975, 17 pp., free. Government Printing Office, Washington, D.C. 20402. Provides tips on educating and training mentally retarded individuals in search of employment. Useful for teachers, guidance counselors, and job seekers.

Respond to Workers with Epilepsy. Epilepsy Foundation of America. President's Committee on Employment of the Handicapped, 1978, leaflet, free. Government Printing Office, Washington, D.C. 20402. Provides facts about epilepsy and reasons to employ persons with epilepsy.

Selling to Industry (for Sheltered Workshops). Social and Rehabilitation Service, 1973, 28 pp., free. Government Printing Office, Washington, D.C. 20402. Provides easily implemented ideas for expanding and upgrading workshop contract promotion.

Sheltered Workshop Study: A Nationwide Report on Sheltered Workshops and Their Employment of Handicapped Individuals. Vol. 1: Survey. Claude W. Whitehead, U.S. Department of Labor, June 1977, 127 pp., free. Government Printing Office, Washington, D.C. 20402. Report of a survey of policies, programs, and services of sheltered workshops. Includes handicaps served, analysis of wages and fringe benefits, and of financial and personnel structure. *Statistical Appendix to Vol. 1* is also available.

So You're Going to Hire a Mentally Restored Person. President's Committee on Employment of the Handicapped, 1977, leaflet, free. Government Printing Office, Washington, D.C. 20402. Provides information for employers who have decided to hire a mentally restored person.

So You've Hired Someone with a Hearing Impairment. President's Committee on Employment of the Handicapped, 1977, 5 pp., free. Government Printing Office, Washington, D.C. 20402. Discusses common concerns and special considerations for the deaf employee. Includes the manual alphabet.

Suggestions for Using Interviewing Guides for Specific Disabilities. U.S. Department of Labor, 1969, leaflet, free. A manual on how to use the following interviewing guides published by the Department of Labor (Government Printing Office, Washington, D.C. 20402):

Alcoholism. 1969, 10 pp., free.

Diabetes. 1969, 8 pp., free.

Epilepsy. 1969, 8 pp., free.

Hearing Impairments. 1969, 17 pp., free.

Heart Disease. 1969, 8 pp., free.

Legal Blindness and Blindness. 1969, 18 pp., free.

Mentally Restored. 1969, 16 pp., free.

Mental Retardation. Rev. 1974, 12 pp., free.

Visual Impairments. 1969, 15 pp., free.

Supervising the Mentally Handicapped: The Procedures, the Rewards. Howard F. Rudd, Jr., President's Committee on Employment of the Handicapped, December 1976, 4 pp., free. Government Printing Office, Washington, D.C. 20402. Provides guides to developing an effective training program for slow learners and mentally retarded employees.

These, Too, Must Be Equal: America's Needs in Habilitation and Employment of the Mentally Retarded. President's Committee on Mental Retardation and President's Committee on Employment of the Handicapped, 1974, 22 pp., free. Government Printing Office, Washington, D.C. 20402. Guide to education, training, and employment of the mentally retarded. Includes proposals for curriculum design, grants, information sources, medical rehabilitation, and living facilities.

Workers Certification under Section 14 of the Fair Labor Standards Act. U.S. Department of Labor, April 1976, 77 pp., free. Government Printing Office, Washington, D.C. 20402. A report on the law's requirements.

Workers Compensation: Some Facts for Deaf People. Gallaudet College. President's Committee on Employment of the Handicapped, 1977, 8 pp., free. Government Printing Office, Washington, D.C., 20402. General explanation of workers' compensation and what it can mean for the deaf worker.

Yes, You Can Get A Job. President's Committee on Employment of the Handicapped, 1976, 8 pp., free. Government Printing Office, Washington, D.C. 20402. Provides information about employment training or retraining for disabled individuals.

Your New Blind Secretary. National Association of Blind Secretaries. President's Committee on Employment of the Handicapped, 1976, leaflet, free. Government Printing Office, Washington, D.C. 20402. Gives the employer aids in orienting the new blind secretary.

Federal publications can be ordered directly from the sponsoring office or committee:

President's Committee on Employment of the Handicapped
1111 20th Street, N.W.
Washington, D.C. 20210

Office of Personnel Management
Bureau of Recruiting and Examining
1900 E Street, N.W.
Washington, D.C. 20415

Office of Personnel Management
Office of Selective Placement
Room 6514
1900 E Street, N.W.
Washington, D.C. 20415

Office of Human Development
Publications Distribution Unit
Room G311 Switzer Building
330 C Street, S.W.
Washington, D.C. 20201

Department of Labor
Division of Evaluation and Research
200 Constitution Avenue, N.W.
Washington, D.C. 20210

Department of Labor
Employment Training Administration, Inquiries
601 D Street, N.W., Room 10225
Washington, D.C. 20213

Department of Labor
Employment Standards Administration
200 Constitution Avenue, N.W.
Washington, D.C. 20210

NEWSLETTERS ON EMPLOYMENT AND VOCATIONAL REHABILITATION

Clearing House Memo
National Clearing House of Rehabilitation Materials
Oklahoma State University
Stillwater, Oklahoma 74074
Quarterly, free, professional audience.

It's About Time
Joseph Bulova School of Watchmaking
40-24 62nd Street
Woodside, New York 11377
Irregular, free, general audience.

MDC Information Newsletter
Materials Development Center
Department of Rehabilitation and Manpower Studies
University of Wisconsin—Stout
Menomonie, Wisconsin 54751
Bimonthly, free, professional audience.

NRCA News
National Rehabilitation Counseling Association
1522 K Street, NW
Washington, D.C. 20005
Bimonthly, free, professional audience.

JOURNALS ON EMPLOYMENT

Achievement
Achievement Disabled Action Group, Inc.
925 N.E. 122nd Street
North Miami, Florida 33161
Described as "the voice of the handicapped," *Achievement* is a newspaper
by and for handicapped persons. Provides much information on current and
proposed legislation, advocacy efforts, and consumer activities. Publication
began in 1969.
Monthly, $2/yr, general audience.

American Rehabilitation
Rehabilitation Services Administration
Superintendent of Documents
Government Printing Office
Washington, D.C. 20402
Publishes articles on current issues, new programs and services, RSA activities, and model state programs. Publication began in 1975.
Bimonthly, $11.75/yr, professional audience. Former titles: *Social and Rehabilitation Record, Rehabilitation Record.*

Disabled USA
President's Committee on Employment of the Handicapped
1111 20th Street, N.W.
Washington, D.C. 20210
Monthly, free, general audience.

International Rehabilitation Review
Rehabilitation International
122 E. 23rd Street
New York, New York 10010
Reports news of meetings and events of interest to the international rehabilitation community. Publishes articles on services in member countries, in addition to reports on special programs in barrier-free design and recreation. News from the International Center on Technical Aids, Housing and Transportation is a regular feature. Published since 1949. Quarterly, $5/yr, professional audience. Former title: *Bulletin of the International Society for Rehabilitation of the Disabled.*

Journal of Applied Rehabilitation Counseling
National Rehabilitation Counseling Association
1522 K Street, N.W.,
Washington, D.C. 20005
Serves the needs of the counselor in the vocational rehabilitation setting. Articles deal with current theoretical or professional issues, innovative rehabilitation counselor techniques, integrative reviews of the rehabilitation literature, and research having primary significance for the practitioner. Published since 1970. Quarterly, $8/yr, professional audience.

Rehabilitation
British Council for Rehabilitation of the Disabled
Tavistock House
Tavistock Square
London WC1
England
Publishes original articles on all aspects of rehabilitation of the disabled. Some topics discussed are housing, vocational rehabilitation, innovative programs in Great Britian and other countries, voluntary services and psychological adjustment. Published since 1948. Quarterly, $6/yr, general audience.

Rehabilitation Gazette
4502 Maryland Avenue
St. Louis, Missouri 63108
Published once a year by a volunteer staff. Contains information about available devices, guided tours and vacations, residential communities, barrier-free design, and employment. Back issues are available. Published since 1971. Annual, $2 for disabled, $4 for nondisabled, general audience. Former title: *Toomey Journal Gazette*

Rehabilitation Literature: For Use by Professional Personnel and Students in All Disciplines Concerned with Rehabilitation of the Handicapped
National Easter Seal Society
2023 W. Ogden Avenue
Chicago, Illinois 60612
Publishes original articles and "identifies and describes current books, pamphlets, and periodical articles pertaining to the care, welfare, education, and employment of handicapped children and adults." Reprints of original articles are available. Abstracts are especially useful in keeping up with the literature of disciplines related to all facets of the disabled person's life and needs. Many articles are of interest to the lay as well as professional person. Published since 1940. Monthly, $12.50/yr, professional audience.

Rehabilitation World
Rehabilitation International USA (RIUSA)
17 E. 45th Street
New York, New York 10017
Designed to disseminate topical and relevant international rehabilitation information to the U.S. rehabilitation community. Foreign programs are described, and opportunities for international cooperation are investigated. Published since 1975. Quarterly, $15/yr, free to members, professional audience.

BOOKS

Herrman, A., and Walker, L. *Handbook on Employment Rights of the Handicapped.* Washington, D.C.: George Washington University, Regional Rehabilitation Institute, 1978.
Malikin, D., and Rusalem, H., eds. *The Vocational Rehabilitation of the Disabled.* New York: New York University Press, 1969.
Sale, Richard T. "Employment." *Awareness Papers.* White House Conference on Handicapped Individuals. GPO No. 232-034/6199. Washington, D.C.: Government Printing Office, 1977.
Stolov, Walter C., and Clowers, Michael R. *A Handbook of Severe Disability: A Text for Rehabilitation Counselors, Other Vocational Practitioners, and Allied Health Professionals.* U.S. Department of Education, Rehabilitation Services Administration, Stock No. 017-090-00054-2. Washington, D.C.: Government Printing Office, 1981.

Wehman, Paul. *Competitive Employment: New Horizons for Severely Disabled Individuals.* Baltimore: Paul H. Brookes, Publishers, 1981.

Wright, George Nelson. *Total Rehabilitation.* Boston: Little, Brown and Company, 1980.

5 PERSONAL AND FAMILY COUNSELING

June Isaacson Kailes

Although many people in modern society suffer from psychological tensions and difficulties, it is widely recognized that being physically disabled imposes some extra challenges. The sufferer and his or her next intimates, in the first instance the immediate family, are affected not only by the general pressures of complex social forces, but by the particular and special tasks of making an adaptation to social life that will maximize the capacities and abilities of people with disabilities. Overcoming the stigmatizing, negative effects of stereotyping and discrimination sometimes presents particular problems of attaining and maintaining mental health through the development of a positive self-image. Much modern thinking has concluded that the barriers to effective functioning of people with disabilities come from negative social arrangements and attitudes that the person with disabilities comes to internalize through his or her life experiences. These considerations lead us to definitions of mental health and of the kinds of resources that can aid in its enhancement.

MENTAL HEALTH DEFINED

Mental health is defined as "a state of emotional well-being in which a person is able to function comfortably within his society and in which his personal achievements and characteristics are satisfactory to him."[1] Mental health is thus summed up by competence in dealing with one's environment. How a person adjusts to life, whether the going is rough or smooth, is one criterion of the state of mental health; another crucial and related factor is the way relationships with other people are handled. Taking the definition further, "Mental Health is part of a continuum. There are degrees of mental health just as there are degrees of mental illness."[2] No one is worry free. Various life events cause distress, anxiety, fear, distrust. We all encounter a variety of problems in daily living; some problems are more difficult to handle than others and require some form of outside help. Sometimes such assistance can be obtained through formal mental health services. Common symptoms, such as anxiety, depression, or substance (drug or alcohol) abuse, frequently occur in persons with generally good mental health. Although the occurrence differs from that in the "technically" mentally ill, the only difference in symptoms is often in intensity, frequency, and duration.[3] Mental health services can help a person deal with these symptoms. These services should not be thought of as being only for the mentally ill; they are also meant for mentally healthy people who are experiencing periods of distress.

This chapter will discuss the nature of mental health resources, what is meant by psychotherapy and counseling, how one may choose among various forms of counseling and psychological help, where to locate such help, alternative resources such as peer counseling, and questions about duration, costs, and confidentiality.

PSYCHOANALYSIS, PSYCHOTHERAPY, COUNSELING

The terms "psychoanalysis," "psychotherapy," and "counseling" are often confused. Psychoanalysis is a therapeutic approach offered by an analyst, psychiatrist, social worker, or psychologist who has had special training in psychoanalysis from a psychoanalytic institute. It is one technique and form of psychotherapy. The basic method used by an analyst is free association, a process in which a patient, usually in a relaxed state, talks about whatever comes to mind. After some time, patterns of the patient's preoccupations begin to appear, and the analyst interprets them. This approach requires a person's going to the analyst four or five times a week, and it usually stretches out over a period of years. This approach, which derives from Freud and his followers, is far less common today than other psychotherapy and counseling approaches because of the tremendous amount of time and expense involved.

Although much has been written in the attempt to distinguish between counseling and psychotherapy, there is no valid, agreed-upon distinction between them, and the terms are used interchangeably in this chapter. Psychotherapy can be viewed as an educational and growth process whereby an individual (often referred to as a therapist, psychotherapist, counselor, or mental health professional) has the opportunity to explore feelings, situations, and events that are causing distress. A therapist helps the client look beyond the issues and problems at hand and explore feelings that may be contributing to them. Therapy is a process by which individuals gain new insights into their difficulties, reevaluate those ways of feeling, thinking, and behaving that have led to problems, and find new and more effective ways of coping. The goal is not to change an individual's personality but to assist the person in making a more satisfactory and comfortable adaptation to life. In order for therapy to work, there must be mutual trust and respect between the therapist and the client.

PSYCHOTHERAPY/COUNSELING FOR PERSONS WITH DISABILITIES

The counseling process can provide useful approaches both to the general problems all people face and to those additional and particular psychosocial situations faced by people who have disabilities and their families.

Parents of congenitally handicapped children or of children who acquire a handicap through illness or accident often need mental health services in order to come to terms with the special problems presented by the child. Common emotional reactions are guilt, self-blame, disappointment, shame or feelings of social stigma, and feeling singled out by bad luck or for special punishment because of personal failure. The variety of reactions is vast, but studies have shown that most parents need some help in getting through the difficult months after the birth or diagnosis of a child with some form of disability. In the past well-meaning professional workers often advised parents to "put away," or institutionalize, a child with severe impairments. This advice overlooks two important points: (1) parents typically love and are attached to their child no matter how impaired the child is, and (2) whether or not institutionalization is ultimately desirable, the child will profit from a period of time in a warm, supporting family environment if it is available.

As the individual with disabilities proceeds through life, he may encounter stress for reasons that a normal person experiences stress—separation from parents, entry into an unfamiliar situation such as school, lack of acceptance by peers, adolescence and identity establishment, sexuality, vocational choice, and setting up an independent living arrangement. Although each of these lesser or greater psychosocial transitions is difficult, for people with disabilities, they can have an especially stressful character. The material and social resources of the person with a disability and his family *may* be adequate to cope with such life problems. Frequently, however, they are not, and some form of outside aid is important. Such aid must be premised on both an understanding of general social forces and psychological reactions and a realistic knowledge of the special problems, fears, reactions, and aspirations of this population.

THE USE OF MENTAL HEALTH SERVICES

For the general population, the terms "mental health" and "mental illness" carry with them many myths, half-truths, stereotypes, and misinformation. Many people believe that the only persons who need mental health services are "crazy" people who have lost touch with reality and are severely confused and disturbed. Mental health services are, indeed, appropriate for such persons, but psychological services are also appropriate and available for people who do not have severe problems or symptoms.

Like the able-bodied population, people with disabilities often stereotype those who seek psychotherapy. Disabled people, as has been made clear, are often the subject of stereotyping by the able-bodied population. They have a continuous struggle against negative attitudes and myths, such as the beliefs that they are mentally retarded, incompetent, or helpless, that they are burdens to society, or that they have no sexual drives or feelings, in other words, that they are asexual. Thus for some people with disabilities, choosing to seek mental health services implies accepting another whole set of stereotypes. The thinking may be, "It's enough that I am disabled, don't tell me I'm crazy too!" Such attitudes need combating on both intellectual and emotional levels. Seeking counseling can and should reflect an individual's *strength* rather than weakness — strength in the ability to recognize conflicts and problems within oneself and to take positive actions to deal with those concerns.

Like all people, the disabled can and do seek mental health and counseling services for a variety of reasons. Some persons seek outside help because they have a problem to solve, others because they are not happy or want to learn more about themselves, some because they have to make an important decision regarding personal relationships, education, or career goals. Decisions regarding educational and vocational goals can be especially complex for the disabled person, who has to weigh more variables than the able-bodied individual. Financial disincentives, physical limitations, and misinformed employers with negative attitudes and discriminatory practices are all issues to be considered and managed.

People with disabilities and their families often need assistance in learning to cope with a difficult situation brought out by the limitations of the specific disability. For many, learning to cope can be an overwhelming and long-term experience. Coping with disability is difficult and presents unique problems in terms of mental health. In learning to live with, understand, and accept one's physical limitations, many emotional and psychological issues may arise. Sometimes one needs help even in acknowledging that one has a disability, and then one may need help with sorting out what one can and cannot do, with recognizing and/or reevaluating and rediscovering skills, strengths, and weaknesses, and with setting realistic life, educational, and career goals.

People often seek out mental health counselors during a crisis. A crisis can be personal or environmental. Environmental crises are usually temporary and include such natural disasters as fire, flood, earthquake or accident. A personal crisis may be the ending of an important relationship as in divorce, the loss of a loved one, the loss of a job, or the loss of a physical function such as the ability to walk. Crises range from mild and transient to severe and enduring. Adjusting to a sudden and profound change sometimes triggers harmful emotional reactions, and these can be eased by a professional mental health counselor.

When the effects of crisis are continuing, individuals may seek help because they are experiencing depression. Some degree of depression is to be expected in everyone's life, since it is a normal and natural response to experiences of loss, failure, and unexpected bad luck. Depression can be caused by such events as divorce, moving, the death of a loved one, or the onset or worsening of a physical disability. Many disabled people experience depression as they go through the process of acknowledging and adjusting to their disability. During depression, prompt, gradual, or intense lowering of mood can occur. Sometimes the feelings subside without outside interaction, with the individual resuming her or his usual frame of mind.

In some cases, however, a depression involves more than feelings of sadness and disappointment. Some depressions get worse, last longer, and are accompanied by such symptoms as a loss of self-esteem (which brings on a continued questioning of one's self-worth), changes in eating habits, problems in sleeping, decreased sexual interest, a desire to withdraw and be alone, inability to concentrate (reading, writing, and conversation become difficult), difficulty in making decisions, feelings of pervasive hopelessness and helplessness, and a tendency to blame oneself for common faults and shortcomings that become exaggerated. Prolonged depression can be debilitating. A person who experiences these warning signs over a period of time should by all means seek professional assistance and should be encouraged to do so by those close to him.

Similarly, people should seek help, or be encouraged to seek it, if they are experiencing excessive and uncontrolled anxiety for no specific reason, or if they seem to be experiencing such anger and fear that they may act out the anger or fear in a violent way. Victims of violent crimes, such as rape, mugging, or other assaults, can experience profound and lasting emotional distress. Such experiences often affect a person's total outlook on life and future functioning, and mental health services can be particularly beneficial in these cases.

Somatic or physical complaints, such as headaches, stomach problems, and heart palpitations, should always be checked by a physician. If a doctor can find no organic cause for the problem, the symptoms may be a sign of unrecognized conflicts, stresses, and/or tensions. When feelings such as anger go unexpressed or are kept within, the body can react in physical ways. In other words, problems that are emotional and psychological at base can present themselves as physical problems.

At times, whole families may need to be involved in counseling. Families may seek counseling for the same reasons individuals do. When one member of a family undergoes change or experiences difficulty, whether emotional, social, physical, or environmental, these changes almost always affect the entire family. Just as a disabled person needs to acknowledge and adjust to physical limitations, so must his or her family acknowledge and adjust to the change. Necessary changes of role within the disabled person's family need to be acknowledged and worked out through the expression and discussion of feelings. The understanding and adjustment of partners, children, parents, and siblings can be a crucial ingredient in a disabled person's ability to cope. Family reactions to a disabled member can show a wide range from guilt, irritation, hostility, and overprotection to rejection. All these are common family reactions. They particularly affect the disabled member's mental health, but they can be devastating to the entire family's psychological health and functioning. Early and adequate counseling services can prevent what might later turn out to be severe adjustment difficulties affecting all members.

SEXUALITY AND MENTAL HEALTH

The area of sexuality in disability warrants separate treatment, since it has been too long ignored as a part of a disabled person's life. The perceptions and feelings about one's body, and the related ability to seek, establish, and experience social and sexual intimacy, are of tremendous importance for everyone's mental health, but they are especially crucial for disabled persons. The capacity to view and experience oneself as a social and sexual being is of vital importance to mental and emotional well-being.

Why has the area of sexuality in disability been ignored? The entire subject of human sexuality has been filled with myths, half-truths, warped thinking, prudishness, anxiety, embarrassment, and guilt. In the past fifteen years or so, a new openness has evolved in U.S. society regarding sexual interests, discussion, and expression. Various aspects of sexual functioning and preferences are problematic for many people in general; they may be even more of a problem for people with some kinds and degree of physical disability. Unfortunately, the myths, misconceptions, and inhibitions that have applied to sexuality in general are stronger, and have prevailed longer, for the disabled population. For many years, the disabled population was generally seen and treated as an asexual or nonsexual group. Because the physically disabled may be limited in some functions, many persons have assumed that their needs and interests, including sex, were not the same as those of the able-bodied. Tragically, some people with disabilities have incorporated this myth into their own self-concepts.

Because the disabled were seen and treated as a generally asexual group, the feeling has existed among health professionals that repressive psychological processes should be encouraged to hold down the disabled patient's thoughts, feelings, and expressions of sexuality. This attitude may have been somewhat effective in dealing with past generations of the disabled, when punitive attitudes toward sexuality were a part of the prevailing mores. The present generation, including the disabled, has been raised in an atmosphere of fewer inhibitions and less repression of sexual thought and feeling. Although in some cases sexual drive and means of expression may be altered, sexual activity and desire are generally of vital importance in the lives of disabled people. Sex should be viewed as a normal, pleasurable, and bonding experience that all people, regardless of physical limitations, can enjoy.

Many professionals who work with the disabled were educated and trained prior to the more recent open discussions of sexuality, and they conformed to the mores of a society where open expression of sexual interest and desires was inhibited. The repression was perpetuated by the lack of specific professional training in the area of the sexuality of people with disabilities. Thus, until recently, few therapists routinely included sexual material in their clinical assessments of disabled persons, either because of lack of knowledge or because of their own misconceptions, discomfort, and anxiety. When combined with general social attitudes toward the disabled client, such an approach may make it difficult for the client to request help with a sexual problem. The problem can become intensified, with a cycle of silence ensuing in which little is expressed and nothing done. If the client cannot discuss these problems with his sexual partner or with a therapist, the troubling and unresolved issues may assume great proportions. Unattended sexual concerns thus may take a great toll on a person with disability.

Sexual difficulties for both the able-bodied and the disabled frequently are related to earlier experience. Thus, persons who acquire a physical disability in adulthood usually have established earlier sexual patterns to which they can return, depending, of course, on the degree and type of disability. Resumption of sexual activity after acquisition of a disability may also depend on the individual's psychological and emotional response to the limitations and the ability, if necessary, to depart from previous sexual habits and forms of expression and to find new options for satisfying sexual activity. People who experienced physical disability prior to becoming sexually active may never have had the opportunity to develop a sense of themselves as a social and sexual being. Prolonged hospitalizations, limited mobility, inaccessible public transportation, and overprotective parents during childhood and adolescence can all contribute greatly to a deficit in interpersonal and social, including sexual, skills. Additionally, many adolescents with physical disabilities have not been provided with sex education, covering reproductive health care, sexual expression, dating, contraception, and interpersonal relationships. Lack of information, compounded by a lack of social experience, frequently leads to social awkwardness and psychological anxiety.

No matter when the disability was incurred, physical factors may interfere with a disabled person's sexual functioning. Lack of sensation, paralyzed limbs, catheter management, bowel and bladder care, lack of coordination, muscle contractions, spasticity, pain, and problems with positioning can all affect sexual activity. Sexual difficulties and consequent performance anxieties related to these factors can often be worked through adequately, with the aid of accurate information and specific suggestions from a knowledgable person. Most often, intensive sex therapy à la Masters and Johnson is not required.

Even when a person's ability to engage in sexual activity is not impaired by a physical disability, concerns may arise from such psychological factors as fear, lack of confidence, and problems with body image (one's ability to see oneself as a desirable sexual partner). A fear of being embarrassed, ridiculed, rejected, or alienated from friends is common among the nondisabled. It is especially common for the physically disabled to struggle with body image issues and to wish they could live up to the idealized "perfect" body type of TV commercials. For people with disabilities, as well as the able-bodied, sexual difficulties may also arise and persist because of difficulties of communication with the sexual partner. For any of these concerns, counseling by mental health professionals may be appropriate and helpful.

Physicians are often perceived as being well-trained and equipped to handle the sexual concerns of their patients. In fact, however, some physicians have no specific competence, and they may be anxious and extremely ineffective in discussing sexual issues with their patients. If a trusting relationship exists with other health and mental health professionals, such as a physical therapist, occupational therapist, nurse, social worker, psychologist, or speech therapist, they may be satisfactory sources of aid or of referral to sources where sexual concerns can be dealt with more adequately. The professional associations listed near the end of this chapter can also be called on to assist in finding a professional who is comfortable and knowledgable about the sexual concerns of people with disabilities.

Family-planning agencies are in the process of making their services more available and accessible to people with various disabilities. As yet, however, many clinics are not accessible and/or prepared to provide these services to the disabled community. It may be necessary to call several family-planning services, such as the Planned Parenthood organization, in order to ascertain whether they are able to meet a disabled person's specific needs. The national policy of nondiscriminatory services in all fields should be interpreted to include the right of everyone to reproductive health care and family-planning services, regardless of ability to pay. Peer counselors, discussed later in this chapter, can also be very helpful in the area of sexual concerns.

MENTAL HEALTH SERVICES

Mental health professionals work in a variety of community facilities as well as in private practice. Agency-based professionals are most frequently found in community mental health centers, family service agencies, health and social service agencies, outpatient clinics of general and psychiatric hospitals, and in counseling centers on college and university campuses. Local community mental health centers are required to provide a full array of services from emergency, partial hospitalization, and inpatient facilities to community consultation and education and outpatient counseling.

Family service agencies have as their purpose the strengthening of family life by assisting families and individuals in coping with problems or crises of daily living. The agencies assist people in coping with stress situations, such as interpersonal, family, and marital conflicts, illness and/or disability of family members, and parenting problems. General services are given to families and children of all ages and include individual, marriage, family, and group counseling. The agencies also provide information and referral to appropriate community resources, financial and budgeting counseling, and advocacy services. Some family service agencies, such as Catholic Family Service and Jewish Family Service, concentrate on serving specific religious groups, while others are nondenominational.

Helplines and hotlines, another form of assistance, are found in many cities. These telephone counseling services offer anonymous, often twenty-four-hour, assistance for problems related to substance abuse, rape, suicide prevention, child abuse, and many other situations. In addition to giving counseling on the immediate crisis, these services often refer callers to sources of longer-term assistance.

Holistic health centers provide a newer form of assistance for health, including psychological health. A holistic approach to health and mental care takes into account the whole person — body, mind, and spirit. These centers treat emotional and physical symptoms as inseparably related. Treatment is focused on the interdependence of the various components of one's life and the way imbalance among these components affects health. Health is viewed as a positive state of physical, emotional, and spiritual well-being, which can be nurtured, developed, and enjoyed. The holistic approach encourages the development of a life-style that leads to personal self-development and optimal health.

Local mental health associations are voluntary citizens' groups that help people obtain information regarding mental health and illness and where mental health services can be obtained. To locate counseling services in one's community, one can also consult the community's guide to mental health, counseling, and social services. Such a guide or directory is frequently published by such community organizations as United Way,

Community Chest, Council of Social Agencies, or the local Welfare Planning Council.

TYPES OF COUNSELORS

Disabled persons should understand the types of therapists available and have some knowledge of their educational and training backgrounds. Social workers, psychologists, and psychiatrists are the three types of professionals most often encountered in the various mental health agencies. Members of these three professions work together in almost every kind of mental health facility, and their mental health roles and activities greatly overlap, although only psychiatrists can prescribe medication and administer certain medical treatments. Other professional counselors include psychiatric-mental health nurses, marriage and family counselors, sex therapists, rehabilitation counselors, and pastoral counselors.

CLINICAL AND PSYCHIATRIC SOCIAL WORKERS

Clinical and psychiatric social workers are usually trained in individual, group, marital, and family therapy, as well as in diagnosis, referral, consultation, and community organization. In the process of obtaining a Masters Degree in Social Work, they must complete two years of field-work experience in health and mental health settings. In many states, they must be licensed in order to practice psychotherapy privately.

PSYCHOLOGISTS

Clinical psychologists are trained to provide therapy to individuals and groups. In addition, most psychologists are skilled in the use of psychological tests, which aid in diagnostic assessment as well as in measuring personality and intellectual traits. Most practicing psychologists have a doctoral (Ph.D.) degree in psychology, but some function with a master's degree.

PSYCHIATRISTS

A psychiatrist is a medical doctor who has completed three years of specialty training in psychiatry and is licensed to practice medicine. A board-certified psychiatrist has practiced for two years and has passed the written and oral examinations of the American Board of Psychiatry and Neurology.

PSYCHIATRIC-MENTAL HEALTH NURSES

Psychiatric-mental health nurses have received specialized training in the prevention, treatment, and rehabilitation of mental-health-related problems. These practitioners have received advanced academic and professional training and hold a master's or higher degree. They conduct individual, family, and group therapy and also assume roles in mental health consultation, education, and administration.

MARRIAGE AND FAMILY COUNSELORS

For marriage and family counselors, the focus is on interpersonal relationships and family dynamics. Training requirements vary from state to state, and in some states they are specifically licensed. Academic requirements for clinical membership in the national organization, the American Association of Marriage and Family Therapy, is a master's or doctoral degree in social work, psychiatric nursing, clinical psychology, or a closely allied field. Clinical members must also complete supervised experience.

SEX THERAPISTS

Any of the above professionals may also do sex therapy provided they have some additional special training. There are at present no laws to *enforce* minimum standards of education and experience for sex therapists, but recently two national organizations, the American Association of Sex Educators and Counselors and Eastern Association of Sex Therapy, have established certification standards for sex therapists.

REHABILITATION COUNSELORS

The rehabilitation counselor's focus is on the client's desire to work, the kind of work the client is able to do, and the type of work the client prefers. Although there are no licensing requirements for rehabilitation counselors in the United States, the counselor may be certified by the Commission on Rehabilitation Certification, formed by the American Rehabilitation Counseling Association. To be eligible for the certification examination, a candidate must have a master's degree and one to five years of rehabilitation experience or a bachelor's degree and four to five years of related rehabilitation experience.

CLERGY OR PASTORAL COUNSELING

Traditionally, the clergy have done spiritual counseling as part of their religious responsibilities. Some clergy, however, have additional training in counseling beyond their religious training, and many of these individuals are certified by the American Association of Pastoral Counselors.

A professionally trained counselor, psychotherapist, or mental health professional can practice psychotherapy, but not all people who label themselves counselors or psychotherapists have adequate training. People seeking counseling should check a professional's qualifications. State licensing and certification ensures minimum standards of competency and protects the public. Any doubts concerning the credentials of a counselor can be checked with the following professional associations:

Marriage and Family Counselors

American Association for Marriage and Family Therapy
924 West Ninth
Upland, California 91786

Pastoral Counselors

American Association of Pastorial Counselors
3000 Connecticut Avenue, N.W. Suite 300
Washington, D.C. 20008

Physicians

American Medical Association
535 North Dearborn St.
Chicago, Illinois 60610

Psychiatric-Mental Health Nurses

American Nurses' Association, Inc.
2420 Pershing Road
Kansas City, Missouri 64108

Psychologists

American Psychological Association
1200 Seventeenth St., N.W.
Washington, D.C. 20036

Rehabilitation Counselors

American Rehabilitation Counseling Association
1607 New Hampshire Ave., N.W.
Washington, D.C. 20009

National Rehabilitation Counseling Association
1522 K Street, N.W.
Washington, D.C. 20005

Sex Therapists

American Association of Sex Educators Counselors
5010 Wisconsin Avenue, N.W. Suite 304
Washington, D.C. 20016

Eastern Association of Sex Therapy
10 East 88th Street
New York, New York 10028

Social Workers

National Association of Social Workers
1425 H Street, N.W., Suite 600
Washington, D.C. 20036

The National Federation of Societies for Clinical Social Work
c/o Charles Triller
2727 Marshall Court
Madison, Wisconsin 53705

PEER COUNSELING

A highly important, newer resource for disabled people is peer counseling, an approach that is in line with recent emphasis on self-help. The Little People of America, Ostomy Associations, and centers for independent living are examples of mutual aid or self-help groups. Each such group is made up of people who are seeking, by cooperative effort, to reduce, cope with, and surmount some personal, physical, environmental, or social problem affecting each of their lives. In most cases their mutually shared concern is one that is also addressed by professionals. "But members of these groups often find, in the concept of people who have 'been there' helping others like themselves, something beyond anything a professional could give them."[4] A growing number of professional agencies refer their clients to self-help groups because they recognize that these groups have been effective in dealing with behaviors and problems that have been resistant to professional interventions.[5] "Peer rather than professional counseling is being used in many places now, sometimes because it is the treatment of choice. Mentally healthy people adjusting to unusual situations often need tutorial more than therapeutic services—an experienced person to teach them how to traverse difficult terrain."[6]

In the disabled community, the self-help movement has taken shape in several forms, two of which are peer counseling programs and peer-conducted centers for independent living. In the latter, supportive services for the disabled, such as attendants' referral, housing assistance, transportation, job development, advocacy, information and referral, as well as peer counseling, are found. Peer counseling programs for people with disabilities also exist on some university and college campuses. The term "peer counselors" refers to people who have experienced a physical disability themselves and have achieved an emotionally sound adjustment to their limitations, as well as a substantial degree of independence in daily living. They are people who utilize their own experience in living with a disability, plus their training in counseling skills, to provide supportive guidance and information on a variety of areas of interest to the disabled.

Peer counseling is a self-help process, taking place in a person-to-person or group setting, in which people with similar life-experience problems share with each other. Like any good counseling, peer help involves both feeling and intellectual elements; concerns and coping methods for dealing with emotional, social, and sexual adjustment are shared. Unlike professional "help," peer counseling usually also provides a mutual support system, in which people can comfortably relate to and support others with similar problems. Peer counselors can provide practical information, emotional support, and role models, or "living proofs" of successful adjustment by individuals who have experienced similar physical limitations. Success in having coped with a similar disability gives the peer counselor credibility, as well as a deeply felt empathy that often allows him or her superior understanding and genuine inspiration to other persons with disabilities. A peer counselor is thus often able to help in ways that the able-bodied professional cannot.

OBTAINING SPECIALIZED GENERAL COUNSELING

Some therapists are not knowledgable about the special psychological and emotional concerns and problems a person with physical limitations faces. When seeking a therapist for a person with a disability, one should be aware of the therapist's experience and background, and the potential counselee may ask the therapist about his or her experience working with people who have a disability. However, it is not always necessary for the therapist to have had prior experience working with the disabled. Some therapists who have little or no such prior experience are able to understand the disabled person's unique concerns and problems. One can often sense this ability in an initial contact.

If the physically disabled person is homebound, the task of locating a therapist is difficult, but not impossible. Some mental health centers have homebound programs, in which counselors are available to go to the client's home. Some therapists in private practice also make home visits. Helplines and hotlines can also be useful for the homebound.

Other persons with physical disabilities and self-help organizations are excellent sources of referral. Agencies that focus on serving the disabled are also good sources for locating therapists who are familiar with and experienced in working with the disabled. For specific disability categories, social agencies and self-help groups are good sources of information about therapists experienced in working with that population. For example, agencies serving the deaf and the hard-of-hearing should be able to refer an inquirer to a therapist who can sign and is comfortable and experienced working with the deaf population; organizations serving the mentally retarded population are a good source of referral for counselors experienced with this population.

SOME PROBLEMS OF MATCHING

An individual may not "click" with a particular therapist, and in that case he may want to ask the therapist for referral to another mental health professional. Although the counseling relationship should be given a fair chance, of at least two or more sessions with the therapist, it is all right to change therapists if a patient is unhappy with a particular one. Like all people, therapists have different personalities and styles of relating. They also have differences in their levels of skill and competence, and some are better suited for particular clients than others. If the patient does change therapists, it is usually beneficial for him to discuss his feelings with the current therapist before changing. Frequent changes or desires to change counsellors, however, should lead the individual and the therapist to take a careful look at what is going on and to discussion of these negative feelings.

Therapists in private or publicly funded agencies are also open to "consumer" questioning and matching. Their patients can ask for another therapist if they are truly unhappy. Some people are reluctant to make this request if they are not paying or are paying very little for the counseling services. The agencies are supported by taxes and community subsidies, however, and their clients have contributed to their support and have the same rights as private clients.

CONFIDENTIALITY

It is very important to note that counseling records are confidential. Information contained in personal records cannot be released to anyone, including a new therapist. The former therapist must have a written consent from the patient before he can release records. Separate consents have to be signed for every person who wishes to obtain information from a therapist, since a "consent-for-release-of-information" is good only for the specific person or insurance company designated on the consent form.

THE DURATION OF THERAPY

The time needed for therapy varies from a single session up to several years' duration, depending on the individual's needs, desires, and financial resources. The length of time a person is in therapy does not necessarily indicate the severity of the problem. Some people achieve all they want and need in just a few sessions; others choose to continue for a longer time because they feel they can benefit from extended counseling. Sometimes individuals begin therapy with one goal in mind and find that, after a certain period of time, they really want something else, since therapy can open up many unexplored areas. Some therapists operate on a contract basis and agree to meet with their client for a certain number of sessions; others do not specify the length of therapy. Questions must be asked of a therapist if there is any uncertainty on this point or if it is felt that goals have been accomplished and it is time to discontinue therapy.

Traditionally, a therapy session lasts about forty-five to fifty minutes. Not all therapists, however, follow this timing. Some choose to see clients for *longer* periods of time, for example, for 1 1/2-hour or 2-hour sessions. Perhaps these clients come only twice a month. Clients should know, however, that if they are seeing a therapist for only five minutes, perhaps once a week in a clinic, they are not receiving psychotherapy. Often a psychiatrist will see people for a few minutes a week to check on how they are doing with medications. This checkup is not and should not be confused with psychotherapy. Patients who want psychotherapy should ask for it.

WHO CAN AFFORD TO BE IN THERAPY?

The fees of many public and private mental health agencies are based on an individual's ability to pay. Theoretically, no one should be prevented from obtaining mental health services because of inability to pay. Most agencies not only consider the individual's income, but also the available insurance benefits, such as Medicare, Medicaid, and private insurance. Although some private therapists are expensive, others base their fee on an individual's ability to pay and will also accept such insurance payments as those mentioned above. A particular therapist should not be ruled out until an investigation is made of these points.

ARE MENTAL HEALTH SERVICES ACCESSIBLE?

The answer to this question depends on the physical structure of the clinic or agency. Disabled persons, like anyone else, have the right to mental health services. Under Section 504, of the Rehabilitation Act of 1973, discussed in chapter 3, they are entitled to all medical and mental health services. Any agency, clinic, or hospital that receives any federal funds must serve them and cannot deny them admission because of a disability or because they use a wheelchair. If such rights have been violated because of a disability, or if an individual has been denied services from a facility that receives federal assistance, then the agency is in violation of Section 504. For redress, the Regional Office of Civil Rights, Department of Health and Human Services should be contacted.

NOTES

1. Alfred M. Freedman, Harold Kaplan, and Benjamin Sadock, *Modern Synopsis of Comprehensive Textbook of Psychiatry* 3d ed. (Baltimore: The Williams & Wilkins Co., 1980), p. 803.

2. Merrit Eaton, Jr., and Margaret Peterson, *Psychiatry, Medical Outline Series*, 3d. ed. (Flushing, N.Y.: Medical Examination Publishing Co., 1976) p. 94.

3. Ibid.

4. Roger Corn, ed., *Aiding Adjustment to Physical Limitation: A Handbook for Peer Counselors*. (Columbia, Md.: Howard Community College, August 1977).

5. Frank Riessman, "How Does Self-Help Work?" *Social Policy* September/ October, 1976, p. 41.

6. Corn, *Aiding Adjustment to Physical Limitations*, p. 53.

6 | SPECIAL SERVICES FOR CHILDREN

The most visible and commonly available programs for handicapped children are those that deal with their educational and health needs. Schools throughout the nation have special education units. Each state has a diagnostic and treatment program expressly for children with orthopedic and other medical problems, and another for children with a developmental disability.

From a slow and spotty beginning, special education programs have expanded to become one of the distinctive features in each state's public school system. During 1981, the number of children receiving special education services averaged about 8.5 percent of the school-age population. Nearly 3.94 million children received special training and instruction under the nation's major program of education for the handicapped: Public Law 94-142, the Education for All Handicapped Children Act. An additional 260,000 severely disabled children received educational services from miscellaneous programs financially supported by the federal government, such as deaf-blind centers conducted by the Department of Education under the provisions of Public Law (P.L.) 91-230, or state-operated schools provided by P.L. 89-313. The number of impaired children who will receive special educational assistance in 1982 is predicted to decline. The President's Office of Management and Budget estimates that 3,802,500 children will be enrolled under P.L. 94-142, and slightly more than 200,000 others will receive educational help from other programs. With some exceptions, all states have been required since 1980 to make a free, appropriate public education available to children between the ages of 3 and 21 who suffer from any health problem or learning impairment. However, federal, state, and local budget cutbacks are now seriously affecting the nation's 16,000 local public school districts that provide the bulk of special education services. Unless this situation is reversed, the total number of young, disabled students in 1983 is expected to remain close to the levels predicted for 1982.

Each state conducts two distinct medically related and social service programs for children. One is the Crippled Children's Program, better known as Crippled Children's Services (CCS) that in 1981 provided medical treatment and rehabilitation to nearly 700,000 children. This program originated as Title V of the Social Security Act's provisions for maternal and child health and is the oldest and most prevalent public medical care system for disabled children in the nation. In many respects it is apt to be the most rigid and conservative as well. Developmental disability programs also exist in every state. These differ from CCS in that, as the name implies, the focus is on individuals whose normal sensory, intellectual, or physical development was inhibited or prevented. Enormous variances among these state programs and shifts in eligibility definitions account, in part, for probably less than one-third of the nation's estimated two million developmentally handicapped children receiving needed health services in 1981. A handful of states conducts an elaborate and comprehensive array of services, but the majority have services of considerably lesser scope. The breadth of these programs seems to be more related to the strength and vigor of organized parental groups in lobbying for legislated services than to the size of the disabled population or to the richness of the state's tax base. The nature of these state programs also reflects the continuing philosophical conflict of institutional care versus community-based care.

Although none of these three types of programs—special education, CCS, and developmental disability programs—is precisely duplicated from state to state, the programs tend to be more alike than different. Those aspects of the programs that should be standard throughout the nation will be described, and the range of services that one might reasonably expect to find will be explored, along with new developments and trends in the services. Some attention will be given to ways in which the consumer can deal effectively and successfully with these educational and health systems.

SPECIAL EDUCATION SERVICES

BACKGROUND OF SERVICES

The term "special education" is used to describe the instructional services a school offers for children with an exceptional physical, emotional, intellectual, or perceptual malfunction. Despite the widespread acceptance of the term and the prevalence of services today, both the concept and the services implied largely developed during the past thirty years. There have, of course, always been some educational provisions for the disabled. But American society generally has been indifferent, if not unsympathetic, to the needs of the handicapped child and his family. Many schools were developed during the 1890s, but these were residential institutions and asylums for the mentally retarded (then called feeble-minded or idiots), and "institutions" for the deaf. A few public school special classes were organized at the turn of the century, largely instigated because of Alexander Graham Bell's radical proposal in 1898 that programs for handicapped children should be part of the public school system and that children should not be sent away from their home because of their blindness, deafness, or mental deficiency. Beginning in 1920 and continuing until 1960, a variety of trends developed throughout the nation, primarily, if not wholly, attributable to the phenomenon of special reimbursement formulas created by the states to offset the costs incurred by local school districts in establishing and maintaining special programs and classes. By 1930 nearly every large American city had some type of educational service for disabled children. Examples of some of these early trends remain evident today: self-contained classes for the educable mentally retarded in local public schools, state residential schools and hospitals for children with retardation or hearing impairment, special classes in local schools for children who are physically disabled, and remedial classes in speech correction or speech therapy.

The greatest impetus to the development of locally based special education occurred in the mid-1960s when parents of exceptional children, activated by mounting national concern over many civil rights issues, demanded alternatives to institutional placement for their children and educational opportunities equal to those provided for nonhandicapped children. Some strides were made; nevertheless, by 1970 only one-third of the states mandated public schools to provide special classes. Recourse to the courts proved to be a highly effective tool for obtaining these goals. Several suits involving the right of the handicapped to a free, public education were filed, but two were of unusual importance. In an action filed against the Commonwealth of Pennsylvania in 1971, the Pennsylvania Association for Retarded Children successfully contended that mentally retarded children could learn if an appropriate education program were provided, if education were viewed more broadly than the traditional academic program, and if educational training were started early in the child's life. The court's formal approval of a consent agreement firmly established the legal right of mentally retarded children in that state to an appropriate education at public expense. Additionally, the court required that schooling be provided in the least restrictive environment. Other litigation in the District of Columbia, occurring almost simultaneously with that in Pennsylvania, was of even greater significance because it applied to *all* handicapped children and was argued on constitutional grounds. Declaring for the plaintiff in a class action suit, *Mills v. the Board of Education of the District of Columbia*, the court ruled that public schools were constitutionally required to provide for handicapped children, even if these children did not fit the traditional educational mold.

Judicial decisions in other states, particularly California, and the legislative advocacy efforts conducted nationally by the United Cerebral Palsy Association, National Association for Retarded Citizens, Council for Exceptional Children, and the American Association on Mental Deficiency led to the passage of the Education for All Handicapped Children Act in 1975. This act, popularly known as Public Law (P.L.) 94-142, is the nation's major statement of public policy for the handicapped.

Despite the assurances and hope brought by the law to so many, it was neither wholeheartedly nor uniformly endorsed. President Ford, reluctantly signing the legislation after overwhelming congressional approval, called the act inflationary and an administrative nightmare. His reservations were based on doubts concerning attainment of the act's mission and on its projected costs:

> Unfortunately, this bill promises more than the Federal government can deliver and its good intentions could be thwarted by the many unwise provisions it contains. Everyone can agree with the objective stated in the title of this bill—educating all handicapped children in our Nation. The key question is whether the bill will really accomplish that objective.
>
> Even the strongest supporters of this measure know as well as I that they are falsely raising the expectations of the groups affected by claiming authorization levels which are excessive and unrealistic.
>
> Despite my strong support for full educational opportunities for our handicapped children, the funding levels proposed in this bill will simply not be possible if Federal expenditures are to be brought under control and a balanced budget achieved over the next few years. (From the Veto Message signed November 29, 1975.)

DESCRIPTION OF P.L. 94-142

The primary goal of the Education for All Handicapped Children Act is to give every disabled child the learning opportunities needed to achieve personal and economic self-sufficiency and productivity. The legislation expanded Part B of the less encompassing Education of the Handicapped Act of 1969, P.L. 91-230, by mandating that a *free appropriate public education* was to be made available, by 1980, for all handicapped children between the ages of 3 and 21. The general guarantee applies to all handicapped children regardless of the severity of their disability or their families' ability to pay for services. There are, however, exemptions to the age eligibility requirements. States are not required to make educational provisions for children between the 3 to 5 and 18 to 21 age ranges if (a) state law expressly prohibits or does not authorize the expenditure of public funds to provide education to nonhandicapped children in either of these age groups, or (b) the federal requirement conflicts with a court order that governs the provision of free public education to handicapped children in that state.

Nor does the inclusive age range of 3 to 21 mean that handicapped children are legally compelled to attend school until they reach the maximum age. It means, rather, that educational programs *must be made available* by all states for handicapped children falling within that age group. State laws defining the upper age limit for compulsory school attendance by nonhand-icapped children must be the same as for children who are handicapped. The thematic phrase is also subject to misinterpretation. The term "all handi-capped children", in the act's title and appearing throughout the statute, carries the literal interpretation that an infinite number of handicapped children will be guaranteed a federally mandated educational program. The law, however, limits the number of handicapped children to 12 percent of the entire school-age population of the state between the ages of 5 and 17. This limitation was included to avoid the potential threat of "over-counting" children as handicapped in order to generate the largest possible federal allocation. States may, of course, provide educational services to as many handicapped children as they wish; but not with funds derived from P.L. 94-142 when the number of children totally or in defined categories of impairment, with the exception of learning disability, exceeds the 12 percent limitation. The total number of handicapped children served is now about 8.5 percent of the nation's school-age population. The ceiling for learning-disabled children is based on a percent of the estimated prevalence. The proportion of children with this problem reached the upper limit of the currently used prevalence rate of 3 percent in January 1982. "All handi-capped children" refers more precisely to the inclusiveness of disabilities covered under the act, and means that states must provide specialized education for children with *all types* of impairment.

ADMINISTRATION

At the federal level, P.L. 94-142 is presently administered by the Office of Special Education within the Office of Special Education and Rehabilitative Services in the Department of Education. At the state level, the state's educational agency (SEA) administers the program and is responsible to the U.S. Department of Education for ensuring that educational provisions exist for disabled children and that the state's educational plan conforms with the federal law. Congress deliberately established this line of responsibility so that one agency would be "squarely responsible" for the failure to deliver services or for violating the rights of handicapped children.

To receive federal financial grants under the act, states must comply with

six conditions, even if state and local funding must be increased to
do so:

1. States must locate, identify, and evaluate every handicapped child within their
    jurisdictions (the "child find" system) and devise methods for determining
    which children are not receiving needed services to which they are entitled.
2. Evaluations of handicapped children must be conducted in a nondiscrimin-
    atory manner.
3. Children must be placed in the least restrictive environment consistent with
    their special needs.
4. Parents or guardians must be given fundamental due process rights, includ-
    ing an impartial hearing on any matter concerning the evaluation, place-
    ment, or provision of a free appropriate education for their children.
5. States must establish inservice training for general and special educational,
    instructional, related services, and support personnel.
6. States must pay for all educational services and guarantee all rights to
    handicapped children in private schools or facilities as well as for those in
    public schools.

These requirements make P.L. 94-142 unique among federal educational
grant programs. Although many others also have detailed prerequisites on
the use of federal funds, this act goes one step further by requiring states to
guarantee certain rights to handicapped children and their parents. Local
school agencies (LEAs), or districts, are responsible for designing and
providing special education and related services, and for implementing the
guarantees and assurances.

PATTERN OF FUNDING

Although responsibility for funding is shared among the federal, state,
and local governments, the major strength of P.L. 94-142 lies in the federal
funding formula that was included as an integral part of the law. This
formula is based on the number of handicapped children served in a state
multiplied by a percentage of the average amount spent annually by all the
states for each public school pupil. This percentage, the federal contribution,
was stipulated in the law to be 5 percent in 1978, 10 percent in 1979, 20
percent in 1980, 30 percent in 1981, and to maximize in 1982 at 40 percent.
Thereafter, the federal percentage would remain at 40 percent. The share of
federal participation is, however, now lagging far behind these levels. In
1978 and 1979, Congress appropriated the authorized amounts of 5 and 10
percent. Twelve percent was appropriated for 1980 and 1981, respectively,
compared with the authorized levels of 20 and 30 percent. The appropriation of $931 million for the 1982 school year was less than one-fourth of the

nearly $4 billion required to maintain the original formula of federal partici-
pation. New major cutbacks proposed by the federal administration for 1983
not only would further reduce the government's share of financing, but also
would eliminate categorical, or separate, funding of the program. Instead,
Congress has been asked to consolidate this program with over a score of
others that would share a total Local Education Block Grant of $3.6 billion.
Additionally, the president has proposed that the Department of Education
be abolished.

ASSURANCES, TARGET POPULATIONS, AND SERVICES

REQUIREMENTS AND GUARANTEES

Public Law 94-142 makes a number of stipulations which must be
adhered to by both the state and local school systems. These requirements
are given as assurances and guarantees to the parents and children for whom
the law was enacted:

1. Assurance of extensive child identification procedures.
2. Assurance of "full service" goals with detailed timetables.
3. A guarantee of complete due process procedures.
4. Assurance of regular parent or guardian consultation.
5. Assurance of special education being provided in the least restrictive
    environment.
6. Assurance of nondiscriminatory testing and evaluation.
7. A guarantee of policies and procedures to protect the confidentiality of
    student data and information.
8. Assurance of the maintenance of an individualized instructional plan.
9. Assurance of an effective policy guaranteeing the right of handicapped
    children to a free, appropriate public education, at no cost to parents or
    guardians.
10. Assurance of a surrogate to act in behalf of any child whose parents or
    guardians are either unknown or unavailable, or when a child is a legal
    ward of the state.
11. Maintenance of programs and procedures for the comprehensive inservice
    training and professional development of all school personnel.

DISABILITY DEFINED

The main difference between traditional definitions of handicapped children and that found in P.L. 94-142 is that the latter uses two criteria for

determining disability. First, whether the child has *one or more* of specifically listed disabilities; and second, whether the child *requires special education* and *related services*. Eleven handicapping conditions are mentioned in the act. Special education, educational tools, and related services must be provided to children who are mentally retarded, hard of hearing, deaf, deaf-blind, speech impaired, visually handicapped, seriously emotionally disturbed, orthopedically impaired, other health impaired, multihandicapped, or who have learning disabilities. Preliminary statistical reports for 1981 indicate that the greatest majority of children, 85 percent, were receiving special education programs because of learning and communicative handicaps. Thirty six percent, or 1,410,000 children, had a learning disability; 1,200,000 (30 percent) were speech impaired, and 750,000 (19 percent) were diagnosed as mentally retarded.

Variations from the basic terminology used in the act to define disability may be discovered in different parts of the nation. Some state and local educational agencies follow the popular trend of referring to disabled children as "individuals with exceptional needs." Although this terminology started with the good intention to avoid labeling children, it has been reduced to the acronym IWEN. In the jargon of the educational system IWEN fall into four categories:

1. Communicatively handicapped, which includes the deaf, deaf-blind, severely hard of hearing, severely language-deprived (including aphasic), and children with other language and speech deficits.
2. Physically handicapped, which includes blind, partially seeing, orthopedically handicapped, and other health-impaired children (including drug-dependent and pregnant minors).
3. Learning handicapped, which includes children with learning disabilities and behavior disorders and educationally retarded children.
4. Severely handicapped, which includes developmentally disabled, trainable mentally retarded, autistic, and seriously emotionally disturbed children.

Frequently, many school districts describe impairment in terms of levels or degrees, such as severe, moderate, and mild. Using these broad categories, of the 3.94 million children enrolled in special educational programs during 1981, 13 percent had severe handicaps, 36 percent had moderate impairments, and 51 percent had mildly handicapping conditions. For all children who meet the disability criteria of P.L. 94-142 the school must accommodate the child's special needs, develop goals and a written plan for achieving them, and provide related or supportive services necessary for the child to benefit from the individualized instruction program.

APPROPRIATE EDUCATION, SPECIAL SERVICES, AND RELATED SERVICES

Adaptive planning, or educational programming, to meet the educational needs of handicapped children did not originate with P.L. 94-142. During the 1960s, many public school districts and all university teacher-training schools were successfully adapting their facilities, procedures, and teaching methods to reenter handicapped children into various regular education programs. By 1970, the practice of integrating mild and moderately disabled children into the mainstream of educational activities was firmly established and well on its way to becoming a national trend. The impelling requirements of the 1975 legislation did, however, make integration a prevasive characteristic of special education programs nationally since all programs were to be based on the concepts of an *appropriate* education in the *least restrictive setting*.

APPROPRIATE EDUCATION

A written individualized education program (IEP) is the foundation of an appropriate education for each handicapped child. Although the entire law has often been called "a revolutionary approach to special education," it is the mandatory IEP requirement that may be considered the most radical feature. Traditionally, special education has been dominated by a categorical approach. This approach assumed that children having a similar problem or bearing the same label, such as "mentally retarded" or "speech handicapped," also shared the same needs, and that these needs could be met with standard programming in a common setting. Prior to the passage of P.L. 94-142 however, this traditional approach was being abandoned and replaced by an educational programming system that was based on an evaluation of the individual child's needs. The IEP mandate sped up this trend and created homogeneity among the nation's special education programs by requiring that planning for children be based on IEPs that contained: (1) the child's present levels of educational performance, (2) annual goals, (3) short-term objectives for achieving the identified goals, (4) special education and related services to be provided, (5) a statement of the extent to which the child will be able to participate in regular education programs, (6) the projected dates for the initiation and anticipated duration of services made available, and (7) objective criteria, evaluation procedures, and schedules for determining, at least annually, whether short-term objectives are being achieved.

Initially, schools had much difficulty in arriving at a satisfactory IEP format since none was stipulated by the law, and in 1977, the year the legislation took effect, many varieties of IEPs were being used. Uniformity has increased steadily, largely due to the efforts of commercial publishers in marketing standardized forms, and some general tendencies in IEPs are now evident. Typically, IEPs are two or three pages long, but 7 percent extend to 11 pages. In one exceptional instance noted by the U.S. Department of Education in 1980, the extensive educational needs of one child required an IEP of 47 pages. Far from restricting themselves to the mandated IEP requirements, most of the nation's schools include additional data. Much is routine information that the law does not require, such as age and sex, but other IEPs contain more complex additions. The majority list placement recommendations and the personnel who will be responsible for providing services to the child. Over one-half require specific information concerning recommended instructional materials, resources, strategies, or techniques. One-third of the IEP forms ask for assessment data to support statements of the child's current levels of performance, and one-fourth also focus on student strengths.

Of the schools that conduct special education programs, approximately 7,500, most show a remarkably high rate of compliance with the requirements mandated in P.L. 94-142. Virtually all IEPs of public school-handicapped students, 99 percent, state the specific educational services to be provided and the projected date for starting them. Ninety-five percent include annual goals and the anticipated duration of specific services. Over 90 percent indicate a child's present level of educational performance, short-term objectives, and proposed evaluation procedures. Annual reviews are conducted on 88 percent of the IEPs, and a similar number are monitored periodically throughout the school year. Less frequently, however, do the IEPs define the extent to which a handicapped child will participate in the normal school routine. In 1980, only 62 percent of the IEPs indicated that children were receiving any services in the least restrictive educational environment. The absence of planned reentry or socialization opportunities for nearly 40 percent of handicapped students emphasizes the complexity of issues involved in determining what constitutes the least restrictive environment, and the many continuing problems encountered by schools, teachers, and parents, in assimilating disabled children into the school's mainstream.

Much controversy and debate has centered on the meaning of the term *least restrictive environment*. The concept originated from court decisions in several states during the 1970s banning the complete segregation of handicapped children from the regular school population. Congress was motivated to include this provision in P.L. 94-142 because of the legal principles already established by the courts, and because of general concerns related to (a) inadequate or biased assessment methods used to classify children as "handicapped," (b) placement of students in special classes as a substitute for the development of other school programs or for the failure of schools to modify their physical facilities to accommodate disabled children, and (c) the broader social and educational benefits brought to handicapped and nonhandicapped children alike through interaction and shared social experiences. The congressional intent appeared to be the expression of a belief that handicapped children should be educated in the regular classroom with normal peers whenever this was feasible or appropriate. Unfortunately, the vagueness of the terminology led to many conflicting interpretations. One interpretation, known as *mainstreaming*, generated a ground swell of conviction and emotion among many parents and special educators that any segregation of handicapped children was inhumane, unwarranted, and also prohibited. The coined word, mainstreaming, described both the elimination of any separate educational programs, and the process by which this goal would be accomplished—the rapid integration of all handicapped children, regardless of degree of severity, into the normal classroom.

Some schools experimented with this approach when P.L. 94-142 became effective in 1977, but for several reasons their efforts mostly resulted in disappointment and frustration for everyone concerned. Regular classroom teachers were inadequately prepared for the diversity of need manifested among severely or multiply handicapped children, and the cost of providing the large number of special instructors, resource teachers, and support staff exceeded budget limitations. The most decisive reason, however, was demonstrated evidence that severely handicapped children did not effectively learn basic skills when placed in the regular classroom. Emulation of children with higher ability occurred only when the disparity between a handicapped child and the group was sufficiently narrow as to hold hope for bridging the distance. For most mildly and moderately handicapped, mainstreaming now is interpreted as education within the regular classroom, at least for a portion of the day. Placement of more severely handicapped children within the normal classroom, even for carefully selected activities, is generally an unrealistic expectation.

As the result of much trial and error in creating an *appropriate* education, most of the nation's school districts now have numerous program alternatives for disabled children. Depending upon the number and scope of programs available, these alternatives are known either as a limited or full *continuum of services*. The concept of a full continuum is based on the varying degrees of severity which a handicapped child experiences at different times, on the different amounts and types of assistance required at various age levels, and on the different combinations of assistance that may be required. These services may range from education in the regular classroom for students with mildly or moderately handicapping conditions to separate programming for children with severe disabilities. Figure 2 illustrates one possible upwardly flowing continuum, ranging from nonparticipation to full participation in the regular classroom. Occasionally a full continuum of services may be available within a single school district. More often, however, a number of districts, each providing one or more components of a service continuum, combine their special education resources and group together as a special education consortium.

FIGURE 2. A CONTINUUM OF SPECIAL EDUCATION SERVICES.

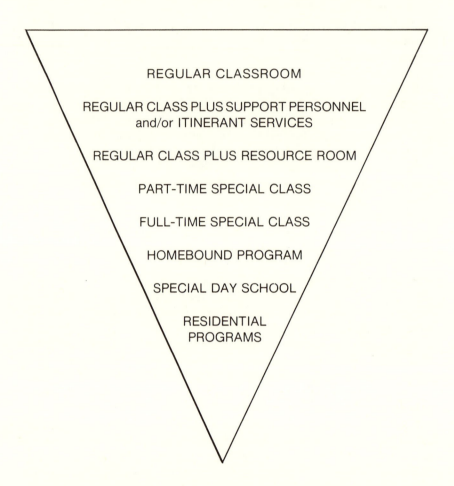

REGULAR CLASSROOM

REGULAR CLASS PLUS SUPPORT PERSONNEL
and/or ITINERANT SERVICES

REGULAR CLASS PLUS RESOURCE ROOM

PART-TIME SPECIAL CLASS

FULL-TIME SPECIAL CLASS

HOMEBOUND PROGRAM

SPECIAL DAY SCHOOL

RESIDENTIAL
PROGRAMS

SPECIAL EDUCATION AND RELATED SERVICES

Schools are required to provide specially designed instruction and related services. The former consists of (a) any school instruction (b) designated as "special education" under the state's educational code, that is (c) "specially designed" to meet the unique needs of a handicapped child, and (d) is provided at no cost to the parent. Federal regulations define related services broadly as supportive, corrective, and developmental assistance that will help a handicapped child to benefit from special instruction. Specifically, these will include early identification and assessment of disabilities, counseling, medical diagnosis and evaluation, psychological services, physical and occupational therapy, recreational activities, school health services, social work services when conducted in the school, parent counseling and training, special transportation to school and within the school, speech pathology, and audiology. Other activities such as dance or music therapy, and artistic and cultural programs may qualify as related services if they are required to assist the handicapped child. Special education and related services needed by a child are determined by parents, teachers, other school personnel such as a psychologist or nurse, and, when appropriate, the child, when the individualized education program (IEP) is being written.

Differences between the two types of services appear to be clear and distinct, but this apparent clarity is sometimes blurry. Definitions used in the various states' educational codes, or those required by the reimbursement formulas of other federal educational programs administered by the states, often differ from the service classifications used in P.L. 94-142. Many states, for example, categorize speech pathology as a special education service. Although federal regulations list this as a related service, the government will accept this service as special education because it is so defined under state standards. Other states classify speech pathology as a related service, and this is accepted as well. Because of the wide variation among the states in defining instructional and supportive, or therapeutic, assistance, the U.S. Department of Education is permissive in accepting services as either educational or related. The difference in definitions occasionally becomes a hotly disputed issue because service definition is another critical feature in the funding formula of the Education for All Handicapped Children Act. States and local school districts receive federal funds for special education services but not for related services.

In general, children's educational needs differ by age group. In 1980, about 63 percent of all children received special education in reading and in both oral and written English. Approximately 46 percent received training in mathematics, and 28 percent required speech rehabilitation. The needs of younger children tended to reflect communicative and motor impairments. At the preschool levels, 60 percent of the children needed speech services, compared to 28 percent of the entire handicapped group; and 38 percent of preschoolers, compared to 13 percent of all handicapped children, required motor training. Emphasis shifted to more academic subjects as children got older. Nearly 36 percent of children in the 3-to 5-year age range were taught reading and English, and 28 percent received arithmetic instruction. The predominant focus in children 13 years and over was in reading, writing, or speaking. Seventy-three percent received this instruction, and an average of 57 percent of children in the 13-to-21 year group also received special training in mathematics. Physical education was specified for about 8 percent, and 31 percent of older handicapped children received vocational or prevocational services.

For the most part, severely and multiply handicapped students require more supportive assistance than do those who are mildly or moderately impaired. However, in 1980, about 13 percent of all handicapped children received related services. Ten percent received a single related service, and the remaining 3 percent received two or more services. The most common related services were transportation and medical assistance, such as school nurse care, visual examinations and diagnostic evaluations.

Although many successes have been claimed for P.L. 94-142, the act's most impressive accomplishments have been in unifying the basic elements of special education, the involvement of parents in special education decision making, and in focusing national attention on the needs of young handicapped children. These achievements do not, however, overshadow the number of unserved children, management variances among the states, and the lack of adequate funding. Educational disparities continue to exist between the handicapped and nonhandicapped school age population. Less than half of all handicapped children were receiving educational services, the U.S. House of Representatives Subcommittee on Select Education found, in 1981. Progress toward the act's goal of full educational opportunities for children aged 3 to 21 by 1980 was slow and irregular, and even with adequate funding, most school districts do not expect to realize this goal until 1984.

Nonuniformity among state programs is also a cause of concern and particularly so in view of the president's desire to eliminate the federal Department of Education. States have varied widely, since the act was implemented in 1977, in defining and assessing specific handicaps, especially learning disabilities, emotional disturbances, and mental retardation. As a result of these discrepancies, a child may qualify for special education and related services in one state but not in another. The classification of mental retardation, the major cause of child impairment, fluctuates greatly among the states. Current figures indicate, for example, that the diagnosis of mental retardation is made far more frequently in some southeastern states than it is in other parts of the nation. Although the variation may reflect a truly different prevalence, it also may occur because of the use of culturally biased tests, overreliance on one measure of function, or racial discrimination. A 1982 study by the U.S. General Accounting Office (GAO) found, for example, that a disproportionate share of minority children were participating in some special education programs. The GAO also reported that participation in special education depends on a set of interrelated factors such as the state in which the child lives, the child's handicapping condition, sex, minority status, and programs available in the school district. Although these factors reduce equal access to special education, the GAO concluded that "those most in need of services have received them under P.L. 94-142." Thus, the priorities to serve first the unserved and second the most severely handicapped children may have been realized.

Variances in state administration and deficiencies in child outreach program alternatives tend to pale, however, beside other critical issues. The federal proportion of funding has fallen significantly behind the original formula, and it is doubtful if state and local governments can absorb this additional financial burden. Changes in the Education for All Handicapped Children Act, proposed by the president, would further weaken the nation's commitment to providing fully accessible and available education services. In early 1982, the administration identified 16 "targets of opportunity" for deregulation. These statutory and regulatory targets were selected, the administration explained, because of complaints and litigations, difficulties in compliance, and paperwork demands. If accepted by Congress, nearly all aspects of P.L. 94-142 would be altered, including: definition of special education and handicapped children, related services, specific learning disabilities, free appropriate public education, individualized education programs, services provided to children placed in private schools by their parents, comprehensive development of school personnel, due process procedures, nondiscrimination in evaluation procedures, confidentiality of information, and, the least restrictive environment.

CRIPPLED CHILDREN'S SERVICES

A good deal of public medical care for disabled children in the United States is provided through the system known as Crippled Children's Services. As the plural ending of the name suggests, there is no single, nationwide program. Rather, each state conducts a separate but similar program. These, in aggregate, comprise the national system. The purpose of Crippled Children's Services is to provide specialized medical care and rehabilitation for handicapped children whose families are unable to meet the total cost of these expensive services.

The name Crippled Children's Services can be confusing, since it is used in at least four different ways. Broadly speaking, Crippled Children's Services refers to the federal government's policy for the welfare of the nation's handicapped youngsters. Often it is used to denote the program of a specific state, sometimes to describe the kinds of medical services needed by an impaired child, and in most states it is used to identify the agency responsible for dispersing the services, although some states use a different name, believing CCS is an anachronistic and no longer accurate title. When the program or service elements are discussed, the full name and the initials CCS are used interchangeably. The agency, however, is always referred to as CCS.

Crippled Children's Services are found in every state and the District of Columbia, as well as in American Samoa, Guam, the Northern Mariana Islands, Puerto Rico, the Trust Territory, and the Virgin Islands. Together they represent one of the nation's oldest, most widespread, and, at least until recently, most respected public social and health service systems. Administration of the CCS program follows the familiar pattern of federal and state participation. The program is now administered federally by the Office for

Maternal and Child Health within the Department of Health and Human Services' Public Health Service. State administration of the program is the responsibility of the Maternal and Child Health (MCH) unit within each state's health agency. One-fifth of the programs are, however, administered by other state agencies, including welfare departments, social service departments, and, in three instances, state universities. Locally, CCS programs are generally operated by local health departments, but sometimes they are conducted by other community agencies under contractual arrangements. Variant patterns may include state-operated CCS programs in rural areas, and locally operated programs in urban regions. Both the federal and state governments are involved in establishing objectives, eligibility criteria, services to be provided, and standards for quality control.

DESCRIPTION

Since its origin, over fifty years ago, the CCS program has had surprisingly little change in mission and objectives. Many states developed their own system of health services for disabled children as far back as the early 1920s, but the federal program is a product of the Great Depression. During the period of recovery from that crisis, President Roosevelt requested a small but highly regarded government agency, the Children's Bureau, to make recommendations for legislation that would benefit children. The Bureau made proposals for the use of federal tax funds to improve state services to children, giving particular attention to expanding maternal and child health programs, child welfare services, and medical care for crippled children. Services for crippled children were included as Title V in the nation's basic charter of social policy, the Social Security Act, which was enacted in 1935 and became operative January 1, 1937.

AIMS OF THE PROGRAM

Present-day objectives of the CCS program are a blend from several sources. Although the original congressional mandate laid the foundation, subsequent alterations, geared toward expanding the program, have been made by directives and regulations from federal agencies, and from the creation of new separately funded programs affecting maternal and child health. State legislatures are involved in setting the program's objectives only when they expand upon the minimum requirements set by the federal government. Typically, each state program is designed to (1) locate physically handicapped children who may be in need of medical care, (2) provide health care services to physically handicapped children, (3) provide financial assistance to families to pay for medical treatment, (4) rehabilitate children with severely handicapping physical conditions, (5) prevent handicapping conditions in children through early diagnosis and treatment, and (6) set standards and maintain high-quality medical care for all handicapped children, including the development of facilities and new services.

FEDERAL FINANCING

CCS is a tax-supported program that receives funds from federal, state, and usually county sources. The quality of a state's CCS program is directly related to the source of funding. When supported by federal grants-in-aid and matched by state funds in the minimum amount stipulated by formula, services are minimal and eligibility curtailed. The range of services is widened and eligibility is expanded when more money comes from more sources or when state appropriations are enlarged.

The basic Social Security Act did not merely state that Congress hoped and recommended that states would provide services for crippled children. A dangling carrot of generous federal funds, known as grants-in-aid, gave states a strong incentive to participate. The financial dilemma of the 1930s made most state legislatures eager to accept any available federal funds, even when there were several strings attached. In accepting federal money, states were required to match certain federal appropriations. Additionally, states were required conscientiously and zealously to implement programs for finding and serving crippled children.

The federal financial formula has continued through the years with few changes. Congress makes appropriations, called grant funds, and then distributes them to the states in two portions, Fund A and Fund B. Under Fund A, each state receives both a flat grant and a variable grant. The amount of money contained in the variable portion is based on the percentage of children under 21 throughout the nation who live in that state. States must match dollar for dollar the funds allocated to them under Fund A. A percentage of Fund B is apportioned according to each state's need for financial assistance in administering the CCS program. Funds remaining in this purse are called "special project funds." They are awarded to colleges and universities for financing "special projects of regional or national significance which may contribute to the advancement of services for crippled children." States are not required to match Fund B allocations.

No part of the grants-in-aid, Fund A, may be paid to children or their parents. The funds are to be used solely to pay for professional services for children. The larger federal grants go to rural states and was the original intent of Congress. As a rule, states with low per capita income receive more federal funds than richer states. Although each state is required to have some kind of case-finding and treatment program for crippled children, states have the option of developing their own programs without federal financial involvement. After holding out for many years, Arizona has now joined the rest of the nation in obtaining the Title V grants, as they are called. Previously, its crippled children's program was financed primarily with state taxes and with some assistance from the Federal Bureau of Indian Affairs.

In 1980, the federal grant to the states for Part A funds was $102,100,000, and $105,700,000 in 1981. Rather than merely matching the annual grant, the states and territories exceeded their required contribution by $200 million for each of those years. Thus, in 1981, the total amount spent for CCS nationally was over $300 million. For both years, federal appropriations to the individual states ranged from about $150,000 to $3 million. The average grant to a state was $1 million. Categorical, or separate, funding for this national program would be eliminated if proposals submitted by the Reagan administration are accepted by Congress. The president has asked that CCS be consolidated with five other large government children's and mother's programs sharing a total Maternal and Child Health Service Block Grant appropriation of $347,524,000 in 1982.

STATE AND LOCAL FINANCIAL ROLES

Compared to the intricacies involved at the federal level, funding by the states is a smooth and simple budgetary process. There are three sources in most states: (a) appropriations by the state legislature, (b) county funds, and (c) parental contributions. However, on a national scale, repayments from families of physically handicapped children and local revenues are only a small percentage of the CCS budget. Sixty-one percent of CCS funding comes from state appropriations, 31 percent from federal grants-in-aid, and 8 percent from county and parental reimbursement funds combined.

The amount of money that the state legislature appropriates determines whether the state's CCS program will only meet minimum federal standards or will excel them. In most states, the legislature determines what medical conditions will be covered by CCS. Where this occurs, legislators find themselves in the uncomfortable position of being responsible for some children's exclusion from the program. Perhaps that is the reason many states delegate this responsibility to the CCS agency. Legislative appropriations to CCS are usually divided into three categories:

1. Diagnostic Services. Diagnostic services are paid for entirely out of state funds to comply with the federal requirement that such services be given without regard to residence, income status, or source of referral.
2. Treatment Services. State and county funds are combined to pay for these services.
3. State Nonresidents. State funds are used for the treatment of children who are in need and whose county, state, or nation of residence, is in question.

Funds for crippled children are used to provide direct services in one of four ways: (a) state-operated and staffed clinics, (b) local health departments, under contract with the state, (c) fee-for-service arrangements with private physicians, or, most often, (d) a combination of full-time state staff and part-time private physicians working together in state clinics. State and locally operated programs nearly always employ psychologists, nurses, and physical and speech therapists to implement physicians' recommendations.

Predicting expenses is a difficult problem for all CCS programs. The seeking out and locating of crippled children is a costly service, although it is now shared with school districts under the P.L. 94-142 law. Yet, this activity often appears to be phlegmatic and uneven, primarily because too many unanticipated clients can severely tax budgets. Unexpected events may also create unmeetable financial demands. Several years, ago, for instance, a major voluntary health agency, the National Foundation (now the March of Dimes Birth Defects Foundation) ceased paying for the care of polio patients, and state legislatures everywhere had to make special appropriations so that CCS programs could meet their unusual and extraordinary expenses.

ADMINISTRATIVE STRUCTURE

Despite its birth in federal law, CCS is actually a state-conducted program. The way local programs operate is determined, almost entirely, by state law. Each state CCS agency is given wide latitude to interpret the legal guidelines established by the local legislature and to discern the legislative intent. These interpretations are developed in the form of departmental policies, rules, regulations, and procedures. Over the years, CCS administrators at both state and local levels, have gained the unpleasant reputation of being slaves to their procedure manuals, rather than using them as operational tools to smooth the flow of services to the community. Evidence of a tendency toward a "bureaucratic mind-set" in CCS programs has been apparent for a long time. As far back as 1953, the Children's Bureau, which was in charge of CCS at the time, was apprehensive over the trends to rigidity. The Children's Bureau's qualms were expressed as reminders to CCS personnel that (1) people have a right to know about services available through public agencies, (2) diagnostic services should be readily available to all children in CCS programs without charge, without restriction, and without referral requirements, (3) children should be treated as children, not as disease entities or handicaps, (4) treatment of the individual should be given with respect and with feeling for his dignity and worth as a human being, (5) parent-child relationships should be maintained during periods of enforced separation caused by hospitalization of the child, (6) the agency's staff should work as a team and in cooperation with other agencies, and (7) quality and continuity of care are a means toward accomplishing community service and not an end in themselves.

ELIGIBILITY REQUIREMENTS

Since the origin of CCS, the program network has cherished and promoted a reputation for nationwide consistency in eligibility requirements. Changes in administrative accountability and levels of funding, starting in 1974, have greatly changed this uniformity. There are wide differences in the number and types of medical conditions covered by the states' CCS programs. Often these variations reflect lobbying and pressure on state legislators by parent groups. In all CCS programs, eligibility is always complicated and is an interplay of three main factors: (1) the medical conditions that are covered, or "medical eligibility," (2) the type of service that is desired or required, diagnosis or treatment, and (3) the financial ability of the family to pay the estimated costs of treatment. Age is also a consideration. It is the most clearly defined, readily determined, and least complex.

ELIGIBLE HANDICAPPING CONDITIONS

All states follow the federal guidelines in defining a physically handicapped child as a person under twenty-one years of age who has physical defects resulting from congenital anomalies or from disease, accident, or faulty development. The types of conditions generally recognized are (1) conditions of an orthopedic nature caused by congenital malformation, infection, disease, or injury, (2) central nervous system defects, such as paralysis from polio or injury, cerebral palsy, spina bifida, and hydrocephalus, (3) defects that require plastic surgery, such as cleft palate, severe burns, and other major disfigurements, (4) eye conditions leading to a loss of vision but excluding ordinary refractive errors, (5) ear conditions leading to a loss of hearing, (6) rheumatic or congenital heart disease, and (7) other specified conditions, such as cystic fibrosis, phenylketonuria, and nephrosis. Since any addition to this disease roster requires an additional state appropriation of funds, the list varies. Some states have more extensive coverage and include such conditions as diseases of the blood and blood-forming organs, endocrine and metabolic diseases, and digestive, respiratory, and genitourinary system disorders. Nearly every state includes neoplasms, and there is a trend, particularly among those states where legislative funding is less frugal, to cover injuries caused by serious accidents, poisonings, and acts of violence. In all, there are 125 established diagnostic categories. But there are enormous variations in coverage among the states. Children with chronic otitis media, for example, may be covered under CCS in some states and in others they are ineligible. In a few rare but noteworthy instances, genetic evaluations and amniocentesis are offered, but CCS agencies are typically reluctant to get embroiled in the political controversies that usually accompany services dealing with fetal intervention. In general, the entire CCS program is geared more to medical treatment of existing conditions than to medical prevention.

TYPES OF SERVICE

There are two basic types or phases of services: diagnostic and treatment. Diagnostic service is available to children if they have or are suspected of having one of the specified handicapping conditions. Referrals may be from anyone. A physician, parent, social worker, nurse, teacher or concerned friend may refer a disabled child to the local Crippled Children's Services agency for consideration for diagnostic workup. The word "consideration" sounds a cautionary note. Eligibility is not automatic on application. An employee of CCS, who may be a clerical intake worker, a nurse, or social worker, reviews medical records, usually interviews the parents, and then decides whether or not the child's problems appear to fall within the confines of CCS's list of medically eligible conditions. If the decision is "yes," as it is more often than not, an appointment is scheduled. This screening is called the "presumptive evidence of an eligible handicapping condition."

At some CCS agencies a staff physician will conduct the examination. As a rule, however, it will be performed by a physician in private practice who, because of recognized professional ability, is considered to be a specialist in the field of the child's disorder. Diagnostic services must be provided without cost to the family. Federal regulations also strictly prohibit any residence requirement. Only when the child's medical needs are obviously not within the scope of CCS services is the request for diagnosis denied. *If the child's condition proves to be ineligible under CCS, the agency is required to assist the family in obtaining treatment from other sources.* This is sometimes termed "medical case management."

Treatment services are limited to children (1) who are diagnosed as having a condition covered by the program, (2) whose parents or guardians need help in paying for the recommended care and who request assistance from CCS, and (3) who are under 21 years of age and reside permanently in the particular state. Even when these criteria are met, CCS has a set of rules for "limits of service." For example, when the only treatment indicated is custodial or palliative, CCS will generally not accept the child. When a child who is receiving treatment reaches the point where he needs only custodial care, CCS will often discontinue service, although only when alternative sources can be arranged. Service is also likely to be limited to children who have a prognosis of cure. The availability of an accepted form of treatment is also a factor. Experimental drugs or plans of treatment for research purposes are usually not authorized by CCS.

When budget constraints of CCS require cuts in service, the medically eligible conditions are ranked according to priority. These additional criteria are always part of the internal policies of any CCS agency. Because they are not well publicized, a great deal of misunderstanding surrounds them.

Parents often harbor suspicion that these limitations are a secretive means of excluding a child's entry into the program, but this is not the case. The restrictions are based upon federal guidelines, and their intent is to maintain the overall objectives of CCS: first, to enable a child to attain his greatest physical, social, and mental potential as he reaches adulthood, and second, not to deplete the financial resources of a CCS program for one child at the expense of many others.

FINANCIAL ELIGIBILITY

By law, diagnostic services must be available to all children at no charge; however, states and even localities are free to set their own income eligibility requirements for treatment services. If, after the diagnostic studies are completed, the estimated cost of care turns out to be within the family's budget, the child will remain under private care. The family's financial eligibility is worked out on an individual basis. It is determined mainly by the total cost of the recommended treatment and the ability of the family to pay that cost. Each state sets a maximum income ceiling for financial eligibility that is usually based on the family's adjusted gross income as reported on state income tax forms. The maximum income allowed may extend from a few thousand dollars to generous amounts. In California, for example, the income limitation in 1982 was an amazingly liberal $147,000. The family's adjusted gross income is used to determine the share of treatment costs a family must bear, or reimbursement obligation. The underlying philosophy is that care should be made available to all disabled children, particularly when families are unable to provide it, and that families should contribute a portion of their resources, if they can, toward the cost of the care. There is an equally strong conviction that the living standards for families with moderate or lower incomes should not be reduced to the point of privation. At all levels of the CCS program, there is awareness that the costs of caring for a child with a long-term condition can be a financial hardship or catastrophe for the family. Before CCS treatment services are started, there is a financial eligibility interview with the family. It is, to say the least, an intricate and time-consuming procedure and one that families should prepare for—both psychologically and in accumulating the answers to questions they are likely to be asked. In the majority of CCS programs, this interview goes under the heading "family intake and eligibility process" or "comprehensive family assessment." The interviewer's questions, requests for financial information, and observations follow a common pattern:

1. *Social Assessment.* This portion of the interview includes collection of information on the family's cultural background, its social, educational, and economic strengths and weaknesses, and the attitude of family members toward the child's disability that may affect treatment.

2. *Program Interpretation.* The interviewer will also discuss (a) the types of cases and families for whom the program is intended, (b) the services that are provided and limitations, (c) the family's responsibilities, such as keeping appointments, following through with treatment recommendations, and informing the agency about any change in residence or in financial circumstances, (d) facts relating to financial eligibility standards, repayment procedure, and annual reevaluations of the family's finances, and (e) the nature of the appeals procedures.

3. *Treatment Plan.* A public health nurse usually conducts this part of the interview, explaining to the parents what the course of treatment will be, the kinds of surgery or therapy involved, special equipment that the child will require, and what results are anticipated. CCS offices feel very strongly about the importance of close involvement with the family.

4. *Family Finances.* The letter notifying families of their appointment with CCS ordinarily includes instructions about the kind of information and documents they should bring with them. These are (a) their latest federal and state Income Tax Returns (not the W-2 form), (b) current paycheck stubs of three or four months so that average earnings can be calculated, (c) health insurance papers, since CCS policies require that all insurance benefits be used before its own funds are spent, and (d) information regarding unusual and extensive expenses of child care, medical and dental bills, alimony, or child support payments and educational costs.

The final decision about financial eligibility comes down to whether the amount of a family's tax reported income is sufficient to pay all or part of the treatment expenses for their disabled child. With this in mind, families should bring other financial data, even though these may not have been requested, including bills for taxes or assessments, bills for insurance premiums, home upkeep and major repairs, mortgage payments, and utility costs. CCS agencies may also inquire about current savings, bank balances, and any investments a family might hold. Generally, the portion of medical expenses families must pay is based on a percentage, often 200 percent, of their state income tax liability. If, for example, a family paid $500 in state income taxes during the previous year, their payment obligation is $1,000. This amount is payable in twelve monthly installments, and the total liability is redetermined annually. All CCS agencies are firm about full disclosure of family finances and increasingly are becoming more adamant as federal and state allocations are tightening. Spot-checks may be conducted to verify earnings and expenditures. Paradoxically, CCS has not vigorously sought repayment from families in the past, but this laxity will likely change since President Reagan has urged that repayment be pursued more actively.

The costs of professional care are analyzed just as rigorously. They are based on the estimated costs of physician office visits, laboratory and x-ray services, surgery, physician's hospital visits, hospital care, prosthetic equipment, occupational and physical therapy, and in a few states, transportation expenditures connected with these services.

AGE ELIGIBILITY

To be eligible, a child cannot be any older than twenty-one. Even an individual over twenty-one whose condition stemmed from childhood is not eligible.

BENEFITS

The range of benefits depends upon the type of service for which a child is medically eligible and the family financially eligible. All states provide two broad categories:

1. Diagnostic services for children suspected of having physically handicapping conditions. At the minimum, these services will consist of medical examinations, necessary laboratory and x-ray tests, and family consultation.
2. Treatment service for the handicapping condition, including physician services; hospital and surgical care; physical, speech, and occupational therapy; laboratory tests, x rays, appliances; equipment; and any other needed service.

CCS agencies often provide two other services:

1. Medical therapy services for children with neuromuscular and orthopedic handicaps, including (a) clinic services of a pediatrician and orthopedic surgeon and (b) physical and occupational therapy, as prescribed by the clinic or private physicians. In many states this CCS program is conducted jointly with local school districts. The intent is to provide a combined medical-educational approach, using the special professional skills of teachers, social workers, therapists, parents, nurses, and physicians. The medical-therapy team is responsible for the physical and occupational therapy needs of the child. These may consist of therapy evaluations and reevaluations, individual and group therapy, consultation with parents in developing a home treatment plan, and social work support counseling. Where CCS offers this adjunctive service, it is provided without charge to all children with eligible conditions.
2. Medical case management in the development of a medical treatment plan. This activity is an essential element of good medical care. The program assists families in identifying the appropriate medical and therapeutic specialists and institutions that may help a child, and in coordinating with other professional workers such as public health and school nurses, social workers, and advocacy agencies. The program also helps families resolve problems involved in keeping complicated appointment schedules, arranging for transportation, transferring medical records, and locating new facilities and services when the family moves. In some states, such as Michigan and

Indiana, transportation for medical and therapeutic care is paid for by the program.

USEFUL INFORMATION

Few, if any, programs operating throughout the United States have had as salutary an impact upon as many physically disabled people as the Crippled Children's Service. For the majority of the disabled population now living, it was the single agency that most affected the way their lives would develop and the avenues for growth that would be open. The program is unparalleled in terms of national scope, historical origin, extent of care, its traditional insistence upon the highest quality of medical standards, and probably its public and professional acceptance. It is the nation's bedrock public medical program for children.

Ironically, many of the same elements for which it is praised have become the cause for controversy and condemnation. Questions have been raised about the program's internal rigidity, the conditions of eligibility, and even the program's level of concern for the population it was created to serve. For the most part, these criticisms are directed at services, financial and medical eligibility, and the way CCS agencies operate. Two of these problem areas will be reviewed and some suggestions given for circumventing them. The most realistic way of approaching any agency is to know beforehand what to expect and then develop a plan for obtaining services in the most painless way possible.

ELIGIBILITY

The conditions of both financial and medical eligibility are, frankly, onerous. Short of pressing for legislative change in eligibility standards, however, there is little that can be done on an individual scale. For most parents, the major problem lies in understanding and accepting restrictions of medical eligibility. Mental retardation, for example, is almost uniformly excluded from CCS coverage. The explanation is scarcely satisfactory, but most states have distinctly separate programs for mental retardation, mental illness, and crippled children. Unless the child has another condition, such as heart disease or cerebral palsy, that falls under the CCS umbrella of handicapping conditions, he is forthrightly ineligible. However, handicaps rarely occur singly or in isolation, and often in the case of mental problems, there is an accompanying physical deficit. Parents might be aware of other difficulties the child presents and could describe them to the CCS intake interviewer. There might, for instance, be observations about the child's unusual gait, physical clumsiness, or distorted perception. Parents could try taking this approach because the policies and regulations of CCS agencies invariably contain "exceptions" for noneligible conditions. Equally present, though less tangible, are the interviewer's personal feelings and the program's general humanitarian commitment. Neither workers nor agencies like to reject persons who apply for service.

If eligibility or services are denied, an appeal for reconsideration can always be made, as with any publicly funded organization. Agencies do not like appeals. They are costly in staff time, preparation, and the mental ordeal for personnel. If an agency receives numerous grievances or complaints over a period of time, there is always a governing board or higher administrative office that starts asking why. Most agencies, including CCS, find that accepting the appealing potential client is, in the long run, the most efficient way of resolving disagreements over eligibility. Before filing a formal appeal, the family should present the problem to successively higher supervisors and authorities within the office. If results are ineffective, a written request for review can be filed.

Redeterminations of financial eligibility are an accustomed part of any program that is supported totally or partly by tax funds. In CCS they are conducted annually. Redetermination is minor, however, compared to the screening that is done to establish financial eligibility in the first place. There is no sidestepping this procedure, but it will be expedited if parents carefully scrutinize their income and expenses, compile these into an accurate list covering the past three months, and bring these records to the redetermination interview.

AGENCY OPERATIONS

Parents who have had experience with CCS are apt to point out problems that seem endemic to all CCS programs. These relate to (1) excessive waiting periods for therapy programs, (2) lack of medical, nursing, social service, and therapy personnel, (3) inconsistency in the CCS programs from state to state and, frequently, from county to county, (4) constant changes in administrative policies and regulations, and (5) reliance upon administrative interpretations of eligibility and treatment policies. The difficulties that have been described may beset any medical or human service agency and are not specific to CCS. Furthermore, national labor statistics paint a gloomy picture of job turnover in human service fields; for example, the annual displacement of nurses soars in many agencies beyond 100 percent. All CCS programs report a shortage of qualified therapists, primarily because of the higher salaries offered by hospitals and the allure of private practice. Nationwide surveys indicate that social workers tend to move on to other job opportunities after two years.

APPEALS PROCEDURE

There should never be any reluctance to file an appeal after all preliminary attempts to correct a problem have been exhausted. Filing an appeal should not be viewed as an indictment of any one staff member but as an opportunity courteously given by the agency to review its standards and method of operation. However, not all CCS agencies have formal appeal procedures, even though federal regulation requires them. Complaints, in this event, should be registered with the agency's highest authority and with both state and national legislators. This procedure takes time, but it is effective. The request should be made in writing; usually the agency will have a form that can be filled out.

Aside from questions about eligibility, the right of appeal may be used when there is any dissatisfaction because of (1) unreasonable delay in an agency's acting upon an application for services, (2) refusal of the opportunity to apply for services, (3) possible erroneous interpretation or application of state standards, (4) the lack of services or the kind of services provided, (5) personal differences with the interviewer, or (6) the estimate of the annual cost of care and the applicant's ability to pay any or all of these costs.

WHERE TO GET CCS SERVICES?

The best way to locate services is to inquire at the county welfare or health department. CCS programs operate throughout the nation, but there has been a recent trend toward changes in name. Some states, in attempting to develop a more positive image for the program, have erased the term "crippled children" in the belief that it is somewhat stigmatizing. In Colorado and Massachusetts, for example, the name has been changed to the Handicapped Children's Program. In California, the initials are the same, but the name is now California Children Services.

DEVELOPMENTAL DISABILITY SERVICES

Since 1963, Congress has directed attention repeatedly toward a vulnerable subset of the handicapped population, now known as the developmentally disabled, that often has been slighted, and that requires detailed planning and orchestrating of available services and resources at the state and local levels. Developmentally disabled persons comprise about 9 percent of the millions of physically and mentally handicapped people in the country. The original legislation dealt exclusively with the mentally retarded, but three subsequent amendments have greatly expanded the range of disabilities covered. Beginning in 1970, program eligibility was expanded to include cerebral palsy, epilepsy, and autism, in addition to mental retardation. Although these impairments still account for about 70 percent of the population classified as being developmentally disabled, the present law, the Developmental Disabilities Assistance and Bill of Rights Act of 1978 (P.L. 95-602), discarded categorical eligibility and now as many as 200 different disabilities could be covered—providing they are severe and that other criteria are met. In comparison to federal financial participation in the handicapped children's education and crippled children's programs, developmental disability grants are small. The national DD program, as it is called, was intended, however, only to supplement state-supported programs. It was not intended to relieve states of their responsibility to maintain and expand existing services, or to create other needed ones. Because developmentally disabled persons require a wide number of critical services on an intermittent or continuing basis, and often over an entire lifetime, Congress took the unusual approach of gearing the federal program around existing generic organizations at state and local levels.

BACKGROUND OF SERVICES

President Kennedy's appointment of a National Panel on Mental Retardation in 1961, which was charged with outlining a national plan to combat mental retardation, was the second in a series of important steps which eventually culminated in a national developmental disabilities program. The foundation had been laid three years earlier with the enactment in 1958 of Public Law 85-926 which provided higher education grants directly to states and universities for the training of college instructors who, in turn, would train teachers of the mentally retarded. More significantly, however, the act confirmed the principle of federal categorical assistance to groups of persons with various handicapping conditions. Confirmation of the targeted assistance principle, initially established in the Social Security Act's crippled children's program, paved the way for landmark legislation in 1963 for the mentally retarded and the mentally ill, and for numerous later programs which were part of the Great Society era. The National Panel's report to the President in 1962 included ninety specific recommendations. Many of these were incorporated by Congress into the lengthy Mental Retardation Facilities and Community Mental Health Centers Construction Act of 1963 (P.L. 88-164). The act contained a comprehensive program of prevention, treatment, and rehabilitation services for the mentally retarded, and a strategy for implementation involving federal, state, and local levels of government. For two decades, this act and the report upon which it was based, have been the nation's chief blueprints for constructing a national program for the developmentally disabled.

A high level of federal and public concern for the mentally retarded continued to be maintained during the Johnson administration. The national Head Start Project was formed in 1965 as an attempt to intercept the development of retardation in children who came from impoverished or disadvantaged backgrounds. Other early intervention and compensatory education activities, which were part of the War on Poverty program, also had the auxiliary purpose of stemming social causes of retardation. In 1966, the

President's Committee on Mental Retardation was appointed as a permanent and central position for exerting continued leadership and policy direction. Two years later, the Joseph P. Kennedy, Jr. Foundation established the Special Olympics, a highly visible, creative, and well-publicized method for sustaining public attention on the retarded.

Responding to allegations that the term "mental retardation" was scientifically inexact, and charges that the mental retardation act discriminated against children with related problems, Congress revised the original mental retardation statute and enacted the Developmental Disabilities Services and Facilities Construction Amendments in 1970 (P.L. 91-517). Further amendments in 1975, primarily stimulated by intense parental concern over the civil rights of handicapped children in general, were enacted as Public Law 94-103, the Developmentally Disabled Assistance and Bill of Rights Act. The most recent, and drastic, overhaul of the legislation occurred in 1978 when Congress evaluated the traditional categorical approach to funding and found serious drawbacks. Although the grouping of many children into one broad classification of developmental disability was found to reduce the prominence of any one group, this tended to be at the expense of severely and multiply handicapped children whose needs were based on the services they required rather than on the categories of their impairment. In the government's first major departure from the conventional method of fund allocation, the categorical definition was changed to one emphasizing the handicapped person's functional limitations and the services needed to surmount those barriers. The resulting legislation, Public Law 95-602, is comprised of two sections: the Developmental Disabilities Assistance and Bill of Rights Act, and the Developmental Disabilities, Rehabilitation and Comprehensive Services Amendments of 1978.

At the federal level, the program is administered by the Administration of Developmental Disabilities that is part of the Office of Human Development Services, in the Department of Health and Human Services. Three agencies are involved at the state level. State-wide planning is conducted by the state's developmental disabilities council, and protection of rights and guarantees of service are provided by the protection and advocacy agency. Direct services are usually administered by the state health department, but sometimes states have a separate developmental disabilities agency. Locally, the health department is frequently responsible for the delivery or coordination of services, although often welfare departments or a specific developmental disabilities agency may have this responsibility.

DESCRIPTION OF THE PROGRAM

The general purpose of the federal law is to establish basic uniformity among state programs by increasing the availability of services. More specifically, the goals are to improve the availability, quality, and coordination of services, encourage deinstitutionalization, assure that a individualized habilitation plan is devised for each client, define the individuals who may be classified as developmentally disabled, and establish standards for the quality and appropriateness of services. Prime responsibility for attaining these goals is delegated to two state agencies, a developmental disability planning council and a protection and advocacy office. The state agency directly concerned with the delivery of services may also be involved. As one condition for receiving the federal allocation, the state planning council is required to develop an annual plan describing needs, objectives, coordination of existing services, and the use of federal allotments in filling gaps in the state's panoply of services. The planning council is also required to monitor the effectiveness of other state agencies, such as the departments of education or health, in providing services to the developmentally handicapped.

The protection and advocacy office (P&A), which must be separate and distinct from any other state agency, is empowered to pursue legal and administrative remedies in protecting the rights of the developmentally disabled. The federal legislation, echoing the phraseology of P.L. 94-142, stipulates that care and services should be given in a setting that is the least restrictive of personal liberty, and that all programs must meet standards assuring the most favorable outcome for these services. The law enlarges upon the due process guarantees of the Education for All Handicapped Children Act by meticulously specifying the rights of the developmentally disabled, and in demanding annual reports from the protection and advocacy agency as another prerequisite for federal funding. Congress was led to take these explicit measures because of the scandalous history of many states in routinely violating the civil rights and constitutional guarantees of the mentally impaired.

STANDARD SETTING AND INDIVIDUAL PLANNING

Few of the federal requirements have been as enthusiastically and uniformly met as those relating to the setting of standards. Frequently, however, the states' scrupulous concern over this obligation has focused on those aspects of care that are easily measurable, objectively determined, and can be quantitatively established by regulations. All states, for example, have been diligent in assuring that institutional or other residential programs follow minimum standards on diet, prohibit unnecessary physical or chemical restraint, allow visits from relatives and friends, and comply with fire and safety standards. Less tangible components of care are less easily assessed. Although the federal law requires that each client's program be based on a highly individualized rehabilitation plan, and has established guidelines, there remains wide variation among the states in the format of these plans, in the extent of detail, and in follow-up. Parents will likely find various names given to the plans throughout the states. Some plans follow the federal designation, individual habilitation plan (IHP), but variations may be individual program plan (IPP), or, less frequently, problem-oriented record (POR). This latter term has largely fallen into disfavor, however, because of its pessimistic implication.

The concept of individual plans was borrowed from the nation's education program for handicapped children and, in many ways, is identical. The individual programs plans are prepared jointly by representatives of the state or local agency that has the legislated responsibility for providing or coordinating services to the developmentally disabled, the child's parents or guardian, and, if appropriate, the child. The program plan will usually consist of (a) an assessment of the disabled child's specific capabilities and problems, (b) a statement of specific, time-limited objectives for improving the capabilities and resolving the problems of the child, (c) a schedule of the type and amount of services required to achieve program plan objectives, including identification of the provider or providers of service responsible for attaining each objective, (d) a schedule of periodic reviews and assessments to ascertain that planned services have been provided and that objectives have been reached within the time frames, and (e) a provision for annual review. The problems generally encountered by the states have been in developing plans that fix on a child's developmental progress yet accommodate frequent, and often prolonged, deviations from this expected pattern, and in providing the great number of therapeutic and training services that will lead a child to normal growth and development.

POPULATION SERVED

The functional and conglomerate term, developmental disability, was popularized in 1970 when an earlier statute for the mentally retarded was amended and renamed. The Developmental Disabilities Services and Facilities Construction Act (P.L. 91-517) extended eligibility coverage to a wider population of individuals with neurologically linked impairments similar to mental retardation. The name change also reflected scientific and educational consensus on the developmental nature of intelligence. Two later amendments, in 1975 and 1978, successively redefined the term and in 1978 the federal government eliminated the categorical approach to developmental disability. Nevertheless, many states retain categorical terminology, such as mental retardation or cerebral palsy, in their statutes but the terms are used synonymously with the federal definition.

From 1963 until 1978, the number of individuals covered grew as the federal eligibility criteria expanded. However, the 1978 shift in eligibility definitions reversed this pattern. Formerly the developmentally disabled included anyone with one of four major handicaps—mental retardation, cerebral palsy, epilepsy, and autism. Since 1978, developmental disability has meant (1) any severe, chronic disability (2) attributable to a mental and/or physical impairment (3) manifested before age 22 that is (4) likely to continue indefinitely and causes a (5) substantial long-term barrier (6) in three or more areas of life activity—communication, self-care, learning, mobility, self-direction, independent living, or economic self-sufficiency, and (7) requires a combination or sequence of extended services that are individually planned and coordinated.

Expectedly, the impact of the definitional change has significantly affected the types of impairment and the numbers of individuals eligible for coverage under the present Developmental Disabilities act. Overall, the number of covered people decreased from 5.3 million to 3.9 million, or 27 percent, between 1978 and 1981. Ten percent of mildly retarded persons and 5 percent of people with medically controlled seizures were dropped from the original target population. In contrast, the most visible increase occurred among those individuals whose disabilities fell outside the original four primary categories. Under the new definition, 11.8 percent of people described as developmentally disabled had conditions such as cystic fibrosis, deafness and blindness, osteogenesis, Tourette's syndrome, tuberous sclerosis, and spina bifida. In releasing the 1981 report, the Administration on Developmental Disabilities noted that "while the number of the population served may be shrinking, those now covered represent those most in need of the services provided." The administration's optimistic report contrasted sharply, however, with findings by another government agency. The National Center for Health Statistics estimated in 1981 that 9.6 million Americans were developmentally disabled and that 3.4 million of these were school-age children. Of the total number, nearly 3.5 million adults and slightly over 2 million children were described as being substantially handicapped because of their immense and extensive service needs. Official estimates of the number of developmentally disabled children who received services also tends to be contradictory. The Administration's claim that over one million children received assistance in 1980 was countered by the Select Panel for the Promotion of Child Health that reported to the Secretary of Health and Human Services, that direct assistance was provided to about 300,000 children in that year.

GRANT FUNDING FOR STATE PROGRAMS

Grants are authorized by the federal statute for the purpose of developing and implementing a comprehensive and continuing system of state services. There are four types of grants: basic services, protection and advocacy, special projects, and university affiliated facilities. *Basic service* grants provide minimal assistance to the states in coordinating and obtaining services from all agencies, and in developing services that other generic agencies cannot provide for developmentally disabled people. Although the states have, in general, made great strides in developing and coordinating existing services, much of the original impact of the national legislation has diminished since 1981 because of reduced social and health program budgets at all levels of government. For the most part, individual state programs for the developmentally disabled are included in this trend. The pattern is irregular, however. In some states, attempts to cut government spending by curtailing services to the developmentally disabled have been averted — or delayed — primarily because of the success of parent organizations and professional groups in mobilizing public resistance.

Some programs, such as those in North and South Dakota and in the more sparsely populated New England states, appear to be little affected by budget cutbacks occurring in other parts of the nation. This may, of course, be temporary, but more likely it is due to the federal funding formula that favors rural states. Everywhere, however, the low level of federal appropriations reemphasizes the original congressional intention that the federal program would not supplant, nor become a substitute for, state programs. Since 1972, for example, when the federal allotment was $49.5 million, the amount has remained virtually stationary. The total grant for all states in 1980 was $50,680,000, and for 1981 the amount was increased by only one thousand dollars. Grants to individual states ranged, in 1981, from $30,000 to $3.5 million, with the average basic grant being $822,500. The effectiveness of the federal philosophy, however, is reflected in the vitality of state programs nationwide. In 1972, the states spent $800 million, and in 1981 the costs were in the neighborhood of $5 billion. One state, California, expended $420 million in 1981 on hospital and community-based services, and projected a $450 million budget for 1982–1983. The president's first 1982 budget requested Congress to consolidate appropriations for developmental disability services in the Social Services Block Grant. This position was reversed, however, and the administration later proposed a categorical allocation of $51,293,000 for basic support of the states' developmental disability programs.

Grants for *protection and advocacy* services and for *special projects* have been budgeted for a total of $10.5 million in 1982–1983. The national system of protection and advocacy which has been in effect since 1978, is expected to cost $8 million. The projected budget of $2.5 million for special projects reflects a decline of nearly fifty percent since 1980. The purpose of these funds is to develop new projects that improve the quality of services to the developmentally disabled, and to demonstrate new or improved service techniques and service delivery systems. Twenty-five percent of these funds are earmarked for projects of national significance. In 1980, 24 projects were so designated, most of them in the areas of advocacy, technical assistance, training, and projects for special subgroups of the developmentally disabled population. Two examples of the 37 special projects conducted during 1980 include the development of a model educational program for severely and profoundly disabled adolescents and their parents, and the operation of an innovative training facility for developmentally disabled children whose condition was further aggravated by severe hearing impairment.

Grants for university affiliated facilities (UAFs) have been provided since the inception of the developmental disabilities program to operate demonstration facilities, conduct applied research, establish interdisciplinary training programs for persons who provide specialized services to the developmentally disabled, and to give direct services. Thirty-six UAFs were being funded by the developmental disabilities act in 1982, and $7.5 million was authorized by the president for their continued operation during the next fiscal year.

RANGE OF AVAILABLE SERVICES

Varying programs are available throughout the nation for children who are included under the broad rubric of developmental disability. Although nonhandicapped and developmentally disabled children share common basic needs, impaired children require many specialized services because of the chronicity of their handicapping condition and the fluctuating nature of their impairment. These special services that may be required may consist of intrusive care, such as medical and surgical intervention, or developmental assistance provided by an infant stimulation program or enabling services given in day activity classes, or support services, such as residential care and provisions for income maintenance. The range of services required varies by the child's age, degree of severity, amount of parental involvement, and the array of services available within any community. The extent to which a child has had early socialization experiences is also a relevant factor. Many children, for example, with histories of frequent or prolonged hospitalization, or institutional placement, require a larger and more extensive battery of services than those children who have less complex problems or who have strong bonding attachments with their parents, and brothers and sisters. Each of these variables will affect the extent to which a child depends upon externally provided services, but they do not affect the basic criteria for judging the quality of services. Developmentally disabled children require a *continuity of services provided in the most normal setting which will promote their absorption into the community mainstream.* For most developmentally disabled children there are seven categories of essential services:

1. Identification services, including agency efforts to identify the presence of disability and its probable causes, and to develop, plan, and assess the service needs of the disabled child on a periodic basis
2. Treatment services, including appropriate medical and dental care, prosthetic devices, and periodic health monitoring
3. Residential services, including out-of-home living arrangement if necessary, in settings which approximate normal family life situations, such as foster

homes or small family and group facilities

4. Developmental services, including day activity centers, education, speech and physical therapy, mobility and self-care training programs

5. Transportation services, including transportation to day care centers, schools, training programs, and medical and therapeutic resources

6. Leisure and recreational services, including structured and unstructured leisure opportunities which promote the development of self-reliance as well as socialization skills, and experiences which will permit the child to taste and to desire participation in the broader community life

7. Facilitating services, including counseling, protection of rights, follow-along surveillance for continued review of plans, individual case management to insure that services are appropriately delivered, and guardianship, if needed.

BIBLIOGRAPHY

Brewer, Garry D., and Kakalik, James S. *Handicapped Children*. New York: McGraw-Hill Book Company, 1979.

Brown, Ronald T. "A Closer Examination of the Education for All Handicapped Children Act: A Guide for the 1980s." *Psychology in the Schools*, July 1980, pp. 355-60.

Carpenter, Robert L., and Robson, Donald L. "P.L. 94-142: Perceived Knowledge, Expectations, and Early Implementation." *The Journal of Special Education*, Fall 1979, pp. 307-14.

Cleland, Charles Carr. *Mental Retardation: A Developmental Approach*. Englewood Cliffs, N. J.: Prentice-Hall, Inc., 1978.

Council for Exceptional Children. "Full Educational Opportunities for Handicapped Individuals." *Awareness Papers*. White House Conference on Handicapped Individuals, GPO No. 232-034/6199. Washington, D.C.: Government Printing Office, 1977.

Gearheart, Bill R. *Special Education for the '80s*. St. Louis: The C. V. Mosby Company, 1980.

Geren, Katherine. *Complete Special Education Handbook*. West Nyack, New York: Parker Publishing Company, Inc., 1979.

Hart, Verna. *Mainstreaming Children With Special Needs*. New York: Longman, 1981.

Kneedler, Rebecca Dailey, and Tarver, Sara B., eds. *Changing Perspectives in Special Education*. Columbus, Ohio: Charles E. Merrill Publishing Company, 1977.

Maloney, Michael P., and Ward, Michael P. *Mental Retardation and Modern Society*. New York: Oxford University Press, 1979.

McIntosh, Dean K. "Mainstreaming: Too Often a Myth, Too Rarely a Reality." *Academic Therapy*, September 1979, pp. 53-59.

McPhillips, Regina, ed. *Proceedings of the First National Conference of State Directors for Crippled Children*. Sponsored by the John Hopkins University, School of Hygiene and Public Health, Department of Maternal and Child Health, 1974.

Meisels, Samuel J., ed. *Special Education and Development.* Baltimore: University Park Press, 1979.

Neisworth, John T., and Smith, Robert M. *Retardation.* New York: McGraw-Hill, Inc., 1978.

Paul, James L.; Stedman, Donald J.; and Neufeld, G. Ronald, eds. *Deinstitutionalization.* Syracuse, New York: Syracuse University Press, 1977.

Payne, James S., and Patton, James R. *Mental Retardation.* Columbus, Ohio: Charles E. Merrill Publishing Company, 1981.

Prehm, Herbert J., and McDonald, James E. "The Yet to be Served—a Perspective." *Exceptional Children,* April 1979, pp. 502–7.

Schifani, John M.; Anderson, Robert M.; and Odle, Sara J., eds. *Implementing Learning in the Least Restrictive Environment.* Baltimore: University Park Press, 1980.

Sellin, Donald F. *Mental Retardation: Nature, Needs, and Advocacy.* Boston: Allyn and Bacon, Inc., 1979.

Snell, Martha E., ed. *Systematic Instruction of the Moderately and Severely Handicapped.* Columbus, Ohio: Charles E. Merrill Publishing Co., 1978.

U.S. Department of Education. *Annual Evaluation Report, Vol. II, Fiscal Year 1980.* Office of Evaluation and Program Management, Publication No. E-81-47002-II. Washington, D.C.: Government Printing Office, 1981.

_____. *Programs for the Handicapped.* Office of Special Education and Rehabilitative Services, Office of Information and Resources for the Handicapped. Publication No. E-81-22000. Washington, D.C.: Government Printing Office, July–August 1981.

_____. *"To Assure the Free Appropriate Public Education of All Handicapped Children." Second Annual Report to Congress on the Implementation of Public Law 94-142: The Education for All Handicapped Children Act.* Office of Special Education and Rehabilitative Services. Washington, D.C.: Government Printing Office, 1980.

U.S. Department of Health and Human Services. *Better Health for Our Children: A National Strategy. The Report of the Select Panel for the Promotion of Child Health, Vols. I, II.* Public Health Service, Office of the Assistant Secretary for Health and Surgeon General, DHHS (PHS) Publication No. 79-55071. Washington, D.C.: Government Printing Office, 1981.

_____. *Crippled Children's Services 1980.* National Public Health Program Reporting System, Association of State and Territorial Health Officials, ASTHO Publication No. 58. Washington, D.C.: Government Printing Office, September 1981.

_____. *Human Development News.* Office of Human Development Services, Office of Public Affairs. Washington, D.C.: Government Printing Office, December 1981.

_____. *Maternal and Child Health Services 1980.* National Public Health Program Reporting System, Association of State and Territorial Health Officials, ASTHO Publication No. 59. Washington, D.C.: Government Printing Office, September 1981.

_____. *Mental Retardation: Prevention Strategies that Work.* Office of Human Development Services, President's Committee on Mental Retardation, DHHS

(OHDS) Publication No. 80-21029. Washington, D.C.: Government Printing Office, 1980.

_____. *Public Health Agencies 1980, A Report on Their Expenditures and Activities.* National Public Health Program Reporting System, Association of State and Territorial Health Officials, ASTHO Publication No. 61. Washington, D.C.: Government Printing Office, August 1981.

Wortis, Joseph, ed. *Mental Retardation and Developmental Disabilities, Vol. IX.* New York: Brunner/Mazel, Inc., 1977.

Wyne, Marvin D., and O'Connor, Peter D. *Exceptional Children.* Lexington, Mass.: D.C. Heath and Company, 1979.

Zemzars, Ilga S., and Ritvo, Roger A., eds. *Perinatology: The Role of Social Work in Practice, Research and Professional Education.* Report of a National Conference, 1979, sponsored by the Maternal and Child Health Services, Bureau of Community Health Service, Health Services Administration, Department of Health, Education, and Welfare and by the School of Applied Social Sciences, Case Reserve University.

7 | RECREATION AND SOCIAL ACTIVITIES

Diane Schechter, Susan Sygall,

and Katherine Powell

Recreation, the refreshment of one's mind and body, is as necessary to a full and well-balanced life as breathing is to the body's survival. For all of us, able or disabled, recreation provides a respite from our daily or weekly routines, but for handicapped people it often has the additional significance of being an integral part of their rehabilitation regimen. Recreation activities cover a wide and expansive range. For some disabled people, they consist of sedentary pleasures such as reading a book or playing a table game. For others, recreational activities may be adaptations of action sports customarily enjoyed by the nondisabled population, or visits to parks, libraries, theaters, zoos, and museums. Civil rights legislation and recognition of the importance of normalizing experiences for the handicapped has resulted in a greatly expanded range of recreational opportunities available to people who are disabled. This chapter will offer general guidelines for selecting approp-riate programs, review the legal basis and funding of recreational ser-vices, explore the critical issue of accessibility, and provide a reference of major recreational programs and information sources available throughout the nation.

SELECTING A PROGRAM

The value of any recreational program lies in the opportunities it offers for disabled people to acquire a repertoire of leisure time activities, develop motor skills and abilities, participate in group interaction, and provide enjoyment. Seeking out that program which best provides these long-term benefits is the goal of the selection process. Attainment of this broad goal is based on several factors, but chiefly, accessibility. Secondary considerations are the type of activity in which a disabled individual wishes to participate, the degree to which the individual's physical or mental limitations permit participation in the program, and the extent to which an existing program can be modified or a new one created that will accommodate limitations caused by disability.

Although disabled people may often feel more comfortable in recreational activities which are specifically designed for them, they should remember that assimilation into the larger community is accomplished primarily by social interaction, mutual recognition of human needs, and the sharing of experiences with nonhandicapped people. Thus disabled people should, to the greatest extent possible, attempt to maintain themselves within society's mainstream by participating in the community's traditional programs. For example, if the activity sought is weaving and the disability is paraplegia, any qualified weaving class will do, providing that the program and site are accessible to a wheelchair. However, if the individual's disability restricts the use of hand and arm, special instructors, or therapists and equipment may be needed. The rapid development of specific recreational programs throughout the nation now makes it possible to identify a number of resources for most disabled people. These programs range from theater for the deaf and instruction in the fine arts for the mentally retarded, to golf for the blind and whitewater rafting for the paraplegic. Individual listings and informational sources for these programs are included in the reference section of this chapter.

LEGAL BASIS FOR PROGRAMS

The legal basis of recreational and facilitating programs has become important during the past few years because of the gains made in enacting federal legislation prohibiting discrimination against disabled people in programs that receive any type of federal financial support. All federal agencies, according to Section 504 of the Rehabilitation Act of 1973, must issue regulations implementing the following principles: (1) disabled people must be given an equal opportunity to participate, (2) programs in existing facilities must be made accessible, and (3) facilities must be barrier-free. If a federally supported agency is negligent in any of these areas, a complaint may be filed in the form of a letter, which must include all pertinent details, addressed to the Office of Handicapped Individuals, 330 C Street, S.W., Washington, D.C. 20036. If the complaint is not resolved, Section 504 of the act gives the individual the right to sue. Legal assistance can be obtained from the American Civil Liberties Union, local legal aid societies, and other community advocacy groups.

Section 504 also establishes the Architectural Barriers and Transportation Compliance Board. Regulations formulated by the Board require that all new public construction backed with federal money must be fully accessible to the disabled. This requirement also applies to all buildings leased with federal funds. Although buildings closely identified with federal government activities, such as post offices, first come to mind, national parks, public and private libraries operating with governmental subsidies, nearly all schools, most public transportation systems, and cultural or arts programs receiving financial assistance from the National Endowment for the Arts, are all affected by these regulations. Several cities in the United States have made commendable strides toward making services and programs accessible to the handicapped. Some examples are San Antonio, Texas, where first-hand experience and insight has been provided by a disabled woman member of the planning department, and Seattle, Washington, where 25 percent of the city's bus routes are used daily by nearly eighty severely disabled riders. Other examples include subways in Washington, D.C., Atlanta, and San Francisco which are fully accessible to the majority of handicapped people, and the new system planned for Baltimore.

ACCESSIBILITY

Accessibility is the prime factor in selecting any recreational program for a handicapped person. Even the best activity loses value when it is physically unreachable by the potential consumer. Although accessible transportation has generally been guaranteed to disabled people under the provisions of the Rehabilitation Act, transportation is only one of several criteria that determines program accessibility. Some general points to consider when evaluating a recreational program are: Can a disabled person get to the program's location independently? If not, are special transportation services available? If necessary, is there a friend, relative, attendant, or staff aide available to help the individual move from transport unloading point to program location? Other evaluative criteria are more explicit. For individuals using mechanical aids such as walkers, wheelchairs, or crutches, pertinent questions include: Can the site be entered independently? Ramps, for example, should ascend one foot in twelve—an angle of 4.75 degrees. Is the accessible entry into the building the normal entry or must side or rear entrances be used? Do doors open automatically? If not, do they open easily, and, if there are handles, are they readily manipulated? The texture of floors should be examined also, since some types of carpeting interfere with a wheelchair's movability. Aisles and hallways should be sufficiently wide to accommodate wheelchairs. Accessibility of restrooms requires that stall doors open outward, and that a urinal, sink, mirror, and towel dispenser are at wheelchair height. At least one stall should be large enough to accommodate a wheelchair, and, although there are several ways to transfer, there must be adequate space to transfer from wheelchair to stool. And there should also be grasping bars, firmly anchored in stall walls, to aid in transferring.

The type of impairment also affects the criteria used in determining accessibility. For the visually handicapped, important informational and directional signs, including elevator buttons and controls, should be identified in Braille with the signs prominently placed at an arm level. The overall physical milieu should lend itself to auditory and tactile orientation as well. Variances in floor surfaces, for example, help to identify different general areas. Reading materials should be printed in large type or in Braille, and readers or guides should, ideally, be available for the large number of visually disabled people who do not read Braille. Accessibility for people with hearing handicaps requires other specific considerations. Fire and other emergency alarms should be visual as well as auditory, and at least one staff member should be present during the hours the program is in session who is proficient in manual sign language.

These examples are obviously general, but they are suggestive of the ways by which the accessibility of programs can be evaluated. Most states have stringent codes regulating the design of publicly used buildings, and information about the sizes of doorways, halls, and ramps can be obtained from several state and private agencies. Two examples are the Mobility Barrier Section, California Department of Rehabilitation, 830 K Street Mall, Room 126, Sacramento, California 95814, and the American Institute of Architects, 1735 New York Avenue, N.W., Washington, D.C. 20006.

SPONSORSHIP AND FUNDING SOURCES

Recreational programs designed for the disabled are numerous, conducted by many organizations, and funded in a variety of ways. A few are sponsored by state and local governments. Fees for any of these programs are often based upon the ability of the handicapped person to pay. Some programs offered by local parks, libraries, and community education agencies such as community college districts, receive federal and state financial aid and charge minimal fees for their recreational, social, and educational programs. Fees for programs sponsored by locally based agencies such as the YMCA and YWCA, churches, affiliates of the United Cerebral Palsy Association, National Easter Seal Society, or Services for the Blind, are usually based upon a sliding scale. Often, however, these programs are free and conducted by the agency as part of its ongoing program of community services. In a few states, official mental health and developmental disability agencies purchase recreational therapy services for their clients from nonprofit agencies. This practice is, however, rapidly diminishing because cutbacks in federal, state, and local government budgets for 1982 and those projected for 1983 tend to exclude the purchase of recreational programs for the disabled from private vendors. Many other programs have been developed by groups of disabled people themselves, often as an extension of activities conducted by their own self-help organizations, or as a club activity. Generally, these recreational programs are financed by members, with fees charged for specific activities. There are many organized groups of disabled people throughout the nation that conduct recreational activities, but general information can be obtained from: (1) American Coalition of Citizens with Disabilities, 1200 Fifteenth Street, N.W., Suite 201, Washington, D.C. 20005, (2) Blinded Veterans Association, 1725 DeSales Street, N.W., Washington, D.C. 20036, and (3) Paralyzed Veterans of America, 4350 East West Highway, Suite 900, Washington, D.C. 20014.

REFERENCE GUIDE TO NATIONAL AND LOCAL RECREATIONAL PROGRAMS, PARKS, AND WILDERNESS AREAS

Parklands and wilderness areas are administered by an assortment of public and private agencies that includes federal, state, and local governments, Audubon and botanical societies, and nature conservancies. By contacting the administrative office, or public information or public relations departments of these agencies, disabled people can usually obtain maps of the recreational lands and descriptions of the programs offered. Disabled people should not be hesitant in describing their physical limitations or in asking explicit questions about the accessibility of the park area for handicapped visitors since, when simply asked whether or not a facility is wheelchair accessible, staff members of park agencies may not supply adequate information. Nevertheless, the presence of some physical barriers should not be the sole reason for deciding not to visit a particular parkland. Although disabled people may encounter environmental problems such as a rough terrain that hampers their mobility, difficulty and discomfort are usually completely eclipsed by the thrill of being there to enjoy the park site. An official of the Fish and Wildlife Service of the United States Department of the Interior, in encouraging disabled people to visit national parks, aptly points out the need to "be adventurous and willing to challenge yourself by trying new things." "Obstacles," she observes, "are not as difficult to overcome as they may seem at first and there is no greater joy than to actually be there and to have done it yourself."

It is with this concept in mind that the Special Program and Populations Division of the National Park Service is operated. This agency, through its numerous branches, provides brochures containing information on all parks and lands under its jurisdiction, and agency personnel have been trained to readily identify the most rewarding and accessible places to visit. Trails, historical sites, visitor centers, national monuments, cultural centers, and wildlife refuge areas, which have been so designated by Congress, are among the areas operated by this arm of the U.S. Department of the Interior. Although detailed information on accessibility and special facilities for handicapped people can be provided by administrators of any park or designated site, the best source of general information is from regional offices. Inquiries should be addressed to the Regional Coordinator, Special Programs and Populations Service, U.S. National Park Service, at offices in the following national regions:

Alaska Area:	540 West Fifth Avenue Room 202 Anchorage, Alaska 99501
Mid-Atlantic:	143 South Third Street Philadelphia, Pennsylvania 19106
Midwest:	1709 Jackson Street Omaha, Nebraska 68102
National Capitol:	1100 Ohio Drive, S.W. Washington, D.C. 20242
North Atlantic:	15 State Street Boston, Massachusetts 02109
Pacific Northwest:	Fourth and Pike Building Room 922 Seattle, Washington 98101
Rocky Mountain:	P.O. Box 25287 Denver, Colorado 80225
Southeast:	75 Spring Street, S.W. Atlanta, Georgia 30303
Southwest:	P.O. Box 728 Santa Fe, New Mexico 87501
Western:	450 Golden Gate Avenue P.O. Box 36063 San Francisco, California 94102

Each state has an official agency, usually known as the department of parks or parks and recreation, that administers state parks and recreational facilities. Special efforts to accommodate the needs of the handicapped may be in the form of minimal services such as day use of camp grounds, park sightseeing by motorized excursions or by short walks, or educational exhibits at a visitor's center, or they may be more extensive and consist of specially constructed overnight camping facilities. California's Department of Parks and Recreation, for example, maintains eight wheelchair accessible campsites in its large park system, and reservations for the use of these barrier-free camp units may be made in person or by mail through commercial Ticketron outlets. A factsheet on these facilities is available from the Distribution and Recreation Center, Department of Parks and Recreation, State of California, P.O. Box 2390, Sacramento, California 95811. Park rangers at individual state parks throughout the nation are often excellent sources of information about park-sponsored programs for the handicapped, and they frequently provide physical assistance in helping handicapped visitors. Most rangers have had sensitivity training as part of their agency's staff development program and, experience shows, tend to go out of their way to accommodate the needs of disabled people. Special services such as table extenders and tours for the blind, for example, are usually available when requested. A central information source about all state park recreational programs is the National Recreation and Park Association, 1601 North Kent Street, Arlington, Virginia 22209.

Municipal, county, and regional parks are also good sources of recreational activities. Although not specifically designed to accommodate disabled visitors who have severe mobility limitations, many facilities such as bikeways, pathways, fishing areas, and day camp sites are accessible to the majority of disabled people. There are other park and nature areas in all sections of the country that, although small and frequently unpublicized, welcome handicapped people. Especially in the western states, utility companies have developed many reservoirs and dam sites for public recreational use. Specific information about the facilities and services available in these recreational sites can be obtained from local chambers of commerce or from city and county departments of parks and recreation.

NATURE TOURS, WILDERNESS AND CAMPING EXPERIENCES, AND TRAVEL

Many sources of recreational programs for the handicapped that are often overlooked include local fishing, hunting, and boating clubs. Either as a regular community relations program or as a special service provided upon request, these organizations frequently have sightseeing excursions, nature explorations, or special field days for groups of handicapped children and adults. Names and addresses of these organizations are also available from local chambers of commerce, as well as from most sporting goods stores. One commercial sports outfitter, the American River Touring Association, regularly offers white water rafting activities for the disabled. The address of the Association is 445 High Street, Oakland, California 94601.

National and regional conservation organizations such as Ducks Unlimited, Inc., National Audubon Society, and Sierra Club, have shown increasing interest in providing activities for the handicapped. These organizations publish newsletters, magazines, and brochures that contain announcements of programs or events in various parts of the nation, as well as advertisements of travel tours for the handicapped. Examples of publications are *Audubon Magazine, Ducks Unlimited*, and *Friends O'Wildlife*. Adventurous experiences such as wilderness treks are not only popular with nonhandicapped people everywhere, but now are available to special populations, including the aged and the disabled. Two organizations offering these so-called "highrisk" programs are (1) Minnesota Outward Bound School, 308 Walker Avenue, South Wayzata, Minnesota 55391, and (2) Environmental Traveling Companions, 1739 Taravel Street, San Francisco, California 94100. The latter organization conducts a low-cost wilderness exploration program that includes backpacking, skiing, and rafting for persons with special needs.

Many community social service organizations such as the YMCA, YWCA, Girl Scouts, and Boy Scouts, generally include handicapped people in all their programs, including camping experiences, in a laudable effort to mainstream people who previously had been excluded from many activities available to the nonhandicapped. There is, however, a wide variance in the availability of these programs. The activities of some agencies, although affiliated with national groups, tend to reflect the interests and concerns of the local governing board. Other service groups, such as the Scout agencies, have a national commitment to serve young handicapped people and children and thus display more consistency in the programs that they conduct throughout the country. Comprehensive information about the nation's many camping programs is available from the American Camping Association, Bradford Woods, Martinsville, Indiana 46151. The Association publishes a booklet, "Parents Guide to Accredited Camps," which gives information on programs for the handicapped. It is available for $1.95 plus postage. In addition, national offices of social service organizations also provide camping and recreational program information. Some agencies that conduct camping activities for the handicapped are:

Boy Scouts of America
      Scouting for the Handicapped Service
      P.O. Box 61030
      Dallas-Ft. Worth Airport
      Texas 75261

Campfire, Inc.
      4601 Madison Avenue
      Kansas City, Missouri 64112

Disabled Sportsmen of America, Inc.
      P.O. Box 26
      Vinton, Virginia 24179

Girl Scouts of the U.S.A.
      830 Third Avenue
      New York, New York 10022

National Easter Seal Society
      2023 West Ogden Avenue
      Chicago, Illinois 60612

The Salvation Army
    120 West 14th Street
    New York, New York 10011

Young Men's Christian Association of the U.S.A.
    101 North Wacker Drive
    Chicago, Illinois 60606

Young Women's Christian Association of the U.S.A.
    600 Lexington Avenue
    New York, New York 10022

Camping and wilderness recreational activities are only a small part of the recreational opportunities that are now available in most parts of the nation. During the past five years, probably because of a heightened national awareness of the needs of the handicapped, travel has become a highly popular and realistic activity for many disabled people. Airlines, buses, and Amtrak trains have not only modified the design of coach facilities to accommodate disabled people, but are aggressively seeking handicapped travelers. National offices of voluntary social and health agencies serving the handicapped can provide travel information, and journals aimed at the handicapped population frequently advertise specially designed national and foreign tours. Another source of up-to-date information is the Society for the Advancement of Travel for the Handicapped, 26 Court Street, Brooklyn, New York 12242. An example of one agency that conducts recreational tours and excursions is New Horizons, a project conducted by a local YMCA in southern California. New Horizons conducts trips throughout the continental United States, Canada, Hawaii, and Great Britain, in addition to providing many weekend caravans and week night outings. Although activities are primarily directed toward the needs of persons with developmental disabilities, the program welcomes children and adults who have other types of impairment. Disabled persons who live in far-flung areas of the nation fly into Los Angeles International Airport where they are met and transported to the trip embarkation point. Descriptive tour brochures and a schedule of excursions and fees are available from the originator and director of this innovative project, Linda Wallace, M.A., YMCA/New Horizons, 209 West Civic Center Drive, Santa Ana, California 92701.

SPORTS ACTIVITIES

Many sports and competitive activities are conducted throughout the nation either as special programs for the handicapped or as mainstreaming activities in which handicapped and nonhandicapped people participate together. More and more, however, disabled people are developing their own local sports clubs and associations. Some are organized to provide fun and good times, but many others are serious training programs that prepare participants for national competitions.

Almost any sport or game can be adapted to a person's physical limitations, but if at a loss for ideas, handicapped people will find *The New Games Book* and *More New Games!* to be stimulating resources. They are available from The New Games Foundation, P.O. Box 7901, San Francisco, California 94120. Some of the hundreds of innovative and exciting games these books contain may be played competitively, but most others simply have the objective of getting people together for an enjoyable occasion. Some games are solitary, designed for self-amusement, but others can involve large groups of people of varying ages and abilities. Most of the games do not require special equipment but use common materials like earth or balls. A few, however, require complicated devices such as parachutes. The underlying philosophy of the New Games publications is that everyone participates in having a pleasant and happy time. Disabled people, regardless of their level of disability, can play almost all of these games.

Those handicapped persons who are more interested in action-oriented and competitive sports can obtain general information and a free brochure, "Competitive and Recreational Wheelchair Sports," from the Paralyzed Veterans of America, 4350 East West Highway, Suite 900, Washington, D.C. 20014. Another resource is "Sports 'n Spokes," a bimonthly magazine published by Crase and Company, 5201 North Nineteenth Avenue, Suite 111, Phoenix, Arizona 85015, which contains articles and notices of various sporting events for the handicapped, and the names of sponsoring agencies.

Wheelchair sports activities are among the most widely available recreational activities for disabled persons, and they include marathons, track and field competitions, and square dancing. Organizers and developers of these activities often go to exceptional lengths in adapting traditional sports to the special needs of disabled people. Several activities that can be enjoyed by handicapped persons, having nearly any degree of disability, will be described and sources from which more complete information can be obtained will be listed.

ARCHERY

In competitive archery, disabled persons who have the use of one arm only or quadraplegics with limited hand function are permitted to use adaptive equipment that enables them to shoot arrows. In addition to competition, a few bow and arrow hunting activities for disabled people are being started in various parts of the country. There are several sources of information about these activities, and inquiries can be directed to (1) National Wheelchair Athletic Association, James Polk Office Building, Suite 1800, 505 Deaderick Street, Nashville, Tennessee 37219, (2) Disabled Sportsmen of America, Inc., P.O. Box 26, Vinton, Virginia 24179, and (3) National Archery Association, Ronks, Pennsylvania 17572. The Berkeley Outreach Recreation Program, 2020 Milvia, Berkeley, California 94704, provides information about adaptive archery equipment.

BASKETBALL

Wheelchair basketball can be played recreationally with as few as two people, but, if played competitively, the National Wheelchair Basketball Association leagues require a five member team. Competition ranges from regional and national playoffs to international tournaments, and the rules for wheelchair basketball are similar to those required by the National Collegiate Athletic Association. There are, however, special classification rules that enable people with different disabilities, such as amputations, paraplegia, quadraplegia, and postpolio paralysis, to play competitively. The rules also ensure that competing teams are evenly matched in terms of the players' level of disability. Happily, more and more women are playing wheelchair basketball, and there is now a women's division at the national level. The National Wheelchair Basketball Association, 110 Seaton Building, University of Kentucky, Lexington, Kentucky 40506, can provide information about local organizations and basketball teams throughout the nation.

BOATING

Boating activities are being actively pursued by disabled people all over the world, largely because they do not require much in the way of adaptive equipment. An excellent source of information about various activities, teaching methods, and needed facilities is the publication, *Water Sports for the Disabled*, which was prepared for England's national Sports Council by the Advisory Panel on Water Sports for the Disabled, 5 Buckingham Gate, London, SW1, England. A United States based organization that conducts instructor training in canoeing for the handicapped also provides helpful informational materials for canoers or those interested in this sport. Brochures and guidelines are available from the Mississippi Project Aquatics, Box 172, Southern Station, University of Southern Mississippi, Hattiesburg, Mississippi 39401.

BOWLING

Bowling has long been a popular sports activity in America and one which is thoroughly enjoyed by many handicapped people. It is, for example, a featured recreational activity of affiliates of the National Association for Retarded Citizens, and it is part of the regular games played at Special Olympics meets. Wheelchair bowling has rules identical to those for nondisabled players, and competition bowling events are sponsored by the American Wheelchair Bowling Association. Information can be obtained from the Association, c/o Robert Moran, Executive Secretary, 6718 Pinehurst Drive, Evansville, Indiana 47711. Information on programs for the mentally retarded and developmentally disabled is available from (1) National Association for Retarded Citizens, 2709 Avenue E, East, P.O. Box 6109, Arlington, Texas 76011, and (2) Special Olympics, Inc., Joseph P. Kennedy Jr. Foundation, 1701 K Street, N.W., Washington, D.C. 20006.

FLYING

With the development of hand-operated aviation controls, flying clubs for disabled pilots have begun to appear around the country. Even if there is no club in a particular area, disabled people can obtain adaptive equipment and learn to fly with a "regular" flying school. Information on equipment sources and activities in specific regions can be obtained from American Wheelchair Pilots Association, P.O. Box 1181, Mesa, Arizona 85201.

FOOTBALL

Although wheelchair football is still in the developmental stage, the few games that do exist follow the rules of the National Collegiate Athletic Association with these exceptions: the game is played on a 60 yard hard surface field with 8 yard end zones, and teams are composed of six persons. Rule exceptions also allow double touch tackles, down field throws to simulate a kick, and 15 yards for a first down instead of the customary ten. Copies of wheelchair football rules are provided by the University of Illinois, Oak Street at Stadium Drive, Champaign, Illinois 61820. Because this is such a new adaptive sport, disabled people should also write the National Wheelchair Athletic Association to express their interest and to obtain information about any local activities.

GOLF

Modern technology has made golf an increasingly accessible sport for a large number of people with various disabling conditions. Special sound equipment, for example, now permits golf to be played by the blind or visually handicapped and, when outfitted with special golf carts, the game can be played by people who must use wheelchairs in their daily life. Most frequently, an adaptive seat is used which permits disabled people to drive or putt while remaining in the golf cart. General information is available from the National Handicapped Sports and Recreation Association, Capitol Hill Station, P.O. Box 18664, Denver, Colorado 80218. Information about equipment and golf activities can be obtained from Dennis Walter, 250 Jacaranda Drive, Plantation, Florida 33324. Visually handicapped persons can contact local offices of agencies serving the blind, and by writing to (1) United States Blind Golfers Association, 225 Varoone Street, 28th Floor, New Orleans, Louisiana 70112, or (2) Braille Institute of America, 741 North Vermont Avenue, Los Angeles, California 90029. In California, the

Telephone Pioneers Association has taken active interest in developing special golf equipment for the disabled and this interest appears to be spreading among other chapters of this large organization of retired telephone company employees. Any local telephone company's business office will help locate the group closest to where a disabled person lives.

HORSEBACK RIDING

Riding is approached differently by different groups of handicapped people. Some see it primarily as a type of physical therapy, in which case the horse is used as an aid or tool to do a specific rehabilitative exercise. Others view riding as a recreational activity that provides the same pleasure for them as it does for nondisabled people. There are, however, some special precautions that disabled people may have to take. For example, pressure sores can be prevented by padding the saddle or by using a personal pad directly placed on the saddle. Saddles can be specifically designed or adapted to compensate for a rider's inability to maintain balance. If the balancing problem is slight, for instance, a seat belt which straddles the rider's thighs can be bolted to the seat of a western saddle. Specifications for adaptive saddles can be obtained from the Berkeley Outreach Recreation Program described in the section on archery, or from Grizzly Peak Stables, 271 Lomas Cantadas, Orinda, California 94563. Information on therapeutic riding is available from the North American Riding for the Handicapped Association, an organization that also accredits selected stables throughout the country when deemed qualified to offer horseback riding programs for the disabled. The Association's address is Box 100, Ashburn, Virginia 22011.

In nearly every part of the nation, local equestrian groups have established riding programs or clubs for the disabled. One such program was established by a triple amputee. Requests for information may be sent to Jim Brinnottee, Rancho Kumbya Recreation Ranch for the Handicapped, Creston, California 93432. There are international riding organizations as well. In England, information about riding opportunities for disabled people, special equipment and techniques, can be obtained from the Riding for the Disabled Association, Avenue R, National Agriculture Centre, Kenilworth, Warwickshire, CV8 2 LY, England.

LONG-DISTANCE MARATHON

Long-distance and marathon pushing have become popular among disabled people because of the thrill of participation, the stamina that is involved, and also because of national media attention focused on runner and wheelchair marathons. For many years wheelchair racing and endurance activities were primarily conducted as fund-raising events and public awareness campaigns, but this has changed. As a logical result of the rigorous training programs that dedicated wheelchair pushers undergo, it was inevitable that some would seek to test themselves over the long haul in organized competition. Many venturesome athletes have accomplished marathon distances ranging from 15 to even several hundred miles. The National Boston Marathon always includes a large contingent of wheelchair participants, with both men and women competing in five classes, but in 1981, a specific National Wheelchair Marathon was held in Florida. The annual Boston running and pushing event covers the standard marathon course of 26 miles, 285 yards. For the past four years the number of individual long-distance pushers has rapidly grown throughout the country and, undoubtedly, expanded opportunities to participate in sanctioned meets will be developing in other sections of the nation. Most runner marathons everywhere now have special divisions for both mid-distance and long-distance wheelchair competitors.

As in all wheelchair sports and recreation activities, equipment and training are crucial factors in achieving successful performance. Current equipment standards for the National Wheelchair Marathon specify that maximum tire size be limited to 24 inches, the wheelchair must be capable of safely handling speeds of 20 to 30 miles per hour on the downhills, be light enough to allow maximum pushing effort, and strong enough to withstand the "shakes." Mechanical modifications which are permitted include such common items as pneumatic front casters for smoother rides and small diameter push rims for more efficient strokings. Other allowable modifications consist of moving the front casters forward for greater stability, installing turn-knobs for high-speed coasting and steering, using high-performance bearings and tires, strengthening axles and tire rims, and constructing custom-made chairs with exotic metals and alloys.

In many respects, the training program of wheelchair distance competitors is comparable to that of their nondisabled running counterparts and reflects the same diversity. Some competitors work year-round, traversing distances of 50 or 100 miles each week, undergo special weight training, do high-speed downhill and grueling uphill practice, and all this while following preferred near-race and pre-race diets. The basic factors that result in high performance are those that are common to all athletes—proper equipment, appropriate training, personal health and vigor, a strong determination, and lots of self-discipline. More information can be obtained from the National Wheelchair Marathon, c/o Paul DePace, 380 Diamond Hill Road, Warwick, Rhode Island 02886. Another source is the New England Spinal Cord Injury Foundation, 369 Elliot Street, Newton Upper Falls, Massachusetts 02164. To learn about special modifications for wheelchairs, the best source of information is the manufacturer, but "Sports 'n Spokes" magazine frequently contains pertinent articles and carries advertisements from firms that specialize in wheelchair modifications.

MOTORCYCLE RIDING

The National Wheelchair Motorcycle Association advises handicapped people about adaptations that can be made to improve the versatility and use of motor-driven vehicles. The Association tests equipment on various terrains, and the performance of three-wheeled or multi-wheeled vehicles in sand, water, snow, or under general conditions. The informational source is the National Wheelchair Motorcycle Association, 101 Torrey Street, Brockton, Massachusetts 03401. Printed materials that describe motorized wheelchair or motorcycle activities are also available from the New England Spinal Cord Injury Center.

SKIING

The success that disabled people, including those with multiple amputations, have had in learning to ski was the subject of a major television movie, "A Minor Inconvenience." The film's star, James Stacy, added a special touch of realism since he is not only a skillful skier but is also an amputee. Informational resources for disabled people who want to participate in this exciting sport are (1) National Inconvenienced Sportsmen Association, 3738 Walnut Avenue, Carmichael, California 95608, and (2) Blind Outdoor Leisure Development, Inc., Aspen BOLD, 533 East Main Street, Aspen, Colorado 81611. An instruction manual for disabled skiers is available from Jerry Johnson Ski Enterprises, Box 1373, Banff, Alberta, Canada.

SOFTBALL

The traditional sport of softball is becoming increasingly accessible to a large majority of disabled people. By implanting a special ball with a beeping device, for instance, blind players can identify the location and position of a ball. In some versions of the game, a sighted runner accompanies the successful hitter around the bases — if the batter connects with the ball. Softball can also be played by disabled persons who have only moderate mobility skills. In wheelchair softball, for example, all players must play from a wheelchair, whether or not they ordinarily use one. Although the development of this game and its rules are still somewhat formative, a National Wheelchair Softball Association has been organized. The address is P.O. Box 737, Sioux Falls, South Dakota 57101. Information on softball activities for the visually handicapped is usually available from community or governmental agencies that provide services to the blind.

SQUARE DANCING

Of all sports activities, few seem to be enjoyed by disabled people quite as much as square dancing. Nor is any recreational activity for the disabled more prevalent throughout the nation. There seem to be square dance clubs and instructional classes everywhere that have members and learners who are handicapped, and there are any number of dance clubs that are composed entirely of disabled people. Frequently, visits are exchanged between clubs, and dance contests are commonplace. Nearly all affiliates of such national organizations as the National Easter Seal Society, National Association for Retarded Citizens, and United Cerebral Palsy Association conduct square dancing as a regular recreational program activity. Additionally, veterans' groups and community colleges have instructional classes and dance parties. For people who use a wheelchair, information on how to organize a square dance group and how to maneuver and glide the steps is available from the Colorado Wheelers, 525 Meadowlark Drive, Lakewood, Colorado 80226.

SWIMMING

Many handicapped people enjoy swimming purely as a recreational and, often, therapeutic activity, but swimming competition is also part of the annual track and field wheelchair sports competitions that are held in every region of the country. In these competitive events, sponsored by the National Wheelchair Athletic Association, persons with different disabilities compete according to the classification of their skill and degree of physical ability. Competition includes races of different distances, and the strokes include breast, back freestyle, front freestyle, and butterfly. Swimming, of course, does not have to be a competitive sport. Local YMCA's and YWCA's, and numerous organizations such as affiliates of the National Easter Seal Society, sponsor many swimming classes and advanced swimming activities for handicapped and nonhandicapped people alike. A valuable source of information on swimming instruction techniques and program development is *A Swimming Program for the Handicapped*, published by Association Press, Box O, Wilton, Connecticut 06897.

Instructional and descriptive information on several other swimming related sports is also available. Inner-tube water polo, for example, is an activity that can be played competitively or purely for enjoyment. It is also a sport that disabled and nondisabled people can play jointly, or disabled and nondisabled playing teams can challenge each other. Rules and regulations for playing this form of water polo may be requested from Therapeutic Recreation Services, 151 West Mission, Room 203, San Jose, California 95110.

TABLE TENNIS

Table tennis can be played by people with varying disabilities, and may be played by disabled players themselves, or with nondisabled people as either team mates or competitors. Many quadraplegics secure the paddle tightly in their hand and play with remarkable skill. Rules for disabled players are the same as those established by the United States Table Tennis Association for nondisabled players. Competitive matches are held nationally; however, to qualify for national meets, a disabled person must place either first or second in a regional contest. Tournaments, sanctioned by the United States Table Tennis Association, are conducted by the National Wheelchair Athletic Association that also provides information about how this game can be adapted to the physical limitations of handicapped people.

TRACK AND FIELD

Wheelchair track and field competition is governed by the National Wheelchair Athletic Association which regulates competitor eligibility, classification, and equipment standards. All competitors are classed. That is, athletes are grouped into comparable categories, based upon degrees of skill and ability, in order to provide basic fairness in competition. All classes have a slalom event—a race against the clock over a course with required turns, maneuvers, and direction reversals. Penalty seconds are added to elapsed time for errors and faults. The course is entirely flat for severely limited athletes, but obstacles are added for the less disabled and include ramps, curb-type jumps, elevated platforms, and rail bridges. The emphasis is on speed, quickness, maneuverability, concentration, and judgment.

Track events feature short dashes and longer pushes for each class, as well as relays. Quadraplegics, for example, are required to run a 60-yard dash and a 220-yard push. Other classes may compete in a 100-yard dash, or in longer races of 440 yards, 880 yards, or a mile. Relays are 4 × 60, 4 × 100, 4 × 200, and 4 × 400 yards. Field events include discus, shot put, javelin, club throw, and precision club throw. In each of the events the competitor may have the wheelchair held securely in position either by a mechanical holder or by an attendant. The javelin must be at least 220 centimeters in length and weigh at least 600 grams. The discus must weigh a minimum of one kilogram. The shot may be 2, 3, or 4 kilograms, with the specific weight determined by the event's classification level. Athletes from all classes may compete in precision javelin.

The National Wheelchair Athletic Association oversees all competition in track and field events, in addition to swimming, archery, table tennis, and weightlifting, and more detailed information may be obtained by writing directly to that organization. Other sources of information on track and field sports are (1) Canadian Wheelchair Sports Association, 333 River Road,

Ottowa, Ontario, Canada K1L 8B9, (2) Disabled Sportsmen of America, Inc., P.O. Box 26, Vinton, Virginia 24179, (3) National Association of Sports for Cerebral Palsy, United Cerebral Palsy Associations, Inc., 66 East 34 Street, New York, New York 10016, and (4) National Handicapped Sports and Recreation Association, Capitol Hill Station, P.O. Box 18664, Denver, Colorado 80218.

VOLLEYBALL

Volleyball can be played competitively or recreationally by nearly any disabled person. If, for example, players require wheelchairs or have limited use of their lower body, the game can be easily adapted by lowering the net three and one-half or four feet, and letting the participants sit on the floor. Mats, placed on the floor, prevent skin abrasions and prevent injuries when players accidently tumble over. Nondisabled people can also join in and sit, as everyone else does, without having any height advantage over the disabled players.

People with a high degree of mobility can play vollyball at standard net height. Yet mobility can be achieved through practice and determination. People with leg, arm, or below-the-knee amputations regularly—and successfully—play competitions against nondisabled volleyball teams, as the achievements of a team of players from Tel Aviv has strikingly demonstrated. When the game is played on courts with hard surfaces, wheelchair users can join in with nondisabled players. Rules must be firmly agreed upon, however. Nondisabled players, for instance, cannot be permitted to overplay their areas, otherwise their height advantage would unfairly prevent the wheelchair users from full participation.

WEIGHTLIFTING

Weightlifting first became popular with disabled people when paraplegic veterans, returning from World War II, found that residual arm strength could be maintained and significantly augmented by exercising with weights. For a relatively small outlay of money, a set of weights or barbells can be purchased for home exercise or as a body conditioning and recreational activity. Neighborhood gymnasiums and spas, and the athletic departments of community colleges or YMCA's and YWCA's, usually have sophisticated weightlifting equipment that can be adapted to special use. More specific information, and schedules of regional and national competitions, is available from the National Wheelchair Athletic Association. Information on wheelchair weightlifting coaching can be obtained from the British Sports Association for the Disabled, Stoke-Mandeville Sports Stadium, Harvey Road, Aylesbury, Buckinghamshire, England.

WHEELCHAIR TENNIS

Wheelchair tennis is a recently developed sport that has the same rules as regular tennis except for the option of letting the ball bounce twice. Classes for beginners and tournaments for more seasoned and skillful players are springing up all over the country. In one California community, for example, a wheelchair tennis class was started when a group of handicapped people asked their local parks and recreation department to provide instruction. The instructor was first briefed by one of the disabled athletes who had seen a wheelchair tennis tournament played in another part of the country. As with nearly all sports, wheelchair tennis can be played jointly by disabled and nondisabled players. A new organization, the National Foundation for Wheelchair Tennis, can provide additional information about rules, how to form a club, and the location of local tournaments. Inquiries should be mailed to the Association, c/o Brad Parks, 3855 Birch Street, Newport Beach, California 92660.

ARTS AND OTHER RECREATIONAL RESOURCES

Nearly every museum, public art gallery, and publicly-funded theater and library is, because of the affects of Section 504 of the Rehabilitation Act, physically accessible to the majority of handicapped people. In any community there are also any number of informally or formally organized hobby and interest groups and clubs where people of like interests meet to share experiences and to participate in learning. Participation in these activities, such as bridge clubs, travel groups, and chess or photography clubs, to name a few, provide an opportunity for disabled and nondisabled people to interact and share community life. There are, however, specific national organizations that have been established for the specific purpose of bring enriching recreational experiences to the disabled. One example is the Theater for the Deaf sponsored by the University of Montana. This highly professional group consists of both hearing and hearing-impaired actors and has received national acclaim for the excellence of its productions. National tours are conducted annually, and a schedule of performances in various cities throughout the nation is available from Theater for the Deaf, University of Montana, Missoula, Montana 59801. The University also encourages deaf people who aspire to an acting career, to enroll in its theater arts and drama curricula.

Three agencies funded by the federal government have been primarily responsible for stimulating the expansion of arts and other cultural activities for disabled people throughout all parts of the nation. Although Congressional appropriations for these programs has greatly diminished during the past two years, the National Endowment for the Arts, through its National Arts and the Handicapped Information Service, continues to provide financial grants and materials to both public and private agencies for the purpose of making art programs and facilities more accessible to handicapped people. Publications that are available from the Information Service cover such topics as arts for visually impaired persons, arts education for disabled students, and ways in which arts programs and facilities can be made available to the handicapped. Prototypes of model arts programs are also available, and technical assistance is given to cultural resource agencies in altering physical structures and building designs to accommodate disabled people. In addition, the Service has compiled an annotated bibliography on media for the handicapped, including captioned films, Braille arts, and slide-tape presentations. Grants to improve building accessibility have been awarded to numerous institutions and organizations throughout the nation, such as the Metropolitan Museum and Lincoln Center in New York, and the Williamsburg national monument in Virginia. Direct grants are also available to artists and writers. Disabled people who are interested in the arts may ask to be placed on the Service's mailing list and will receive current materials and periodic information, at no cost, about handicapped arts programs. The address is National Arts and the Handicapped Information Service, National Endowment for the Arts, 2401 E Street, N.W., Washington, D.C. 20506.

The National Committee on Arts for the Handicapped, now considerably pressed for funds because of federal domestic budget reductions, offers limited grants, instruction, and resource assistance to schools and community groups that provide arts related programs to the nation's handicapped population. Among its programs are Very Special Arts Festivals where disabled school children and adults can immerse themselves in creative experiences. These festivals are usually one- or two-day affairs where individuals create art work, participate in music and dramatic activities, display their art projects in gallery settings, and generally enjoy themselves. The 1982 Very Special Arts Festival in Anaheim, California, brought entries from the entire state and lasted several days. Nearby Disneyland also joined in the festivities by sending Disney characters to participate in the event. Information about the Very Special Arts Festivals that are held annually in many states and the locations of other arts programs sponsored by the National Committee can be obtained from The National Committee on Arts for the Handicapped, 1825 Connecticut Avenue, N.W., Washington, D.C. 20009.

One of the nation's largest resources of reading materials and reading aids for individuals who cannot hold, handle, or read conventional printed matter is the Library of Congress. A branch of this federal agency, the National Library Services for the Blind and Physically Handicapped, maintains a vast collection of specially produced books, films, magazines, cassettes, and musical materials that are loaned free to handicapped people. The book collection, for example, includes more than 25,000 titles that are available in special formats. The children's collection contains many special books that combine print with Braille, enabling blind and sighted children and adults to read together, and some of the print/Braille books are illustrated with fragrance strips that emit scents when scratched. Seventy magazines on disc, cassette, and in Braille are offered through the program. Subscriptions to many popular magazines, which are produced in electronic or brailled format, are given free of charge to handicapped people. Playback equipment is also available, on a loan basis, to readers for as long as library materials are being borrowed. Reference resources of the Library, which are available, include information on such topics as traveling for handicapped people, and games and sports for disabled persons.

The services of the Library are available throughout the nation by means of a network of 160 locally funded cooperating libraries and agencies which, in turn, circulate materials to handicapped people. Although information about this program can be provided by any local public library, a fuller description of services is available from National Library Services for the Blind and Physically Handicapped, Library of Congress, 1291 Taylor Street, N.W., Washington, D.C. 20542.

BIBLIOGRAPHY

BOOKS

Bucher, Charles A. and Thaxton, Nolan A. *Physical Education for Children: Movement Foundations and Experiences.* New York: Macmillan Publishing Co., 1979.

Clarke, H. Harrison and Clarke, David H. *Developmental and Adapted Physical Education.* Englewood Cliffs, N.J.: Prentice Hall, Inc., 1978.

Complo, Jannita Marie. *Funtactics: Movement and Speech Activities for Special Children.* Belmont, Calif.: Fearon Pitman Publishers, 1979.

Crain, Cynthia D. *Movement and Rhythmic Activities for the Mentally Retarded.* Springfield, Ill.: Charles C. Thomas, Publisher, 1981.

Cratty, Bryant J. *Adapted Physical Education for Handicapped Children and Youth.* Denver: Love Publishing Co., 1980.

Fait, Hollis F. *Special Physical Education: Adapted, Corrective, Developmental.* Philadelphia: W. B. Saunders Co., 1978.

Fluegelman, Andrew. *More New Games!* Garden City, N.Y.: Dolphin Books/Doubleday & Co., 1981.

Fluegelman, Andrew, ed. *The New Games Book.* Garden City, N.Y.: Dolphin Books/Doubleday & Co., 1976.

Geddes, Dolores. *Physical Activities for Individuals with Handicapping Conditions.* St. Louis: The C. V. Mosby Co., 1978.

Geddes, Dolores. *Psychomotor Individualized Educational Programs for Intellectual, Learning, and Behavioral Disabilities.* Boston: Allyn and Bacon, 1981.

Groves, Lilian, ed. *Physical Education for Special Need.* New York: Cambridge University Press, 1979.

Haskins, James. *A New Kind of Joy: The Story of the Special Olympics.* Garden
 City, N.Y.: Doubleday & Co., 1976.
Lear, Roma. *Play Helps: Toys and Activities for Handicapped Children.* London:
 Heinemann Health Books, 1977.
Lovinger, Sophie L. *Learning Disabilities and Games.* Chicago: Nelson-Hall, Publishers,
 1979.
O'Morrow, Gerald S. *Therapeutic Recreation: A Helping Profession.* Reston, Va.:
 Reston Publishing Co., 1976.
Parents Guide to Accredited Camps. Martinsville, Ind.: American Camping Asso-
 ciation, 1982.
*Physical Education and Recreation for Impaired, Disabled, and Handicapped
 Individuals — Past, Present, and Future.* Washington, D.C.: American Alli-
 ance for Health, Physical Education, and Recreation, 1975.
Reynolds, Grace Demmery, ed. *A Swimming Program for the Handicapped.* Wilton,
 Conn.: Association Press, 1973.
Roice, G. Robert, ed. *Teaching Handicapped Students Physical Education.* Washington,
 D.C.: National Education Association of the United States, 1981.
Sherrill, Claudine. *Adapted Physical Education and Recreation: A Multidisciplinary
 Approach.* Dubuque, Iowa: W. C. Brown Company, Publishers, 1981.
Shrivers, Jay S. *Therapeutic and Adapted Recreational Services.* Philadelphia: Lea &
 Febiger, 1975.
Sternlicht, Manny and Hurwitz, Abraham. *Games Children Play: Instructive and
 Creative Play Activities for the Mentally Retarded and Developmentally
 Disabled Child.* New York: Van Nostrand Reinhold Co., 1981.
The Teaching Research Infant and Child Center. *The Teaching Research Curriculum
 for Moderately and Severely Handicapped, Gross and Fine Motor.* Springfield,
 Ill.: Charles C. Thomas, Publisher, 1980.
Vannier, Maryhelen. *Physical Activities for the Handicapped.* Englewood Cliffs, N.J.:
 Prentice-Hall, Inc., 1977.
Water Sports for the Disabled. Advisory Panel on Water Sports for the Disabled.
 London: The Sports Council, 1978.
Wehman, Paul, ed. *Recreation Programming for Developmentally Disabled Persons.*
 Baltimore: University Park Press, 1979.
Wiseman, Douglas C. *A Practical Approach to Adapted Physical Education.* Read-
 ing, Massachusetts: Addison-Wesley Publishing Co., 1982.

BROCHURES AND MAGAZINES

Audubon Magazine. New York: National Audubon Society.
Berkeley Outreach. Berkeley, Calif.: Berkeley Outreach Recreation Program.
Challenge. Santa Ana, Calif.: Chris Collier Publishers.
Colorado Outdoors. Denver: Colorado Department of Game and Fish.
Disabled USA. Washington, D.C.: The President's Committee on Employment for
 the Handicapped.
Ducks Unlimited. Des Plaines, Ill.: Ducks Unlimited, Inc.
Friends O'Wildlife. Raleigh: North Carolina Wildlife Federation, Inc.
Nicosia, Angelo. *Competitive and Recreational Wheelchair Sports.* Washington,
 D.C.: Paralyzed Veterans of America, 1982.
Sports 'n Spokes. Phoenix, Arizona: Crase and Co.

Sports 'n Spokes. Phoenix, Arizona: Crase and Co.
The Conservationist. Albany: New York State Department of Environmental Conservation.

UNPUBLISHED MATERIAL

Edwards, Margie Egbert. "Programming Therapeutic Group Activities for Children." Doctoral dissertation, University of Utah, Salt Lake City, 1976.

Hawkins, Barbara Ames. "Perceptions of Recreation Personnel Toward Mental Retardation Labels and Selected Recreational Experiences." Doctoral dissertation, Indiana University, Bloomington, 1979.

Powers, Patrick James. "Proposed Guidelines for Development of a Backpacking Program for the Mildly Mentally Retarded." Masters' thesis, University of Wisconsin, La Crosse, 1977.

Steadward, Robert Daniel. "Wheelchair Sports Classification System." Doctoral dissertation, University of Oregon, Eugene, 1978.

Thorn, Bernard E. "Normalization and Recreation Service Delivery Systems." Doctoral dissertation, Pennsylvania State University, University Park, 1978.

SOME ARTS AND LIBRARY RESOURCES
FOR THE HANDICAPPED

Association of Foot and Mouth Painters
503 Brisbane Building
Buffalo, New York 10403

Media Access for the Disabled
7551 Melrose Avenue
Los Angeles, California 90046

National Arts and the Handicapped Information Service
Arts and Special Constituencies Project
National Endowment for the Arts
2401 E Street, N.W.
Washington, D.C. 20506

National Committee on Arts for the Handicapped
1825 Connecticut Avenue, N.W.
Washington, D.C. 20009

National Library Services for the Blind and Physically Handicapped
Library of Congress
1291 Taylor Street, N.W.
Washington, D.C. 20542

Performing Arts Theater for the Handicapped
5410 Wilshire Boulevard
Suite 510
Los Angeles, California 90036

Special Constituencies
    California Arts Council
    1901 Broadway
    Sacramento, California 95818
Theater for the Deaf
    University of Montana
    Missoula, Montana 59801

SPORTS ORGANIZATIONS FOR THE HANDICAPPED

Adapted Sports Association, Inc.
    Communications Center
    6832 Marlette Road
    Marlette, Michigan 48453

American Wheelchair Bowling Association
    6718 Pinehurst Drive
    Evansville, Indiana 47711

American Wheelchair Pilots Association
    P.O. Box 1181
    Mesa, Arizona 85201

Amputee Sports Association
    11705 Mercy Boulevard
    Savannah, Georgia 31406

Berkeley Outreach Recreation Program
    2020 Milvia
    Berkeley, California 94704

Blind Outdoor Leisure Development, Inc.
    Aspen BOLD
    533 East Main Street
    Aspen, Colorado 81611

British Sports Association for the Disabled
    Stoke-Mandeville Sports Stadium
    Harvey Road
    Aylesbury, Buckinghamshire, England

California Wheelchair Athletic Association
    P.O. Box 26483
    San Jose, California 95159

Canadian Wheelchair Sports Association
    333 River Road
    Ottowa, Ontario, Canada K1L 8B9

Colorado Wheelers
    525 Meadowlark Drive
    Lakewood, Colorado 80226

Disabled Sportsmen of America, Inc.
    P.O. Box 26
    Vinton, Virginia 24179

International Foundation for Wheelchair Tennis
    1909 Ala Wai Boulevard
    Suite 1507
    Honolulu, Hawaii 96815

National Amputee Golf Association
    P.O. Box 9426
    Solon, Ohio 44139

National Association of Sports for Cerebral Palsy
    United Cerebral Palsy Associations, Inc.
    66 East 34 Street
    New York, New York 10016

National Foundation for Wheelchair Tennis
    c/o Brad Parks
    3855 Birch Street
    Newport Beach, California 92660

National Handicapped Sports and Recreation Association
    Capitol Hill Station
    P.O. Box 18664
    Denver, Colorado 80218

National Inconvenienced Sportsmen Association
    3738 Walnut Avenue
    Carmichael, California 95608

National Wheelchair Athletic Association
    James Polk Office Building
    Suite 1800
    505 Deaderick Street
    Nashville, Tennessee 37219

National Wheelchair Basketball Association
    110 Seaton Building
    University of Kentucky
    Lexington, Kentucky 40506

National Wheelchair Marathon
    c/o Paul DePace
    380 Diamond Hill Road
    Warwick, Rhode Island 02886

National Wheelchair Motorcycle Association
    101 Torrey Street
    Brockton, Massachusetts 03401

National Wheelchair Softball Association
    P.O. Box 737
    Sioux Falls, South Dakota 57101

New England Spinal Cord Injury Foundation
    369 Elliot Street
    Newton Upper Falls, Massachusetts 02164

North American Riding for the Handicapped Association
    Box 100
    Ashburn, Virginia 22011

Riding for the Disabled Association
   Avenue R
   National Agricultural Centre
   Kenilworth, Warwickshire, CV8 2LY, England
Special Olympics, Inc.
   Joseph P. Kennedy Jr. Foundation
   1701 K Street, N.W.
   Suite 215
   Washington, D.C. 20006
United States Association for Blind Athletes
   55 West California Avenue
   Beach Haven Park, New Jersey 08008
United States Blind Golfers Association
   225 Varoone Street
   28th Floor
   New Orleans, Louisiana 70112
United States Deaf Skiers Association, Inc.
   159 Davis Avenue
   Hackensack, New Jersey 07601

SUMMARY AND
CONCLUSIONS

The United States has experienced some important social changes since the 1950s. After the landmark Supreme Court decision of 1954, there ensued the civil rights struggles, led by blacks and followed by other minorities—Hispanics, Asians, Native Americans. These movements for equal rights and enlarged social opportunities are not over; some major objectives have been gained, especially nationally, but on state and local levels continuous battles are still being fought around specific discriminatory practices.

The mid-1960s saw the great expansion of U.S. military actions in Southeast Asia, which brought in its train the major revolution in consciousness of the so-called counter-culture. Women's liberation, student and ecology movements, social protest groups with many and varied objectives were stimulated by and contributed to a pervasive questioning of established beliefs and social institutions. Even though the mid-1970s saw a shift in popular consciousness toward a more conservative political outlook, many of the attitude changes of the preceding decade had been embodied in legislation and thus endure, despite changing political winds. Although the Reagan administration hopes to undo many of these gains, its efforts will not be generally successful.

Probably the least recognized of the spectacular social changes of the past three decades have been the massive alterations in the situation of disabled people in the United States. A movement for public action and legislative changes, led initially by the disabled and their families, culminated in the Rehabilitation Act of 1973. This act, with its subsequent amendments, laid the groundwork for a new deal for the handicapped. It would be too much to claim that a corresponding, broad change in public attitudes has simultaneously occurred. But, just as the 1954 Supreme Court decision gave the civil rights movement legitimacy, so the Rehabilitation Act has provided a legislative framework for the continuing struggle to ensure the rights of the handicapped. Changes in public attitudes will follow. Educational campaigns are no longer merely hortatory and moralistic; they have been sanctioned and empowered by law, and education aimed at changing social attitudes and practices is most effective when conducted in a framework of law. The extraordinary gains of handicapped people in two key areas, the rights to equal employment and to educational opportunities, and their lesser gains in housing and the creation of barrier-free environments could not have been achieved without the legal underpinning. Many well-meant efforts, such as Employ the Physically Handicapped Week and the President's Commission on Employment of the Handicapped, have been ineffective, despite considerable cooperation from the media, because they were based on appeals, not to self-interest, but to philanthropic or moral impulses.

This volume has recorded the advances achieved by disabled people in some critical fields and has sought to reflect both a realistic picture of the present and an optimistic projection of the near future. Yet we do not wish to exaggerate the gains made; nor do we want to underestimate the obstacles that remain. Although the lot of some handicapped persons has improved immeasurably in recent years, many have not yet — for diverse reasons — shared in these gains. To cite an example of a specific disabled group, the 1978 Report of the National Epilepsy Commission estimated an unemployment rate for epileptics of about four times greater than that of the general population. The same report estimated that at least 100,000 epileptics were inappropriately housed in 1977, living either in institutions or in seriously substandard housing, and that they had no choices of alternative living arrangements available and attainable.

Indeed, we are still a long way from the ideal of normalization for disabled people in the United States. Perhaps "ideal" is a misleading, even defeatist term in this connection, for in some countries, notably Sweden where the concept originated, normalization is not an ideal but an established principle and a practical goal that underlies and directs all private and governmental programs. The emphasis in this work has been on facilities, resources, and potentials in the United States and programs in other countries have only been described occasionally and illustratively. In some respects, however, disabled persons have more numerous and more useful supportive services in a number of countries, particularly Sweden and the Netherlands.

In one aspect, however, the United States is quite outstanding, if not unique — that is in the extent and the effectiveness of self-help organizations, such as the Centers for Independent Living, formed by the handicapped themselves. Self-help groups of the disabled, their families, and other supporters should be given a large share of the credit for the achievements made so far. Although self-help groups of the disabled are also relatively active in the United Kingdom and Australia, their most dynamic growth and creativity seems to have occurred in the United States. Perhaps the success of self-help groups in the United States can be attributed to the sparser, less comprehensive governmental provisions for the disabled and to the greater professionalization of services here.

Although for the purposes of this book, we have tended to treat the needs of the handicapped as a special problem in our society, such an abstract treatment should not obscure their interrelatedness to the general social fabric. More adequate and universal medical services and income-payments for the disabled would be best achieved not by separate programs for them, but through the passage of comprehensive national health insurance and some version of an income-maintenance rather than a welfare-based program. Employment of the handicapped is most easily achieved in a vigorous economy and a situation of full employment. An expansion of the housing available for the general population would mean more housing for the disabled. Improvements in institutions and nursing homes in general would also improve the living conditions of the handicapped who reside in them. More money and more adequate facilities for public education would mean better services for the handicapped children who are mainstreamed in them. And so on.

BIBLIOGRAPHY

Bowe, F. *Handicapping America: Barriers to Disabled People.* New York: Harper and Row, 1978.

Bruck, L. *Access — The Guide to a Better Life for Disabled Americans.* New York: Random House, 1978.

Gleidman, J., and Roth, W. *The Unexpected Minority.* New York: Harcourt Brace Jovanovich, 1980.

Goldenson, R., ed. *Disability and Rehabilitation Handbook.* New York: McGraw-Hill Book Company, 1978.

How to Get Help for Kids: A Reference Guide to Services for Handicapped Children. Syracuse: Gaylord Professional Publishers, 1981.

Katz, A. H., and Bender, E. I. *The Strength in Us: Self-Help Groups in the Modern World.* New York: Franklin Watts, 1976.

Kleinfield, S. *The Hidden Minority, America's Handicapped.* Waltham, Mass.: Little Brown, 1979.

May, E., Waggoner, N., and Hotte, E. *Independent Living for the Handicapped and Elderly.* Boston: Houghton Mifflin, 1976.

VALUE-LADEN BELIEFS AND PRINCIPLES FOR REHABILITATION

Beatrice A. Wright

The following principles are excerpted from a longer essay:

1. *Every individual needs respect and encouragement; the presence of a handicap, no matter how severe, does not alter these fundamental rights.*

A person is entitled to the enrichment of his life and the development of his abilities whether these be great or small and whether he has a long or short time to live. He must not be led to devaluate himself, to give up hope, or to remain neglected and deprived. Under no circumstance is he to be treated as an "object" or "vegetable."

Biases that declare some groups to be more worthy or deserving of services than others lead to gross inequities and must be avoided. Life, increased mobility, and better communication skills are just as important to a 72 year old as to a 12 year old, to a mentally retarded person as to an average person, to a Black person as to a White person, to a poor person as to a rich person.

The affirmation of human worth and dignity must not only be kept explicitly in the forefront when allocating limited resources. It should also be reflected in adequate case finding efforts so that no person who has a handicap remains neglected.

2. *The assets of the person must receive considerable attention in the rehabilitation effort.*

A person's healthy, physical and mental attributes can become a basis for

241

alleviating difficulties as well as for providing a source of gratification and enrichment of life. Special care must be taken to avoid over emphasis on the pathologic that leaves one inadequately sensitized to stabilizing and maturity inducing factors. Those attributes of the person that are healthy and promising must be supported and developed.

3. *The active participation of the client in the planning and execution of his rehabilitation program is to be sought as fully as possible.*

Genuine respect for the client leads to the affirmation of his right, within very broad limits, to become actively engaged in the rehabilitation process and to make decisions that affect his life. The client obviously also has information and ideas essential to his rehabilitation progress that are not available to others.

Among the foremost consequences of active involvement on his own behalf are the enhancing of the person's self-respect, his initiative and his responsibility for carrying out decisions.

This principle requires that effort be made to determine the views of every client. Special effort will be necessary in those instances where a major problem of communication exists. Examples of such instances are deafness, aphasia, cerebral palsy, mental retardation, foreign speech, ghetto speech, and stuttering.

4. *The client is seen, not as an isolated individual, but as part of a larger group that includes other people, often his family.*

The problems of the client are intimately connected with those of the larger group of people whose welfare he shares. Therefore, early and active participation of such significant others as spouses, parents, siblings and children is viewed as an important principle in the total rehabilitation process. Where the client is in fact alone, or is resistant towards including other people in his rehabilitation, this principle may remain unactivated.

5. *Because each person has unique characteristics and each situation its own properties, variability is required in rehabilitation plans.*

Grouping persons according to a specific handicap must not lead to stereotyped inferences about them. Differences in the needs, abilities, and circumstances of persons with the same or a similar handicap require diverse approaches rather than the inflexible application of procedures.

Differences in problems that stem from particular characteristics of particular groups further serve to underscore the need for variability in the process of rehabilitation.

6. *Predictor variables, based on group outcomes in rehabilitation, should be applied with caution to the individual case.*

At the present stage of knowledge, the individual, if given a chance, often becomes the exception which, instead of proving the rule, undermines it. Assessment data can, therefore, generally be used more appropriately as an indication of present status and as a *guide to remediation* than as a prognosticator of future performance.

The direct application of group based predictor variables is not questioned in regard to the behavior of groups qua groups, as in voting or consumer behavior, but it is questioned in regard to long-range decisions about a particular individual. Moreover, prediction based on the response of one individual to the rehabilitation process rather than on "group variables" encourages treatment corrections in accordance with continuing evaluation.

7. *The significance of a handicap is affected by the person's feelings about himself and his situation.*

Feelings that often have to be worked through by a person who has suffered a misfortune, such as a disability, are those of resentment, inferiority, guilt, loneliness, and being a burden; doubts about whether one will still be loved and accepted; worries about the future and how one will manage; concern that one will be left behind. Such social-emotional attitudes take time to resolve. When the person accepts his handicap as personally non-devaluating and engages life positively, important rehabilitation goals have been reached.

It is to be stressed that the personal-affective life of the client can generally be most effectively strengthened within the context of dealing with reality problems that exist in his social and physical environment rather than by treating his feelings in an environmental vacuum. Supportive attitudes of family, friends and professionals, as well as opportunities for satisfactory living offered by the community, are main factors that facilitate the person's efforts to come to terms with himself and his handicaps.

8. *The severity of a handicap can be increased or diminished by environmental conditions.*

Although grammatical usage speaks of a "*person's* handicap," the actual severity of a handicap depends to a great degree upon the characteristics of the person's environment. Thus, physical handicaps can be reduced by eliminating architectural barriers, interpersonal handicaps by overcoming devaluating social attitudes, educational handicaps by providing educational and training facilities, economic handicaps by extending work opportunities, emotional handicaps by enhancing family and group support.

It should be stressed that the rehabilitation process itself carries an important environmental impact. Rehabilitation personnel must continuously question whether present methods or systems of operation are always or maximally helpful. They should seek ways to improve the rehabilitation process as well as generally to support environmental changes in the home and community that reduce the severity of handicapping conditions.

9. *It is essential that society as a whole strive continuously and persistently to provide the basic means toward the fulfillment of the lives of all its inhabitants, including those with handicaps.*

Among the obligations of society are the establishment of needed housing, schools, work opportunities, transportation, hospitals, recreation facilities, and other services. Rehabilitation workers bear a responsibility in helping to meet these obligations by initiating and supporting appropriate legislation and programs.

Where national and community resources are limited, ways to make more effective use of them or to expand them must be sought. Inertia and resistance to change lead to ignoring pressing problems and must be replaced by a determined effort to work toward better solutions.

Extending the goals of rehabilitation to its ultimate implications requires that effort be directed toward the prevention of handicapping conditions. Improvement of health care, reduction of accidents, control of pollution, overcoming of prejudice, diminution of poverty, are all major societal responsibilities. Rehabilitation personnel cannot remain indifferent to them.

10. *Provision must be made for the effective dissemination of information concerning legislation and community offerings of potential benefit to persons with handicaps.*

Large numbers of persons who are handicapped remain unaware of the available services from which they could benefit. Professional persons also are often unaware of them and thus do not serve adequately as sources for information and referral. Solution of the problem requires a variety of approaches by which both professional persons and clients can be kept abreast of opportunities that might benefit the client should he choose to avail himself of them.

11. *Involvement of the client with the general life of the community is a fundamental principle guiding decisions concerning living arrangements and the use of resources.*

Under special circumstances, where vital considerations indicate the advisability of some form of institutional living, every effort should be made to help the resident participate in community activities and services. Involvement with the community can also be served by sharing institutional resources and activities with the public. Periodic visits on the part of the resident with his family, friends, or in foster homes, should become established procedure. The location of institutions within rather than outside communities, facilitates such integration.

The development of halfway houses and other interim steps that encourage community involvement is imperative. Housing designed to meet special needs should be available in the community to persons with handicaps.

The client who chooses to avail himself of specialized living arrangements should continue to have the option and opportunity to move elsewhere as circumstances permit. In the interest of life enrichment, the space of free movement of a person should be enlarged rather than constricted.

12. *In addition to the special problems of particular groups, rehabilitation clients share certain problems by virtue of their disadvantaged and devalued position.*

Devaluation and disadvantagement are general life problems experienced by the physically, mentally, socially, economically, and emotionally handicapped; certain minority groups; the public offender; the alcoholic, etc. These common problems give rise to important rehabilitation goals that are shared among diverse handicapped and deprived groups.

Such problems stemming from the particular characteristics of groups are locomotion difficulties of the orthopedically disabled, communication problems of the deaf, addiction of the drug user, malnutrition of the poor, intellectual deficits of the mentally retarded, etc.

13. *Persons with a handicap should be called upon to serve as co-planners, co-evaluators, and consultants to others, including professional persons.*

It is important that the rehabilitation field take advantage of the special knowledge and viewpoints of people who have handicaps. Such persons have had first hand experience with the rehabilitation process itself and are directly involved with problems that personally affect them. Their ideas should be especially sought concerning ways in which rehabilitation services can be improved and the lives of people with handicaps enriched.

Organizations on behalf of the handicapped should make it a point to include representatives of client groups on their advisory boards. Examples of such organizations are rehabilitation centers, private and governmental health agencies, foundations, schools, and hospitals. Rehabilitation agencies should make certain that persons with handicaps serve in professional and non-professional capacities.

With respect to research on problems of rehabilitation, investigators are encouraged to take advantage of the special sensitivities and understandings of persons who have a handicap by having them serve as consultants and co-investigators.

14. *All phases of rehabilitation have psychological aspects.*

The human being reacts cognitively and emotionally to events that involve him. These reactions in turn affect the further course of those events. One is compelled, therefore, to recognize that psychological factors are ever-present and often crucial in all aspects of rehabilitation — medical, surgical, educational, social, vocational, as well as primarily psychological.

15. *Inter-disciplinary and interagency collaboration and coordination of services are essential.*

The needs of individual clients are so diverse, encompassing all problems that one might expect to encounter in human affairs, that a variety of services is necessary. Comprehensive rehabilitation, therefore, requires the effort of many professions, and close working relations among the various kinds of rehabilitation agencies.

There is the persistent danger that the pressure to meet agency and professional needs most efficiently and conveniently will become the principal basis for coordinating services. To guard against this danger, a clear and explicit focus on meeting client needs most effectively is required.

Because of the complexities in the system of services, the client needs a specified person to serve as "coordinator" or "advocate" in providing information and otherwise acting on his behalf. Such a person may come from any of the helping disciplines as appropriate, rather than routinely from a single profession.

16.   *Self-help organizations are important allies in the rehabilitation effort.*

Self-help groups provide important programs and mutual support to persons who are handicapped. They also can aid rehabilitation personnel in the understanding of significant problems and the development of new directions in the rehabilitation field. More extensive collaboration between rehabilitation workers and self-help groups can be expected to further shared objectives.

17.   *Basic research can profitably be guided by the question of usefulness in ameliorating problems, a vital consideration in rehabilitation.*

Basic research can be useful research in the sense of being oriented toward the alleviation and overcoming of problems faced in rehabilitation. The converse is also true: useful research can be basic research in the sense of advancing knowledge through the discovery of general principles that apply beyond the borders of the immediately presenting situation. It is misleading and stultifying to identify basic research with "pure" research, the unwitting assumption being that any guide to research other than that given by "knowledge for its own sake" renders it impure and somehow less basic.

It is, therefore, urged that the question of usefulness be regarded with favor as a guide to research. Basic research can profitably become real-life oriented in its conception and from its inception by considering usefulness as a value in the selection of problems, analysis of data, communication of results, and application of findings.

18.   *Continuing review of the contributions of the rehabilitation effort within a framework of guiding principles that are themselves subject to review is an essential part of the self-correcting effort of professions.*

The values and beliefs expressed in the foregoing set of principles need to be periodically reviewed for two main reasons. First, change in emphasis and content may be indicated by new knowledge and changing times. Secondly, specification as to how the principles can best be implemented requires constant examination and study if their effectiveness as guides in rehabilitation is to be increased.

NATIONAL ADVOCACY, CONSUMER, AND VOLUNTARY ORGANIZATIONS

Affiliated Leadership League of and for the Blind of America
879 Park Avenue
Baltimore, Maryland 21201

Alexander Graham Bell Association for the Deaf
3417 Volta Place, N.W.
Washington, D.C. 20007

American Brittle Bone Society
Cherry Hill Plaza, Suite LL-3
1415 East Marlton Pike
Cherry Hill, New Jersey 08034

American Cancer Society
777 Third Avenue
New York, New York 10017

American Coalition of Citizens with Disabilities
1200 15th Street, N.W.
Suite 201
Washington, D.C. 20005

American Council of the Blind
1211 Connecticut Avenue, N.W.
Suite 506
Washington, D.C. 20036

American Diabetes Association
600 Fifth Avenue
New York, New York 10020

American Foundation for the Blind
15 West 16th Street
New York, New York 10011

American Heart Association
7320 Greenville Avenue
Dallas, Texas 75231

American Lung Association
1740 Broadway
New York, New York 10019

American Parkinson Disease Association
147 East 50th Street
New York, New York 10022

American Veterans of World War II, Korea, and Vietnam (AMVETS)
1710 Rhode Island Avenue, N.W.
Washington, D.C. 20036

Amyotrophic Lateral Sclerosis Society of America
15300 Ventura Boulevard
Suite 315
Sherman Oaks, California 91403

Arthritis Foundation
3400 Peachtree Road, N.E.
Suite 1101
Atlanta, Georgia 30326

Association for Children with Learning Disabilities
4156 Library Road
Pittsburgh, Pennsylvania 15234

Association for Retarded Citizens
National Headquarters
2501 Avenue J
Arlington, Texas 76011

Association for the Severely Handicapped
7010 Roosevelt Way, N.E.
Seattle, Washington 98115

Asthma and Allergy Foundation of America
19 West 44th Street
New York, New York 10036

Blinded Veterans Association
1735 DeSales Street, N.W.
Washington, D.C. 20036

Committee to Combat Huntington's Disease
250 West 57th Street
Suite 2016
New York, New York 10019

Cooley's Anemia Foundation
420 Lexington Avenue
New York, New York 10017

Cystic Fibrosis Foundation
6000 Executive Boulevard
Suite 309
Rockville, Maryland 20852

Disability Rights Center
1326 Connecticut Avenue, N.W.
Suite 1124
Washington, D.C. 20036

Disabled American Veterans
P.O. Box 14301
Cincinnati, Ohio 45214

Down's Syndrome Congress
1640 West Roosevelt Road
Suite 156-E
Chicago, Illinois 60608

Dysautonomia Foundation
370 Lexington Avenue
New York, New York 10017

Epilepsy Foundation of America
1828 L Street, N.W.
Washington, D.C. 20036

Foundation for Children with Learning Disabilities
P.O. Box LD 2929
Grand Central Station
New York, New York 10016

Handicapped Information Resource Center
Center for Architecture and Urban Planning Research
University of Wisconsin—Milwaukee
P.O. Box 413
Milwaukee, Wisconsin 53201

Institute for Comprehensive Planning
151 D Street, S.E.
Washington, D.C. 20003

International Association of Laryngectomees
American Cancer Society
777 Third Avenue
New York, New York 10017

International Association of Parents of the Deaf
814 Thayer Avenue
Silver Springs, Maryland 20910

Jewish Guild for the Blind
15 West 65th Street
New York, New York 10023

Leukemia Society of America
800 Second Avenue
New York, New York 10017

Little People of America
P.O. Box 126
Owatonna, Minnesota 55060

March of Dimes Birth Defects Foundation
1275 Mamaroneck Avenue
White Plains, New York 10605

Mental Health Association
1800 North Kent Street
Arlington, Virginia 22209

Mental Health Law Project
1220 19th Street, N.W.
Suite 300
Washington, D.C. 20036

Muscular Dystrophy Association
810 Seventh Avenue
New York, New York 10019

Myasthenia Gravis Foundation
15 East 26th Street
New York, New York 10010

National Alliance for the Mentally Ill
500 North Broadway
St. Louis, Missouri 63102

National ALS Foundation
185 Madison Avenue
New York, New York 10016

National Amputation Foundation
1245 150th Street
Whitestone, New York 11357

National Association for Hearing and Speech Action
6110 Executive Boulevard
Suite 1000
Rockville, Maryland 20852

National Association for Independent Living
1599 Case Road
Columbus, Ohio 43224

National Association for Sickle Cell Disease
3460 Wilshire Boulevard
Suite 1012
Los Angeles, California 90010

National Association for the Deaf-Blind
2703 Forest Oak Circle
Norman, Oklahoma 73071

National Association for Visually Handicapped
205 East 24th Street
Suite 17-C
New York, New York 10010

National Association of Patients on Hemodialysis and Transplantation
505 Northern Boulevard
Great Neck, New York 11021

National Association of the Deaf
814 Thayer Avenue
Silver Springs, Maryland 20910

National Ataxia Foundation
6681 Country Club Drive
Minneapolis, Minnesota 55427

National Autism Hotline
101 Richmond Street
Huntington, West Virginia 25702
Tel: (304) 523-8269, 525-8014

National Center for Law and the Handicapped
P.O. Box 477
University of Notre Dame
Notre Dame, Indiana 46556

National Committee/Arts for the Handicapped
1825 Connecticut Avenue, N.W.
Suite 418
Washington, D.C. 20009

National Council on Alcoholism
733 Third Avenue
New York, New York 10017

National Council on the Aging
600 Maryland Avenue, S.W.
West Wing 100
Washington, D.C. 20024

National Crisis Center for the Deaf
Box 484
University of Virginia Medical Center
Charlottesville, Virginia 22908
TDD:1-800-446-9876 (except Virginia)
1-800-552-3723 (in Virginia)

National Easter Seal Society
2023 West Ogden Avenue
Chicago, Illinois 60612

National Federation of the Blind
1800 Johnson Street
Baltimore, Maryland 21230

National Foundation for Jewish Genetic Diseases
609 Fifth Avenue
Suite 1200
New York, New York 10017

National Fraternal Society of the Deaf
1300 West Northwest Highway
Mt. Prospect, Illinois 60056

National Genetics Foundation
9 West 57th Street
New York, New York 10019

National Handicapped Housing Institute
12 South Sixth Street
Suite 500
Minneapolis, Minnesota 55402

National Head Injury Foundation
280 Singletary Lane
Framingham, Massachusetts 01701

National Hemophilia Foundation
25 West 39th Street
New York, New York 10018

National Huntington's Disease Association
128-A East 74th Street
New York, New York 10021

National Information Center on Deafness
Gallaudet College
Kendall Green
Washington, D.C. 20002

National Kidney Foundation
2 Park Avenue
New York, New York 10016

National Multiple Sclerosis Society
205 East 42nd Street
New York, New York 10017

National Neurofibromatosis Foundation
340 East 80th Street
Suite 21-H
New York, New York 10021

National Parkinson Foundation
1501 N.W. Ninth Avenue
Miami, Florida 33136

National Retinitis Pigmentosa Foundation
Rolling Park Building
8331 Mindale Circle
Baltimore, Maryland 21207

National Society for Autistic Children
1234 Massachusetts Avenue, N.W.
Suite 1017
Washington, D.C. 20005

National Spinal Cord Injury Foundation
369 Elliot Street
Newton Upper Falls, Maine 02164

National Stuttering Project
656-A Eighth Avenue
San Francisco, California 94118

National Tay-Sachs and Allied Diseases Association
122 East 42nd Street
New York, New York 10017

National Tuberous Sclerosis Association
P.O. Box 159
Laguna Beach, California 92652

Osteogenesis Imperfecta Foundation
632 Center Street
Van Wert, Ohio 45891

Paralyzed Veterans of America
4350 East West Highway
Suite 900
Washington, D.C. 20014

The Phoenix Society for Burn Victims
11 Rust Hill Road
Levittown, Pennsylvania 19056

Prader-Willi Syndrome Association
5515 Malibu Drive
Edina, Minnesota 55436

Rehabilitation International USA
20 West 40th Street
New York, New York 10018

Self Help for Hard of Hearing People
Box 34889
Washington, D.C. 20034

Society for the Rehabilitation of the Facially Disfigured
550 First Avenue
New York, New York 10016

Spina Bifida Association of America
343 South Dearborn Street
Suite 319
Chicago, Illinois 60604

Tourette Syndrome Association
Bell Plaza Building
42-20 Bell Boulevard
Bayside, New York 11361

United Cerebral Palsy Association
66 East 34th Street
New York, New York 10016

United Ostomy Association
2001 West Beverly Boulevard
Los Angeles, California 90057

United Parkinson Foundation
220 South State Street
Chicago, Illinois 60604

Vision Foundation
770 Centre Street
Newton, Maine 02158

Wilson's Disease Association
P.O. Box 489
Dumfries, Virginia 22026

STATE VOLUNTEER— SPONSORED INFORMATION AND REFERRAL SERVICES

ALABAMA

Volunteer and Information Center of Greater Birmingham
3600 Eighth Avenue, South
Birmingham 35222

United Fund Information and Referral
218 St. Francis Street
Mobile 36602

ARIZONA

Community Information and Referral Services
1515 East Osborn Road
Phoenix 85014

Information and Referral Service
2301 East Speedway, #210
Tucson 85719

ARKANSAS

United Way Information and Referral Service
P.O. Box 3257
Little Rock 72203

CALIFORNIA

United Way of Humboldt
P.O. Box 1004
Eureka 95501

Info-Line
3035 Tyler Avenue
Los Angeles 91731

Guideline
7510 Clairemont Mesa Boulevard
San Diego 92111

United Way of the Bay Area Information and Referral Service
410 Bush Street
San Francisco 94108

COLORADO

Volunteer and Information Center of Boulder County
1823 Folsom, #101
Boulder 80302

Mile High United Way Information and Referral Service
1245 East Colfax
Room 311
Denver 80218

CONNECTICUT

Info Line of North Central Connecticut
999 Asylum Avenue
Hartford 06105

Info Line of South Central Connecticut
One State Line
New Haven 06511

Info Line of Southwestern Connecticut
7 Academy Street
Norwalk 06850

DELAWARE

Information and Referral Service
511 West Eighth Street
Wilmington 19801

FLORIDA

Community Service Council of Broward County
1300 South Andrews Avenue
P.O. Box 22877
Fort Lauderdale 33335

Citizens Information and Referral Program
902 Southwest Second Avenue
Miami 33130

Alternative Human Services
3821 Fifth Avenue North
St. Petersburg 33713

GEORGIA

United Way's Information and Referral Service
100 Edgewood Avenue
Atlanta 30303

Help Line
P.O. Box 1724
Augusta 30903

HAWAII

Volunteer, Information and Referral Service
200 North Vineyard Boulevard
Room 603
Honolulu 96817

Maui Kokua Services
97 Mahalani Street
Wailuku 96793

IDAHO

Information and Referral
1365 North Orchard
Suite 107
Boise 83706

Idaho Falls Regional Information and Referral Service
545 Shoup, Room 341
Idaho Falls 83201

ILLINOIS

Central Information and Referral Family Service of Champaign
608 West Green
Champaign 618 20

Community Referral Service
Comprehensive Community Services of Metropolitan Chicago
104 South Michigan Avenue
Suite 1100
Chicago 60603

United Way of Sangamon County
730 East Vine Street
Box 316
Springfield 62705

INDIANA

Community Services Information and Referral
227 East Washington Boulevard
Fort Wayne 46802

926-HELP–LINE
1828 North Meridian Street
Indianapolis 46202

Volunteer Action Center
1509 Miami Street
South Bend 46613

IOWA

Information and Referral of East Central Iowa
712 Third Avenue, South East
Cedar Rapids 52401

First Call for Help
700 Sixth Avenue
Des Moines 50309

A.I.D. Center
722 Nebraska Street
Sioux City 51101

KANSAS

First Call for Help
101 South Walnut
Hutchinson 67501

United Way Information and Referral
420 Insurance Building
212 North Market
Wichita 67202

KENTUCKY

North Kent Aging Information and Referral Services
7410 Highway 42
Florence 41042

United Way Information and Referral
600 South Preston
Louisville 40202

LOUISIANA

South West Louisiana Educational and Referral Center
232-HELP
524 Brook Street
P.O. Box 3844
Lafayette 70502

Volunteer and Information Agency
211 Camp Street
New Orleans 70130

MAINE

Bath Area Information and Referral Service
45 Front Street
Bath 04530

Ingraham Volunteers
142 High Street
Portland 04101

MARYLAND

Information and Referral Service
22 Light Street
Baltimore 21202

Information and Referral of Frederick County
22 South Market Street
Frederick 21701

MASSACHUSETTS

United Way of Massachusetts Bay Information and Referral Service
87 Kilby Street
Boston 02109

Brockton Area Health Line
165 Quincy Street
Brockton 02402

First Call
7 Oak Street
Worcester 01609

MICHIGAN

Community Information Service
United Community Services of Metropolitan Detroit
51 West Warren
Detroit 48201

Information and Referral Center
66 North Division
Grand Rapids 49503

Information and Referral Service
305 Lake Boulevard
St. Joseph 49085

MINNESOTA

Community Services Activities
402 Ordean Building
Duluth 55802

First Call for Help
404 South Eighth Street
Minneapolis 55404

Know Phone
333 Sibley Street
Suite 400
St. Paul 55101

MISSISSIPPI

United Way Information and Referral Office
2315 17th Street
Gulfport 39501

Information and Referral Agency
326 South Street
Jackson 39211

MISSOURI

United Way Information and Referral
915 Olive Street
St. Louis 63101

First Call for Help Community Information and Referral Service
142 Landmark Building
309 North Jefferson
Springfield 65806

MONTANA

Great Falls Crisis Center
P.O. Box 124
Great Falls 59403

NEBRASKA

Grand Island Helpline
222 East Third Street
Grand Island 68801

United Way of the Midlands Information and Referral
1805 Harney Street
Omaha 68102

NEVADA

Voluntary Action Center of Greater Las Vegas
212 East Mesquite
Las Vegas 89101

NEW HAMPSHIRE

Information Outlet
13 South State Street
Concord 03301

Rockingham County Information Center
15 Elm Street
Newmarket 03857

NEW JERSEY

Community Service Council for Monmouth County
601 Bangs Avenue
Room 503
Asbury Park 07712

United Way of Essex and West Hudson
303-09 Washington Street
Newark 07102

Greater Mercer Comprehensive Planning Council
P.O. Box 2103
3131 Princeton Pike
Building #4
Trenton 08607

NEW MEXICO

United Way of Greater Albuquerque
110 Second, North West
P.O. Box 1767
Albuquerque 87103

Self-Help Center
219 North Orchard
Farmington 87401

NEW YORK

United Way Buffalo and Erie County
742 Delaware Avenue
Buffalo 14209

Information Line of United Way
75 Market Street
Poughkeepsie 12601

Life Line
973 East Avenue
Rochester 14607

Information and Referral Service of Volunteer Center
103 East Water Street
Syracuse 13202

NORTH CAROLINA

Information and Referral Service
301 South Breyard Street
Suite 306
Charlotte 28202

Wake County Information and Referral Center
104 Fayetteville Street
Raleigh 27601

First Line
660 West Fifth Street
Winston-Salem 27101

NORTH DAKOTA

Info-Line
305 South Eleventh Street
Box 732
Fargo 58107

Volunteer Services
309 Demers Avenue
Grand Forks 58201

OHIO

Info Line
12 East Exchange Street
Fourth Floor
Akron 44308

Voluntary Action Center Information and Referral
618 Second Street North West
Canton 44703

Community Chest and Council Information and Referral Center
2400 Reading Road
Cincinnati 45202

Community Information Services
1005 Huron Road
Cleveland 44115

Community Information and Referral Service
370 South Fifth Street
Suite G-2
Columbus 43215

OKLAHOMA

Helpline — United Way
601 North Porter
Norman 73071

Helpline Community Service Council of Greater Tulsa
1430 South Boulder
Tulsa 74119

OREGON

Help Line
P.O. Box 1368
Medford 97501

Information and Referral Services
Tri-County Community Council
718 West Burnside
Portland 97209

PENNSYLVANIA

Valley Wide Help
1244 Hamilton Street
Allentown 18102

Contact Harrisburg
P.O. Box 6270
Harrisburg 17112

Community Information and Referral Services
7 Benjamin Franklin Parkway
Philadelphia 19103

Helpline of Information and Volunteer Services
200 Ross Street
Pittsburgh 15219

RHODE ISLAND

Information and Referral Service
229 Waterman Street
Providence 02906

SOUTH CAROLINA

Trident United Way Information and Referral
1069 King Street
Charleston 29403

A.I.D. Assistance, Information, Direction
824 East Washington Street
P.O. Box 1085
Greensville 29302

SOUTH DAKOTA

Volunteer and Information Center
313 South First Avenue
Sioux Falls 57102

TENNESSEE

Family Community Service
93½ Ocoee Street
P.O. Box 2755
Merchants Bank Building
Cleveland 37311

Council of Community Services
250 Venture Circle
Nashville 37228

TEXAS

Information and Referral Service
Community Council of Greater Dallas
1900 Pacific Avenue
Suite 1725
Dallas 75201

First Call for Help
210 East Ninth Street
Fort Worth 76102

Information and Referral Service of Galveston County
4426 Avenue P
Galveston 77550

United Way Information and Referral
1010 Waugh Drive
Houston 77019

Information and Referral
406 West Market
San Antonio 78205

UTAH

Utah County Information and Referral
P.O. Box 1375
Provo 84601

The Information and Referral Center
2900 South Main Street
Salt Lake City 84115

VIRGINIA

The Information and Referral Center
603 East Jefferson
P.O. Box 139
Charlettesville 22902

Information Center of Hampton Roads
101 St. Pauls' Boulevard
Norfolk 23510

Information and Referral Service
United Way of Greater Richmond
2501 Monument Avenue
Richmond 23220

WASHINGTON

Community Information Line
1530 Eastlake Avenue East
Suite 301
Seattle 98102

Information and Referral
West 906 Main
Spokane 99201

Information and Referral for Pierce County
P.O. Box 5007
Tacoma 98405

WEST VIRGINIA

Information and Referral Bureau
P.O. Box 2711
Charleston 25330

Information and Referral Service
109 North Main Street
Wheeling 26003

WISCONSIN

Information and Referral Center in the Fox Valley
600 West College Avenue
Appleton 54911

First Call for Help
1910 South Avenue
P.O. Box 2372
La Crosse 54601

WYOMING

Information and Referral of Natrona County
259 South Center
Room 207
Casper 82601

STATE PROGRAMS FOR CRIPPLED CHILDREN, DEVELOPMENTAL DISABILITY, AND VOCATIONAL REHABILITATION

	Crippled Children	Developmental Disability	Vocational Rehabilitation
Alaska	Division of Public Health Family Health Section Crippled Children Services Pouch H-01 Juneau 99811	Division of Mental Health and Developmental Disability Services Pouch H-01 Juneau 99811	Department of Education Vocational Rehabilitation Division Alaska Office Building Pouch F, M.S. 0581 Juneau 99811
Alabama	Department of Education Division of Rehabilitation and Crippled Children Crippled Children's Services 2129 East South Boulevard P.O. Box 11586 Montgomery 36111	Department of Mental Health Division of Mental Retardation 135 South Union Street Montgomery 36130	Department of Education Division of Rehabilitation and Crippled Children Vocational Rehabilitation Services 2129 East South Boulevard P.O. Box 11586 Montgomery 36111
Arizona	Department of Health Services Family Health Services Arizona Children's Hospital 200 North Curry Road Tempe 85281	Division of Developmental Disabilities and Mental Retardation 1717 West Jefferson Street P.O. Box 6123 Phoenix 85005	Division of Employment and Rehabilitation Service Vocational Rehabilitation Administration 1717 West Jefferson Street P.O. Box 6123 Phoenix 85005

Arkansas

Department of Human Services
Crippled Children Section
Blue Cross-Blue Shield Building
7th and Gainer Streets
P.O. Box 1437
Little Rock 72203

Department of Human Services
Division of Mental Retardation/
Developmental Disability
Waldon Building
Suite 400
Little Rock 72201

Department of Human Services
Division of Rehabilitation
Services
1401 Brookwood Drive
P.O. Box 3781
Little Rock 72203

California

Health and Welfare Agency
Department of Health Service
California Children Services
714 P Street
Sacramento 95814

Health and Welfare Agency
Department of Developmental
Disabilities
714 P Street
Sacramento 95814

Health and Welfare Agency
Department of Rehabilitation
830 K Street Mall
Sacramento 95814

Colorado

Department of Health
Handicapped Children's Program
4210 East 11th Avenue
Denver 80220

Department of Institutions
Division for Developmental
Disability
4150 South Lowell Boulevard
Denver 80236

Department of Social Services
Division of Rehabilitation
1575 Sherman Street
Denver 80203

Connecticut

Department of Health Services
Health Services for Handicapped
Children
79 Elm Street
Hartford 06115

Department of Mental Retardation
Developmental Disabilities
342 North Main Street
Hartford 06117

Department of Education
Division of Vocational Rehabilitation
600 Asylum Street
Hartford 06105

	Crippled Children	Developmental Disability	Vocational Rehabilitation
Delaware	Department of Health and Human Services Division of Public Health Dover 19901	Department of Health and Human Services Division of Mental Retardation Route 1, Box 1000 Georgetown 19947	Department of Labor Division of Vocational Rehabilitation State Office Building 820 North French Street Wilmington 19801
District of Columbia	Department of Human Services Commission of Public Health Crippled Children Services 1875 Connecticut Avenue, N.W. Room 826 Washington 20009	Department of Human Services Commission on Social Services Mental Retardation and Developmental Disabilities Administration 415 12th Street, N.W. Room 410 Washington 20004	Department of Human Services Commission on Social Services Vocational Rehabilitation Administration 122 C Street, N.W. Room 800 Washington 20001
Florida	Department of Health and Rehabilitation Children's Medical Service Program Office 1311 Winewood Boulevard Tallahassee 32301	Department of Health and Rehabilitation Developmental Services Program Office 1311 Winewood Boulevard Tallahassee 32301	Department of Health and Rehabilitation Vocational Rehabilitation Program Office 1309 Winewood Boulevard Tallahassee 32301
Georgia	Department of Human Resources Division of Physical Health 47 Trinity Avenue, S.W. Atlanta 30334	Department of Human Resources Division of Mental Health and Mental Retardation 47 Trinity Avenue, S.W. Atlanta 30334	Department of Human Resources Division of Vocational Rehabilitation 47 Trinity Avenue, S.W. Atlanta 30334

Hawaii

Department of Health
Children's Health Services
Division
Crippled Children Branch
P.O. Box 3378
Honolulu 96801

Department of Health
Waimano Training School and
Hospital
P.O. Box 3378
Honolulu 96801

Department of Social Services and
Housing
Vocational Rehabilitation Division
P.O. Box 339
Honolulu 96809

Idaho

Department of Health and
Welfare
Bureau of Child Health
Statehouse
Boise 83720

Department of Health and
Welfare
Idaho State Council on
Developmental Disabilities
Statehouse
Boise 83720

Board of Education
Vocational Rehabilitation
Len B. Jordan Building
Boise 83720

Illinois

University of Illinois
Division of Services for
Crippled Children
540 Iles Park Place
Springfield 62718

Department of Mental Health and
Developmental Disabilities
401 South Spring Street
Springfield 62706

Department of Rehabilitation
Services
623 East Adams Street
Springfield 62705

Indiana

Department of Public Welfare
Division of Services for
Crippled Children
State Office Building, Room 701
Indianapolis 46204

Department of Mental Health
Division of Mental Retardation
and Developmental Disabilities
5 Indiana Square
Indianapolis 46204

Rehabilitation Services Board
Division of Vocational Rehabilitation
Illinois Building
17 West Market Street
Indianapolis 46204

	Crippled Children	Developmental Disability	Vocational Rehabilitation
Iowa	State Services for Crippled Children University of Iowa Iowa City 52242	Department of Social Services Division of Mental Health Resources Hoover Building Des Moines 50329	Department of Public Instruction Rehabilitation Education and Services 510 East 12th Street Des Moines 50319
Kansas	Department of Health and Environment Bureau of Maternal and Child Health Forbes Field Topeka 66620	Department of Social and Rehabilitation Services Commission of Mental Health and Rehabilitation Services Developmental Disability Section Smith-Wilson Building 2700 West Sixth Street Topeka 66606	Department of Social and Rehabilitation Services Commission of Rehabilitation Services Smith-Wilson Building 2700 West Sixth Street Topeka 66606
Kentucky	Department for Human Resources Bureau for Health Service Division for Maternal and Child Health Services 275 East Main Street Frankfort 40601	Department for Human Resources Bureau for Health Service Division for Mental Retardation 275 East Main Street Frankfort 40601	Department of Education Bureau of Rehabilitation Service Capitol Plaza Tower Frankfort 40601

Louisiana

Department of Health and Human
Resources
Office of Health Services and
Environmental Quality
Handicapped Childrens' Unit
P.O. Box 60630
New Orleans 70160

Department of Health and Human
Resources
Office of Mental Retardation
721 Government Street
Room 308
P.O. Box 44215
Baton Rouge 70804

Department of Health and Human
Resources
Office of Human Development
Division of Rehabilitation Services
P.O. Box 44367
Baton Rouge 70804

Maine

Department of Human Services
Office of Health and Medical
Services
Division of Child Health
State House
Augusta 04333

Department of Mental Health and
Correction
Bureau of Mental Retardation
State Office Building
Augusta 04333

Department of Human Services
Vocational Rehabilitation Services
Operations Unit
State House
Augusta 04333

Maryland

Department of Health and
Mental Hygiene
Preventive Medical
Administration
O'Connor Building
210 West Preston Street
Baltimore 21201

Department of Health and
Mental Hygiene
Mental Retardation
O'Connor Building
210 West Preston Street
Baltimore 21201

Department of Education
Division of Vocational Rehabilitation
301 West Preston Street
Room 1004
Baltimore 21201

	Crippled Children	Developmental Disability	Vocational Rehabilitation
Massachusetts	Office of Human Services Department of Public Health Division of Family Health Services 39 Boyston Street Boston 02116	Office of Human Services Department of Mental Health Division of Mental Retardation 190 Portland Street Boston 02114	Office of Human Services Rehabilitation Commission 296 Boyston Street Boston 02116
Michigan	Department of Public Health Division of Services to Crippled Children Baker-Olin West Building 3500 North Logan Street Lansing 48909	Department of Mental Health Division of Developmental Disabilities Lewis Cass Building Lansing 48926	State Board of Education Bureau of Rehabilitation P.O. Box 30010 Lansing 48909
Minnesota	Department of Health Services for Children with Handicaps Section 717 Delaware Street, S.E. Minneapolis 55440	Department of Public Welfare Mental Retardation Program Division Centennial Office Building Fourth Floor St. Paul 55155	Department of Economic Security Vocational Rehabilitation Division Space Center, Third Floor 444 Lafayette Road St. Paul 55101
Mississippi	Board of Health Crippled Children's Service State Board of Health Building P.O. Box 1700 Jackson 39205	Department of Mental Health Division of Mental Retardation Robert E. Lee Building Jackson 39201	Department of Education Vocational Rehabilitation Division P.O. Box 1698 Jackson 39205

Missouri

Department of Social Service
Division of Health
Crippled Children's Service
Clark Hall, Third Floor
705 South Fifth Street
Columbia 65201

Department of Mental Health
Division of Mental Retardation
and Developmental Disability
2002 Missouri Boulevard
Jefferson City 65101

Department of Elementary and
Secondary Education
Division of Vocational Rehabilitation
2401 East McCarty Street
Jefferson City 65101

Montana

Department of Health and
Environmental Services
Maternal and Child Health
Services
W. F. Cogswell Building
Helena 59601

Department of Social and
Rehabilitation Services
Developmental Disabilities
Division
P.O. Box 4210
Helena 59601

Department of Social and
Rehabilitation Services
Rehabilitative Services Division
P.O. Box 4210
Helena 59601

Nebraska

Department of Public Welfare
Division of Medical Services
301 Centennial Mall, South
Fifth Floor
P.O. Box 95026
Lincoln 68509

Department of Public Institutions
Office of Mental Retardation
P.O. Box 94728
State House Station
Lincoln 58509

Department of Education
Division of Rehabilitation Services
301 Centennial Mall
Sixth Floor
P.O. Box 94987
Lincoln 68509

	Crippled Children	Developmental Disability	Vocational Rehabilitation
Nevada	Department of Human Resources Health Division Bureau of Maternal and Child Health and Crippled Children's Service Capitol Complex 505 East King Street Carson City 89710	Department of Human Resources Mental Hygiene and Mental Retardation Division 1937 North Carson Street Suite 244 Carson City 89710	Department of Human Resources Rehabilitation Division Bureau of Vocational Rehabilitation Capitol Complex 505 East King Street Carson City 89710
New Hampshire	Department of Health and Welfare Division of Public Health Services Bureau of Maternal and Child Health and Handicapped Children Services Hazen Drive Concord 03301	Department of Health and Welfare Division of Mental Health and Developmental Disabilities Office of Developmental Disabilities Hazen Drive Concord 03301	Department of Education Division of Vocational Rehabilitation State House Annex Concord 03301
New Jersey	Department of Health Parental and Child Health Services P.O. Box 1540 Trenton 08625	Department of Human Services Division of Mental Retardation Capital Place One 222 South Warren Street Trenton 08625	Department of Labor and Industry Division of Vocational Rehabilitation Services Labor and Industry Building John Fitch Plaza Trenton 08625

New Mexico

Department of Health and
Environment
P.O. Box 948
Santa Fe 87503

Department of Health and
and Environment
P.O. Box 948
Santa Fe 87503

Department of Education
Division of Vocational Rehabilitation
P.O. Box 1830
Santa Fe 87503

New York

Department of Health
Bureau of Medical
Rehabilitation
Tower Building
Empire State Plaza
Albany 12237

Department of Mental Hygiene
Office of Mental Retardation
and Developmental Disabilities
44 Holland Avenue
Albany 12229

Department of Education
Office of Vocational Rehabilitation
Education Building
Albany 12234

North Carolina

Department of Human Resources
Division of Health Services
Maternal and Child Care Section
P.O. Box 2091
Raleigh 27602

Department of Human Resources
Division of Mental Health,
Mental Retardation and
Substance Abuse Services
Mental Retardation Services
325 North Salisbury Street
Raleigh 27611

Department of Human Resources
Division of Vocational Rehabilitation
620 North West Street
P.O. Box 26053
Raleigh 27611

North Dakota

Social Services Board
Crippled Children's Service
Russel Building
R. R. 1
Bismarck 58505

Department of Health
Mental Health and Retardation
909 Basin Avenue
Bismarck 58505

Social Services Board
Vocational Rehabilitation Services
1424 West Century Avenue
Bismarck 58505

	Crippled Children	Developmental Disability	Vocational Rehabilitation
Ohio	Department of Health Bureau of Crippled Children's Services 246 North High Street Columbus 43216	Department of Mental Retardation 30 East Broad Street Columbus 43215	Rehabilitation Services Commission Bureau of Vocational Rehabilitation 4656 Heaton Road Columbus 43226
Oklahoma	Department of Human Services Crippled Childrens' Unit P.O. Box 25352 Oklahoma City 73125	Department of Human Services Services for Mental Retardation Unit P.O. Box 25352 Oklahoma City 73125	Department of Human Services Division of Rehabilitation and Visual Services P.O. Box 25352 Oklahoma City 73125
Oregon	Crippled Children's Division University of Oregon Health Screening Center P.O. Box 574 Portland 97207	Department of Human Resources Mental Health Division Programs for Mental Retardation and Developmental Disability 2575 Bittern Street, N.E. Salem 97310	Department of Human Resources Vocational Rehabilitation Division 2045 Silverton Road, N.E. Salem 97310
Pennsylvania	Department of Health Bureau of Professional Health Services P.O. Box 90 Harrisburg 17120	Department of Public Welfare Office of Mental Retardation P.O. Box 2675 Harrisburg 17120	Department of Labor and Industry Bureau of Vocational Rehabilitation Labor and Industry Building Seventh and Forster Streets Harrisburg 17120

Rhode Island

Department of Health
Division of Child Health
Service
Cannon Building
75 Davis Street
Providence 02908

Department of Mental Health,
Retardation, and
Hospitalitization
Mental Retardation Services
Aime J. Forand Building
600 New London Avenue
Cranston 02920

Department of Social and
Rehabilitative Service
Vocational Rehabilitation
40 Fountain Street
Providence 09203

South Carolina

Department of Health and
and Environmental Control
Bureau of Maternal and Child
Care
Crippled Children Division
J. Marion Sims and R. J. Aycock
Building
2600 Bull Street
Columbia 29201

Department of Mental Retardation
P.O. Box 4706
Columbia 29240

Department of Vocational
Rehabilitation
Landmark Center
Room 301
3600 Forest Drive
P.O. Box 4945
Columbia 29240

South Dakota

Department of Health
Division of Health Services
Pierre 57501

Department of Social Service
Division of Developmental
Disabilities
Richard F. Kneip Building
Pierre 57501

Department of Vocational
Rehabilitation
Division of Rehabilitation Services
Richard F. Kneip Building
Pierre 57501

	Crippled Children	Developmental Disability	Vocational Rehabilitation
Tennessee	Department of Public Health Crippled Children's Service Program R. S. Gass State Office Building Ben Allen Road Nashville 37216	Department of Mental Health and Mental Retardation Division of Mental Retardation 501 Union Street Building Fourth Floor Nashville 37219	Department of Education Division of Vocational Rehabilitation 1808 West End Building Room 1400 Nashville 37203
Texas	Department of Health Crippled Children's Services Division 1100 West 49th Street Austin 78756	Department of Mental Health and Mental Retardation P.O. Box 12668 Capitol Station Austin 78711	Rehabilitation Commission 118 East Riverside Drive Austin 78704
Utah	Department of Health Division of Family Health Services 150 West North Temple Street P.O. Box 2500 Salt Lake City 84110	Department of Social Services Personal Social Services Developmental Disability/ Mental Retardation Services Unit 150 West North Temple Street P.O. Box 2500 Salt Lake City 84110	Office of Education Division of Rehabilitation Services 250 East South Temple Street Salt Lake City 84111

Vermont

Department of Health
Division of Medical Services
60 Main Street
Burlington 05401

Department of Mental Health
Division of Mental Retardation
and Developmental Disabilities
60 Main Street
Burlington 05401

Department of Social and
Rehabilitation Services
Division of Vocational Rehabilitation
60 Main Street
Burlington 05401

Virginia

Department of Health
Bureau of Crippled Children
James Madison Building
109 Governor Street
Richmond 23219

Department of Mental Health
and Mental Retardation
Division of Mental Retardation
James Madison Building
109 Governor Street
P.O. Box 1797
Richmond 23214

Department of Rehabilitative Services
4901 Fitzhugh Avenue
P.O. Box 11045
Richmond 23230

Washington

Department of Social and Health
Service
Division of Health Services
State Office Building
Mail Stop OB-44
Olympia 98504

Department of Social and Health
Service
Division of Developmental
Disabilities
State Office Building
Mail Stop OB-44
Olympia 95804

Department of Social and Health
Service
Division of Vocational Rehabilitation
State Office Building
Mail Stop OB-44
Olympia 95804

	Crippled Children	Developmental Disability	Vocational Rehabilitation
West Virginia	Department of Welfare Medical Services Handicapped Children's Service State Office Building 1900 Washington Street, East Charleston 25305	Department of Health Mental Retardation Services 1800 Washington Street, East Charleston 25305	Board of Vocational Education Division of Vocational Rehabilitation State Capitol Building Charleston 25305
Wisconsin	Department of Public Instruction Handicapped Children Division 125 South Webster Madison 53702	Department of Health and Social Services Division of Community Services Bureau of Developmental Disability State Office Building One West Wilson Street Madison 53702	Department of Health and Social Services Division of Vocational Rehabilitation State Office Building One West Wilson Street Madison 53702
Wyoming	Department of Health and Social Service Division of Health and Medical Services Children's Health Services Hathaway Building Cheyenne 82002	Department of Health and Social Service Division of Health and Medical Services Division of Community Programs Mental Health Services Hathaway Building Cheyenne 82002	Department of Health and Social Service Division of Vocational Rehabilitation Hathaway Building Cheyenne 82002

INDEX

ABOUT THE
CONTRIBUTORS
AND AUTHORS

Alfred H. Katz is Professor of Public Health and Social Welfare at the University of California, Los Angeles. A specialist in the study of the effects of chronic illness and handicaps, Katz has published six books and over one hundred articles on self-help and self-care in treating these conditions.

Knute Martin is a consultant in health and rehabilitation services. His writings have appeared in *Mental Rehabilitation* (Joseph Wortis, ed.) and *Guardianship Developments.*

June Isaacson Kailes, M.S.W., is a licensed clinical social worker in California and a certified sex therapist. She is Executive Director of the Westside Community for Independent Living, Los Angeles.

Katherine Powell is the Director of Short Center in Sacramento, California, a cultural and fine arts program for developmentally disabled adults.

Diane Schechter, B.A., and **Susan Sygall, M.A.,** were Staff Members of the Berkeley Outreach Recreation Program, Berkeley, California, at the time of writing. Both are now pursuing graduate studies at the University of Oregon.

Beatrice Wright, Ph.D., is Professor of Psychology at the University of Kansas in Lawrence. She is the author of many distinguished contributions on psychology and rehabilitation, among them the classic book *Physical Disability: A Psychological Approach.*